Divining the Weather

About Highland Books

Find out more by downloading our catalogue from www.highlandbks.com. If you find any errors, you can e-mail us at errata@highlandbks.com; we may from time to time publish files on our website concerning this book (such as errors under www.highlandbks/errata).

Divine Weather

A meteorologist looks at the Bible

Jack McGinnigle

Highland Books

Copyright © 2001 Jack McGinnigle

First published in 2001 by Highland Books Ltd

This publication may not be reproduced or transmitted in any form or by any means, electronic or mechanical, nor recorded in any information storage and retrieval system without the written permission of the Publisher. However 'fair use' quotations under 400 words for the purpose of criticism or review do not need permission and licenses permitting limited photocopying are available in the UK from the Copyright Licensing Agency Limited.

Except where otherwise indicated all Scripture quotations are taken from the Authorised Version of 1611, Crown Copyright.

The cover includes files downloaded from the University of Nottingham Meteosat site (www.nott.ac.uk/pub/sat-images/meteosat.html) and from www.corel.com/studio (files number 520027 and 852005). These images are protected by Copyright and used under licence.

ISBN: 1 897913-61-3

Printed in Croatia for HIGHLAND BOOKS
Two High Pines, Knoll Road, GODALM1NG, Surrey GU7 2EP, by Zyrinksi d.d. Printing and Publishing House, Cakovec.

CONTENTS

    Introduction
1. The Essential Environment 12
2. The Weather Rules – OK? 19
3. The Creation 28
4. Weather Creation 47
5. The Flood 68
6. Moses: From Birth to Red Sea 87
7. Elijah, Ezekiel and Jonah 113
8. Galilee and Judea 131
9. A Passage to Rome 147
10. The Unseen God 165
11. The God of Storms 182
12. Expressions and Depictions 195
13. Real Meteorology! 210
14. Patterns of Weather Usage 227
15. In Conclusion... 235

    Postscript
    Should we pray for the weather we want? . . 240

    Appendix 1
    Detailed Methodology of Study 242

    Appendix 2
    Broad-scale weather processes 246

    Appendix 3   Bibliography 250

    Abbreviations used 252

FIGURES, MAPS & TABLES

FIGURES   Page

1. How the sun's power varies during
   the day (near Equator) 36
2. The Earth's movements and the seasons
   (Northern Hemisphere). 37
3. The 'midnight sun' in the Northern
   Hemisphere summer 37
4. The phases of the moon. 40
5. The combined rotation of Earth and Moon. . . 40
6. Tidal formation by Earth and Moon
   gravitation and rotation effects 41
7. The variation of heating due to the shape
   of the Earth (Northern Hemisphere). 52
8. Some atmosphere/surface interactions 53
9. A cumulonimbus cloud seen from afar 121
10. The structure of a desert dust-whirl. 124
11. Cross-section of a sea-breeze. 152
12. Model of the 'Euraquilo' south of Crete . . . 157
13. How the föhn effect works. 172
14. Formation of 'standing wave' cloud 172
15. Mountains and convective cloud. 173
16. How 'banner cloud' forms. 173
17. Frequency of weather-related verses in
    Old and New Testaments 232

18.	*The power and mystery of God (Cats. 1,2,3).*	232
19.	*The contributions of humanity (Cats. 4,5,6)* .	233
20.	*An idealised convection current on a stationary globe.*	248
21.	*The effect of the Earth's rotation on the basic convection model.*	248
22.	*Mid-latitude waves in the upper air wind flow*	249

MAPS

1. A typical North Atlantic weather chart 57
2. The biblical lands 60
3. Possible routes of the Exodus 109
4. Galilee, Samaria and Judea 132
5. The route of Paul's journey to Rome. 149
6. A likely meteorological situation for the journey to Myra. 153
7. The meteorological situation near Cnidus . . . 153
8. An example of weather conditions around an intense low 160

TABLES

1. Weather-related biblical verses categorised. . . 230
2. 'Weather Words' extracted from Cruden's Complete Concordance. 243

Editor's note

Hebrew and Greek words discussed in the text are spelled out phonetically using the English alphabet, (rather than grammatically) except that the Greek 'eta' is written $\bar{e}$ and 'omega' $\bar{o}$.

Introduction

For every book that is written, there is always a 'why' – perhaps, as in this case, more than one. If the subject involves the analysis of a significant amount of data, there needs to be one or more 'hows' as well.

The 'whys'

1. The Bible is filled with weather.

If you start reading from the very beginning of the Bible, you do not have to progress very far before you find a direct reference to weather. The word 'rain' first appears in Genesis Chapter 2 Verse 5 (Ge 2:5): '…for the Lord God had not yet caused it to rain upon the earth…' These words appear immediately after the poetic sequence of the Creation in Genesis (Chapter 1) and refer to the fact that water is essential for all kinds of life and growth.

However, water is such an important substance that there is an even earlier reference. In only the second verse of the Bible (Ge 1:2) the word 'waters' appears: 'And the Spirit of God moved upon the face of the waters' – an immediate introduction to this most important of substances at the very beginning of the Creation description. As we will see, water is one of the fundamentals of our weather wherever we may be on our planet. Thereafter, the pages of the Bible make frequent references to weather concepts and imagery. These are used for a quite astonishing and fascinating range of purposes.

2. People are greatly interested in the weather.

In my life, I have met many people who are fascinated by the weather. When I worked as a meteorologist, I was asked constantly about the workings of the weather – everything from the widest global considerations to the most minute details of micrometeorology. When I lectured on the subject, there was always a barrage of questions at the end of the talk, often excellent and searching enquiries that stretched me to my limit! Everyone recognises that the weather is a major factor in their lives because it is such an important and fundamental part of the human environment in which we all live.

Even if you have not yet been outside in the weather today, it is very likely that you will have seen others battling with it, tolerating it or basking in it, either through your own window or perhaps on your television screen. You may well have read about the weather near and far in your newspaper. You may already have discussed it with someone else. It is rare for anyone to pass the whole day without commenting on the weather.

Today, people know so much more about the workings of the weather. The availability of frequent television broadcasts by weather experts is largely responsible. These broadcasts show colourful weather charts in various scales, cleverly overlaid with radar imagery, satellite pictures and computer predictions of rainfall. Animated picture sequences add to an appreciation of past and future development. All this has raised meteorological expertise markedly and whetted the public appetite for yet more.

The 'hows'

It was the combination of the two 'whys' above that suggested this book should be written. The 'hows' started with the identification of all weather-related biblical texts. This was achieved by applying a special selection procedure, which is described in the next Chapter and more fully in Appendix 1. Every selected reference was then analysed to discover how weather events, concepts and imagery are used in the Bible. The weather aspect of each reference was linked to accepted theological thought to see whether new insights were revealed. The patterns of weather usage through the Bible from Genesis to

Revelation were also examined. Biblical weather wisdom was studied, with some surprising results.

However, this is not a book for the 'expert' – either theological or meteorological! It is a book for anyone who wishes to appreciate how the writers of such an ancient and important document were able to communicate essential meaning by making use of weather events, images and concepts. In the process of this appreciation, the reader will come to understand how today's planetary weather works.

Personally, I have found this unique meteorological journey through the Bible to be a fascinating, exciting and rewarding experience. It has provided me with new and valuable insights into the way God has organised and is organising His World and His people. I hope that you, the reader, will enjoy coming on this same journey and that you too will find it to be of personal interest and use.

I am greatly indebted to those who helped and encouraged me, especially my wife Mai, and my friends Mr Roger Umpleby and the Revd Dr Malcolm White.

Jack McGinnigle   September 2000

1

The Essential Environment

Through the shimmering heat haze we can see the lone shepherd with his flock, inching across the arid slopes. Another figure joins the scene. From the valley below an elderly man climbs towards the shepherd. Their conversation is heated. They move up the slope to the shepherd's tents, set high upon the ridge. The elderly man visits each tent; he seems to be searching for something. The shepherd becomes very angry. He gesticulates wildly; his voice becomes louder and louder. He is complaining about his working conditions as a long-term employee of the elderly man. He cries, 'I've had a terrible time working for you! I've spent every day parched and burnt by the blazing and pitiless sun and every night freezing cold and sleepless in my tent!'

The furious shepherd was Jacob. The elderly man his uncle and employer Laban. The action took place on the slopes of Mount Gilead in the land of Canaan (now in western Jordan). Of course Jacob spoke in Hebrew and a more literal English translation of what he said might have been: 'I have been [thus]: in the day consumed me hath drought, and frost by night, and wander doth my sleep from mine eyes' – that is Ge 31:40 (The Holy Bible, Young's Literal Translation).

This is a particularly significant verse from an early part of the Bible. It is the very first time a biblical character comments directly on the weather and upon the effect it has been having on his life – and we understand, don't we?

We get the picture! Jacob is complaining about the weather, nearly 4,000 years ago. Nothing changes, does it? People have always complained about the weather, frequently tolerated it, sometimes enjoyed it, regularly watched it and made it a constant and favourite topic of conversation and discussion. We all know that weather may be a friend or a foe.

It was Dr. Samuel Johnson who noted, 'When two Englishmen meet, their first talk is of the weather.' Those who live in England may well have to agree with this statement – for it certainly happens many times. However, a visit to anywhere else in the world will very soon reveal that 'weather talk' is popular elsewhere. Even though many places in the world have significantly less variable weather than England does, it is still a constant and favourite topic of conversation.

Strange though it may seem to mid-latitude inhabitants, desert dwellers contrast one very hot and sunny day with the previous day in terms of single degree temperature changes, minuscule variations in humidity or small alterations in wind speed and direction. These small and subtle changes are enough to transform a day from being 'pleasant' to 'completely unbearable'! The fact is, there is some degree of variability in the weather in all parts of the world and these changes, however small, become significant for those who live there.

Of course this is not a surprising conclusion. Apart from those times when we attempt to insulate ourselves in artificial environments (e.g. in buildings or vehicles), we live out our lives in the middle of the weather, minute by minute, wherever we are. People down the ages have recognised the importance of weather in their lives. They found that the weather affected them directly and personally every day of their lives. We are no different.

Divine Weather / 13

Weather in fact and fiction

From ancient works to current publications, detailed descriptions of the weather have often appeared in factual accounts. Quite often the weather is judged to have been such an important constituent of the reported event that it is described and considered in great detail. Everyone is well aware that severe weather has been responsible for many tragic accidents involving damage, devastation and loss; within the reports of such tragedies it is appropriate to describe the sequence of responsible weather in as much detail as possible.

Sometimes the weather itself is the actual news item and so it becomes the subject not only of considerable and prolonged description but also of statistical analysis and learned scientific comment as well. At the other end of the scale, weather, even when not relevant, is often included as background information, as scene setting to help readers imagine the environment of the report.

For the same reasons, weather frequently appears in fictional writing too. Here it is used for similar purposes. The weather may be introduced as an important part of the plot or story; sometimes it is used to stimulate the mood of the reader, to build tension. At other times it seeks to soothe and reassure. Often it is merely to add realism to the scene. All these fictional descriptions of the weather serve the same purpose as non-fictional usage; all are designed to stimulate the imagination of the reader, draw them into the story and enhance realism and participation.

The weather occurs in music and poetry. Certainly Arthur Freed's 'Singing in the Rain' is a song known throughout the world. Furthermore, the weather has provided the inspiration for many other pieces of music. Frederic Chopin's piano composition Opus 28 No.15 is a prelude entitled 'The Rain' and the music weaves a vivid picture of falling raindrops. 'This is the weather the shepherd shuns, and so do I,' says the poet Thomas Hardy. Rossetti, Shelley, Tennyson and many other famous writers have also written poetry about the weather. It is a favourite subject of playwrights, too. 'Blow, winds, and crack your cheeks' says William Shakespeare in 'King Lear'; Shakespeare also wrote a whole play where weather imagery dominated the title – 'The Tempest' promises plenty stormy scenes!

Finally, many famous authors have piquant and amusing weather sayings attributed to them in Quotation Dictionaries. Typical of these quotations, and confirming the universal variability of weather in the world, is this passage by the American writer and humorist Mark Twain. He spoke amusingly (in 1876) of the weather in the north-eastern United States:

'There is a sumptuous variety about New England weather that compels the stranger's admiration – and regret. The weather is always doing something there; always attending strictly to business; always getting up new designs and trying them on the people to see how they will go. But it gets through more business in spring than in any other season. In the spring I have counted one hundred and thirty-six different kinds of weather inside of twenty-four hours.'

The Bible

The Bible really is a most remarkable publication. Experts in the science of textual criticism, whose work includes the authentication of ancient documents, have judged the Bible to be the most authentic collection of ancient writings in the world.

Furthermore, there are few people in the world who are not aware of the existence of the Bible as the book of Christianity, the religion centred upon Jesus Christ. Christianity is calculated to be the World's largest religion with around 1,800 million people out of a world population of over 6,000 million (year 2000 estimate).

Perhaps most remarkably, the Bible is the best-selling book of all time. Every year it sells more copies than any other book in the world. Most households (in the western world at least) will have a Bible somewhere on their bookshelves. Many households have several copies. A survey in a part of the United States revealed (to many people's great surprise) that the average number of Bibles in the households surveyed was seven.

The Bible is a very special book with a number of unique characteristics. It is not one book but a collection of books, bound into one volume, each one the work of different authors and complete in themselves. Its intellectual sweep is incredibly large. It is not a history book, although there is an abundance of history to be found there. It is not a law book although many laws are specified, often at great length. It is not a biography of those who appear in its pages though we are given a great deal of information about the lives of these people. It is not a book of miracle and healing accounts although both are recorded many times. It is not a story-book although there are many stories and illustrations. It is not a poetry book although there is much poetry to be found. It is not a teaching manual although there is plenty of teaching within its pages.

For Christians, it is actually all of these things and much more. Christians believe that the Bible is God-inspired; through these writings God's will and purpose may be revealed. Significantly, many of the writings communicate their points with the aid of weather imagery and concepts.

The use of weather in the Bible

Even those people with little direct biblical knowledge are likely to be aware of some of the more dramatic weather events that are described in the Bible. As children, most will have heard about Noah's Ark through story-books or toys. The dramatic images associated with the Red Sea crossing have long been a favourite of epic film-makers.

The tribulations of poor Jonah and his journey inside the 'whale' are probably equally well known! To add to the many accounts of severe weather and their effects, the Bible proceeds to use weather imagery and concepts in the widest possible spectrum.

The mystery of God is often associated with or described by elements of weather in a most powerful and meaningful way. Also, many other mysterious occurrences are characterised by weather element imagery. This means that the Bible is quite different from the other writings mentioned previously, because it greatly extends the usage of weather to communicate its messages. The Bible employs weather descriptions, concepts and imagery in a great many different situations, ranging from the deepest mystical texts all the way through to simple scene-setting or background storytelling. The inclusion of weather wisdom and early meteorological knowledge is an additional fascination.

How the review was done

The traditional 'King James Authorised Version' (AV) was chosen as the primary Bible source. This is the English translation, which was commissioned by King James I of England around the beginning of the 17th century. After diligent work by a special team of 50 biblical scholars, the AV Bible was published in 1611 and 'Appointed to be used in churches' by the King. It is still in use today.

For this review, the initial procedure involved the identification of all verses containing any reference to weather events, concepts or elements. This was done by recognising occurrences of single or multiple weather-related words ('weather words') within the text of each verse of the Bible. Without computer search facilities, the only way to find such texts would be to read through the whole Bible and pick them out! This would be a vast task constantly prone to error, since it would be very easy to overlook single instances.

Fortunately, Bible computer software provides search routines, which can identify every occurrence of given words throughout an electronic Bible text. Using 116 'weather words', the computer searches presented a rather daunting total 8,000+ occurrences. By examining these, and using a process of amalgamation, it was eventually possible to collect 388 weather-related texts of varying lengths for detailed study. For those who would like to know exactly how this was achieved, the full procedure is given in Appendix 1.

Many passages are found within well-known Bible stories, which involve weather in some way (such as those mentioned at the beginning of this section). These are presented and studied in biblical text order (in Chapters 3 to 9), starting with the Creation and ending with the Apostle Paul's highly eventful sea journey from Jerusalem to Rome. Other passages are grouped appropriately and analysed; results and examples are given in Chapters 10 to 13. A separate statistical analysis of all the data is presented in Chapter 14.

Each weather-related element in the stories is examined and explained from a meteorological point of view. The weather conclusions are then merged with accepted theological understandings, drawing upon a wide range of reference works and biblical translations (see Appendix 3). Where necessary, the original Hebrew and Greek texts were examined to ascertain the full meanings.

The study of weather usage in the Bible requires some appreciation of how our planet's weather works. Weather information is spread throughout the book but Chapters 2 and 4 concentrate on providing an overview of weather generation, starting from first principles. Many people do not realise that familiarity with our weather environment turns us all into remarkably skilled meteorological observers. The next chapter will show you just how much of a scientist you have become, perhaps without knowing it!

2

The Weather Rules – OK?

You've heard them—some people say they do not care what the weather is like. They just ignore it, never letting the weather stop them from doing what they want. But they are wrong: the weather is very important to every human being because it actually controls our lives in some very fundamental ways.

Every time you go outside, the weather determines what clothing and other equipment you will need to maintain your body within the required tolerances for human life. How many layers of what sort of clothing? Will you need a hat? An umbrella? What sort of footwear?

Furthermore, the state of the weather will often contribute to the decisions you make about your outside activities. Your intention to go for that pleasant stroll after lunch may be changed by the onset of heavy rain battering upon your windows! Indeed, there are many recreational outdoor activities, which are cancelled when inclement weather arrives; you may play your game of golf, football or rugby on a rainy day but outdoor tennis or cricket matches will normally be discontinued when the weather turns nasty. 'Bad weather stops play' once again!

In all these examples, bad weather can be inconvenient and frustrating. However the control that weather has on your life will be greatly increased if your planned activities have significant weather-sensitive elements, especially those which carry implications of danger to life and limb. The dinghy sailor has to have full regard for weather developments. Climbing, recreational flying and gliding are other examples of very weather-sensitive activities; there are many others.

However, the people who are most affected, most controlled, by the weather are those whose livelihoods are within weather-sensitive industries. Farmers and fishermen come easily to mind but a great many other activities are weather-sensitive too; commercial and military flying, shipping of all kinds, road transportation, building and construction work, are examples of industries which are affected greatly by poor weather. In addition, economic success will often be involved critically.

Weather is also a significant factor for the first-line emergency services – those who look after the rest of us when things go wrong. Road accidents in fog, and maritime accidents in storms are examples. For the people who work in these services, the weather is an extremely important factor in their lives, to the extent of controlling safety for themselves and for those who work with them.

What's the weather like?

We ask that question many times in our lives – quite often it is addressed to ourselves. It's a simple question but to answer it we actually need to expand it into three other questions. These are: 'How hot is it? How wet is it? How windy is it?' The answers to these three questions will describe remarkably accurately what weather you actually experience when you go out into the open air.

It is to the credit of human beings that they are able to answer these questions with such great efficiency, because the actual processes of evaluation are far from simple. There are a significant number of detailed procedures, which have to be applied before a series of evaluations can be made and a final answer arrived at. This application of weather science is an appropriate place to begin our considerations.

'How hot?'

Temperature

The starting-point of 'How hot' is the temperature of the air relative to your own body temperature. You quickly assess this by the feel of the air upon your skin, although several factors other than pure temperature will also contribute to your assessment of 'hot' or 'cold' or 'warm' or 'cool', etc. Nevertheless, temperature is the important starting-point for the assessment process.

Temperature may be measured by a thermometer, usually a sealed glass tube containing mercury or coloured alcohol, which tells us numerically how hot or cold it is in a scientific temperature scale. Such instruments are common and many people can refer to their own thermometer hanging up on an outside wall. The most used temperature scale these days is degrees Celsius (or Centigrade), although some people may still prefer degrees Fahrenheit. This is a temperature scale that was commonly used in many western countries earlier in the 20th Century. Both these scales were invented almost 300 years ago.

Humidity

Relevant also to the 'how hot' question is humidity, which concerns the amount of water vapour held invisibly in the air. A low humidity means that the sweat on your skin will evaporate quickly. This cools your body down because evaporation requires energy and this is supplied by your store of body heat. This is how human beings (and all other warm-blooded animals) survive when the air temperature is extremely high, even at blood heat or above.

Conversely, a high humidity means much slower evaporation of sweat and you find it hard to cool down. So in times of high humidity you feel it 'muggy' or 'very close' even when the actual air temperature is relatively low.

Humidity may be measured by a hygrometer. There are various types but scientific hygrometers often consist of a 'wet and dry-bulb thermometer' system, usually kept in a white louvred box to allow controlled airflow. One thermometer is designated as the 'dry bulb' thermometer that records the normal air temperature. The mercury bulb of the other thermometer is encased in a muslin pouch which is kept constantly wet by a wick dipped in a reservoir of water. Evaporation takes place continuously from the wet muslin and the heat for this process is extracted from the thermometer, which indicates a lower reading as a result. The greater the difference in the readings of the two thermometers, the lower the humidity. From these two readings it is possible to calculate a very accurate humidity value expressed as a percentage. If the humidity of the air is calculated to be 50% it means that it contains only half the water vapour it could hold invisibly (as a gas). If the humidity is 100%, the readings of both thermometers would be the same, because no evaporation from the wet muslin would take place.

Humidity values can range from a few percent in the driest desert regions of the world up to a maximum of 100%. At 100% humidity, the air contains the maximum amount of water vapour which it can hold invisibly. If the humidity is raised any further, water vapour condenses into water droplets and fog (or cloud) forms.

Sunshine

Sunshine is another factor which affects your assessment of 'how hot' it is. Heat from the sun (which is 150 million kilometres, 93 million miles away) is transmitted as short-wave electro-magnetic radiation. Fortunately, such radiation travels through space and then through our atmosphere without dissipating its energy. When the sun's rays reach the surface of the Earth, the radiation energy is released as heat – and that is why you feel the sun's rays hot on you skin. That, incidentally, is the way in which the

Earth is heated too and this heating process is the beginning of weather generation.

There are scientific instruments to record the intensity of sunshine and also to record its duration throughout the day. Average daily 'hours of sunshine' are a popular measurement offered by holiday resorts in their tourist brochures. These statistics are collected by sunshine recorders which often consist of a glass sphere mounted on a plinth in such a way that sunlight is magnified through the sphere. The sphere acts as a lens and the sun's rays are focused on a card, burning a track across it as the sun moves across the sky. The calibration of the card in hours allows the 'hours of sunshine' to be obtained. Simple but effective!

Wind

And finally, the 'how hot' is affected by the wind. We all create a little climate of heat and humidity in the air close to us, a little personal 'atmosphere', which maintains our body in the correct conditions for its health. In still air, this personal atmosphere becomes relatively stagnant and we can find this uncomfortable; we may find it necessary to remove clothing to increase air movement within our personal atmosphere. On the other hand, a strong wind disturbs our personal atmosphere by turbulence and will normally remove significant body heat unless the wind is very warm and moist. Most times a 'cutting' wind will reduce our assessment of 'how hot?'

'How wet?'

Precipitation

'How wet' includes all types of what is described in meteorology as 'precipitation' – that is drizzle, rain, sleet, snow and hail. The intensity of the precipitation is relevant, as is the perceived duration. 'Hardly wet at all' may be the judgement on a light and quickly passing shower while 'extremely wet' would describe a torrential rainstorm from a leaden sky!

Precipitation is measured by a raingauge, the simplest of which is a funnel collecting rainwater into a bottle. The rainwater is then measured in a measuring glass, which has a direct read-off in millimetres (mm) or inches (in). '10mm of rain' means that there would be rain water 10mm deep over the whole area affected, provided that the surface was completely flat, that it was dry to start with and there was no water drainage or evaporation.

Showers and rain

The term 'shower' is one which causes a good deal of confusion, and meteorologists are often asked to explain the difference between 'showers' and 'rain'. The meteorological distinction lies in the mechanism which produces the precipitation but there are also practical reasons for appreciating the differences between 'showers' and 'rain'.

All precipitation is produced by air rising and cooling. This happens because air pressure decreases upwards and so the air expands as it rises; energy is required for this expansion and the use of energy within the air itself results in a lowering of its temperature. As the air cools, the amount of water vapour (gas) it can hold decreases – in other words the humidity value increases. When the humidity reaches 100% and rising/cooling continues, water vapour condenses into water droplets (or ice crystals) and forms cloud.

These water droplets and ice crystals increase in size due to processes within the cloud and eventually their weight may make them fall out of the cloud. It is then possible for the precipitation to evaporate in the warmer air through which they are falling and sometimes the rain does not reach the ground. When this occurs, you will see *'trailing virga'* which often looks like black or white streaks beneath the cloud. However on many occasions the evaporation will be insufficient to turn all the precipitation back into water vapour and it will arrive on the Earth's surface as rain, drizzle, sleet, snow or hail.

Mass uplift and convection

'Rain' (or drizzle, sleet or snow) is produced by a mass uplift of air and there are various atmospheric mechanisms which cause this. Common among these are 'weather systems' and mountain ranges; these mechanisms will be discussed later. On the other hand, showers (which may also be of rain, sleet, snow or hail) are produced by the generally smaller-scale but often stronger uplift process of convection. You may remember investigating convection in your school science laboratory. A blob of soluble coloured material heated in the bottom corner of a beaker of water caused a trail of colour to spread upwards through the water, move across the surface, sink back and return to the initial point, so creating a fluid circulation. This type of fluid circulation is called a convection current.

This is how convection currents work in the atmosphere and how showers are generated. Air is heated locally, rises to form a cloud (those white rounded 'cumulus' ones) then flows out the top of the cloud to return towards the ground beside the cloud. The sinking air is heated and its humidity decreases, so there will be no clouds in the area of sinking. Meanwhile, precipitation processes within the cloud form 'raindrops' which fall earthwards as showers (and can be frozen precipitation if the temperature is low). As the clouds with their showers move with the prevailing wind direction, the ground surface below is treated to alternating periods of precipitation and dry bright weather. This is why we talk of 'sunshine and showers'.

You may have noticed that 'showers of drizzle' have not been mentioned. By the nature of the stronger up-currents involved with convection, shower precipitation drops are larger than drizzle droplets, which are produced by gently rising air. As a result, 'showers of drizzle' do not occur. At the other end of the scale, violent convection processes can produce huge cumulonimbus clouds (those with a fibrous anvil shape at the top) and very large precipitation drops. It is in such clouds that hail is produced and, in the most violent environments, hailstones can amalgamate to reach great size, sufficient to cause damage to life and property. Lightning and thunder is also a product of strong convection and cumulonimbus clouds; sometimes the huge electrical discharges can cause damage to property or loss of life.

'How windy?'

The question 'how windy' refers to the movement of air at or near the Earth's surface. This movement may range from near stillness to wind flows of great strength and turbulence. Strong winds cause pressure and suction forces around barriers and these can be very destructive. In the media there are frequent examples of the effects of very strong winds, with 'high-sided vehicles' blown over and large structures demolished and carried away by the wind. The wind can blow from any direction and the given direction is the compass point from which it blows. In certain circumstances winds can be extremely variable in direction.

The wind is an important factor in the description of the weather at any place or time and, as already discussed in previous sections of this chapter, is relevant to the 'how hot?' and 'how wet?' questions, which help to define the weather.

Wind speed is measured by an anemometer, the most common of which is probably the rotating cup type that is mounted horizontally at a height of 10m. The stronger the wind, the faster the cup assembly is spun around and the more electrical power it produces from a small generator. The electrical power is fed to a dial (an ammeter) which is calibrated to show the appropriate wind speed.

Wind direction is measured by a wind vane; by means of electrical connections, the position of the vane can be shown on a repeater dial. Thus the wind speed and direction can be read off at any time. If the system is connected to a recorder, mean and extreme fluctuations can also be obtained for any period.

So at the end of all that...

It is really quite incredible that a few seconds of our time will enable us to say what the weather is like. In answering 'How hot', we automatically take into consideration not only temperature but humidity, sunshine and wind. In 'How wet' we include considerations of precipitation type, intensity and persistence and in 'how windy' we take note of wind speed, direction and gustiness. It is an impressive demonstration of our physical sensitivity and analytical brainpower.

The observations of professional meteorologists are little different, except that the elements are measured by scientific instruments and expressed numerically, where possible. Temperature values are read from thermometers, humidity from hygrometers, sunshine from sunshine recorders, wind by anemometers, rainfall by rainguages and precipitation intensity equipment, visibility by transmissometers, clouds by cloud recorders and weather radar. However, even today, parts of professional weather observations (e.g. cloud type) are still a matter for human judgement.

But it all comes back to 'How hot, how wet, how windy?' So what's the weather like outside your door right now? It only takes a few seconds to find out!

3

The Creation

Scientists inform us (positively!) how the Universe came into being and supply us with a timescale for the various events. We are also advised about the origins of our solar system, the way our planet was formed and the development of humanity on Earth. However it is notable that, periodically, all these carefully explained mechanisms and timescales are subject to changes, sometimes changes which amount to a *volte-face;* such is the nature of scientific research.

Likewise, theologians periodically bring new and exciting discoveries to our attention, formulating new truths that may overlap those being addressed by the scientists; despite this, the conclusions from the two groups rarely coincide. Like the scientific discoveries, theological conclusions also keep changing; such is the nature of theological research.

These periodic changes should not surprise us because this is how we extend our knowledge. Research, from whatever viewpoint, will continue to maintain pressure on the boundaries of our knowledge and the inevitable outcome is the replacement of current 'certainties' with new ones.

However most Bible scholars would now agree that the two biblical descriptions of the creation of the Universe, planet Earth and humankind, as recorded in Genesis 1 and then again in Genesis 2, are magnificent poetical representations of a series of fundamental and awesome creation events. Within the poetry of Genesis 1, when the Universe, the Earth and humanity are created in '6 days', there are a number of important references which provide a positive link to the concepts of weather. The rest of this chapter looks at these relationships.

In the beginning ... there was water

According to the story told in Ge 1:1-2:3, immediately after the creation of 'Heaven and Earth' (Ge 1:1), God the Creator set about imposing order upon the formless and chaotic void which included the newly-created Earth. This was achieved by the mysterious imagery of the 'Spirit of God moving upon the face of the waters' (Ge 1:2). It is highly significant that water is introduced right at the beginning of the Bible because, in many ways, it is the substance which is the starting-point of the Earth's weather; indeed it is a fundamental of life as we know it.

Water, consisting of hydrogen and oxygen, is the most common molecular substance on Earth. It has been calculated that 71% of the Earth's surface is covered by water. Water is essential for life and is a substance found in all living organisms. At temperatures common on Earth, water exists copiously in all three forms, that is, solid (as ice), liquid (as water) and gas (as invisible water vapour).

An unusual characteristic of this substance is that the solid form (ice) is less dense than the liquid form. Therefore when water freezes, ice forms on the surface and the freezing process extends downwards. In most cases, this leaves a liquid volume below the ice so aquatic life can continue. The abundant life of the Polar Regions (e.g. seals, fish) is an example. Were it not for that characteristic of density, a good deal of the life we know could not exist.

Another consequence of this unusual characteristic of water is involved with destruction. As ice forms, the decrease in density results in physical expansion and this exerts considerable forces against adjacent solid objects, which are often broken by the pressure. Ice forming in cracks (roads, stonework, wood, etc.) is invariably

Divine Weather / 29

destructive and is an example we can see frequently around us.

With regard to weather, the Earth's supply of water is an essential part of weather generation, since it is the source of all cloud and precipitation. As we will see later, the energy exchanges involved in evaporation and condensation play a very important part in weather development processes over the whole world.

Ge 1:2 is an excellent example of the communication of deep meaning by a superb economy of word. The introduction of water at this point provides a picture of an embryonic world totally inundated by an infinitely deep, chaotic and turbulent liquid. Furthermore the combination of water and darkness – 'darkness was upon the face of the deep' is an intensely powerful concept.

Darkness is a concept linked to our sense of sight, which people use to collect around some 80% of the information they acquire. Without light, our eyes are useless and so in darkness our normal information acquisition is greatly reduced. This is a basis of our fear of darkness. So in verse 2 (v2), the influence of darkness combines with the chaos of the 'deep' to indicate the existence of vast negative forces at that time. Upon this situation the Spirit of God is imposed 'moving upon the face of the waters'. This too is a most powerful image. The Hebrew word for Spirit, *'ruach'* is a most significant one to which we will return throughout the book; the word has a wide meaning ranging from the mysterious to the physical. It can mean wind, air, breath, spirit, soul, life force or simply power.

In this case the *ruach* is moving upon the water and so we are presented with an image of a mysterious wind dominating and imposing order upon the chaos below. Thus the theology links with two meteorological concepts within the first two verses of the Bible. Water is an essential for weather, as is the movement of air, manifested for us as wind.

And then there was light

Ge 1:3 provides God's first command, 'Let there be light and there was light'. Looking at these words logically and scientifically, this means that the Universe was energised, switched on. From a planet Earth point of view, according to the story, the sun started transmitting electromagnetic radiation in all directions as a result of incandescence produced by nuclear fusion reactions deep in its core. 150 million kilometres (93 million miles) distant, some of this electromagnetic radiation would be received at the surface of the Earth, not only as light but, most importantly, as heat.

Electromagnetic radiation is energy transmitted from a hot mass. The wavelength of the energy depends on the temperature of the transmitting body; the hotter the body, the shorter the wavelength. The surface of the sun is estimated to have a temperature around 5,500 DegC and its transmitted radiation has a short wave length. This short-wave radiation has a very important characteristic: Space and the Earth's atmosphere are (almost) transparent to it and so it does not yield up its energy until it impinges upon an opaque object.

Opaque objects (including the human body) register and respond to the energy as heat input and this results in a temperature rise, usually confined to a limited surface depth. Water is a substance which has some degree of translucency to the radiation; it does absorb the energy but spreads it more deeply and so dissipates its effect. In addition, the construction of the eye in many animal forms (including humans) and its associated connections to the brain permit interpretation of part of the radiation as light. Light has only minor import for the weather but heat is a major factor, as we will see.

This first picture of Creation expresses the belief that God had total mastery over all negative and chaotic forces. The force of darkness, with all its implications of fear and helplessness, is totally defeated, routed by the arrival of light. We note that God did not destroy the force of darkness but retained it as the total opposite of light. These two opposites are frequently employed in Christian teaching, where darkness is linked with the forces of evil and light with the forces of good, inextricably linked with the God the Creator.

So this very first command by God was one linked to circumstances which are essential for weather generation. The replacement of darkness with light is a constant source of important imagery within the Christian religion. These two products of electromagnetic radiation, heat and light, are essentials of life as we know it; however heat energy alone is the driving force for weather.

Day and night

In vv4-5, the division of light from darkness produced day and night. There is no indication in these verses how this was achieved but we know it was not done by wiring in a time switch! In fact, God produced day and night for our planet in an elegant way; He caused Earth to rotate on a (near) vertical axis with reference to the sun. As the rotation occurred, each area on the surface of the planet faced the sun's rays for a time during the 'day' receiving light and heat, and then faced away from the sun for the remainder, during which time no light or heat was received.

To achieve this in 24 hours, the Earth has to rotate at considerable speed. When you are standing near the Equator, relative to Space you are actually travelling at almost 1,700 kilometres per hour (kph), that is over 1,000 miles per hour (mph)! The speed decreases as you move away from the Equator but in mid-latitudes you will still be travelling at over 1,000 kph (625 mph).

This realisation raises the next question: 'Why are we not flung into space by the considerable centrifugal force which must exist?' We all know how powerful that force is when our over-enthusiastic bus driver takes a sharp corner rather too quickly! The answer is the force of gravitation. We are kept on the Earth's surface by gravitation, another essential life and weather force. Gravitation is the force of attraction that every body in the Universe has for each other. The larger the body, the stronger the attraction. Despite travelling at great speed, we remain on the surface of the Earth because of the attraction of our body to the centre of the Earth. This force, which acts downwards towards the centre of the Earth, is stronger than the centrifugal force generated by the Earth's rotation. In your bus, the centrifugal force as you turn the corner is parallel to the Earth's surface and so you feel its full effect.

In common with all other objects on Earth, it is gravitation that gives us weight. So we do not see ourselves as travelling at high speed because everything else in the World is moving with us, also held down by gravity. Nevertheless the truth can easily be appreciated in a westward-bound flight in a fast aircraft. You may find that you leave London at 1200 hours and arrive in New York at 1200 hours! The explanation is simple. Your aircraft has actually been stationary in Space (so no time change) and the Earth has obligingly turned around to present you with your destination!

Ge 1:5 gives an essential clue about the creation of day and night by the imposition of rotation, 'And the evening and morning were the first day'. Again we have this incredible economy of word. A day did not arrive like the turning on of an electric light; it came and went gradually.

The mention of morning and evening indicates the effect of our planet's rotation. From an Earth point of view, this rotation causes a weak sun to 'rise' from one horizon, describe an arc across the sky with increasing power until midday, then decrease in power as the arc carries it to its disappearing 'setting' point. God's force of light dominates throughout the day and then he allows darkness to take over for the night-time period. Thus darkness is controlled and becomes part of God's creation.

This variation in heating and light throughout the day is a consequence of a 'fixed' source of radiation shining upon a rotating globe. Figure 1 on page 36 below shows how this works.

The introduction of these creation events is again relevant to forces that are an integral part of the Earth's weather processes. The existence of day and night is one important controlling factor in weather. A final note of absolute authority is communicated with God's action of naming. He created and, to confirm absolute mastery of His creations, He gave them the names they were to have (Ge 1:5).

Land and sea ... and atmosphere

In the following verses, (vv 6-10) the account tells how God imposed further order into the structure of the Universe by inserting a 'firmament' into the waters. It is now that the Earth we know begins to take identifiable shape. The firmament image is an awe-inspiring one. To understand the imagery it is necessary to remember that the writers of this account thought the Earth was flat. The firmament is described as an infinitely vast concave boundary, like a huge inverted plate or bowl, which is inserted by God into the waters to create a large volume of dry space. Some idea of this incredible image can be appreciated if you plunge an inverted glass bowl into a deep basin of water so that the rim of the bowl rests on the bottom. The inside of the bowl remains dry because of the air trapped within. You now have the model which is presented for this part of the Creation. The glass bowl is the firmament (the boundary), the inside volume is the 'dry space' and the bottom of the sink under the bowl is the ground of planet Earth. The water all around is God's domain, the chaotic and turbulent waters calmed and controlled by the *ruach* of God. Once installed, the concept

34 / *The Creation*

is that the firmament becomes the boundary of the Universe. The writers of the account then emphasise how God stamped His authority upon the firmament by naming it Heaven (v8). This really is an amazing concept to be presented so powerfully and succinctly in such ancient writings.

In v9, land and sea were then established and formally named in v10, underlining once again that divine authority. The Biblical imagery used is a gathering of waters to allow dry land to appear. Though not stated, it is clear that the dry land would need to rise so that the forces of gravitation would retain the water (the seas) in the places where God had gathered them. The shape and distribution of land and sea areas have many implications for weather processes throughout the planet; vegetation type and distribution (vv11-12) also contributes to the weather.

According to the first story it was into this vast space above (around) the Earth that the atmosphere was established. Our atmosphere is a fluid (gas) covering around our planet. It is produced from the materials of planet Earth and its environs and is maintained by constant interaction with these sources. This fluid covering is the air we breathe and it consists largely of nitrogen and oxygen. There is also a small and varying amount of water vapour that is highly significant from the weather point of view.

Like everything else, the molecules of the atmosphere are affected by the earth's gravitation and this is the reason they remain held in the vicinity of the Earth. There is a key difference, however. Because the air is a gas, its low density means that it may move more independently of the surface of the Earth. These movements, in addition to affecting us as wind, dominate the weather processes that affect our planet.

Divine Weather / 35

The seasons

In vv14-18 God returns to the subject of lighting the Earth. Light had already been created, day and night established but now there is reference to seasons. Seasons are of course the annual variations of summer, autumn, winter and spring (The AV refers only to summer and winter). The

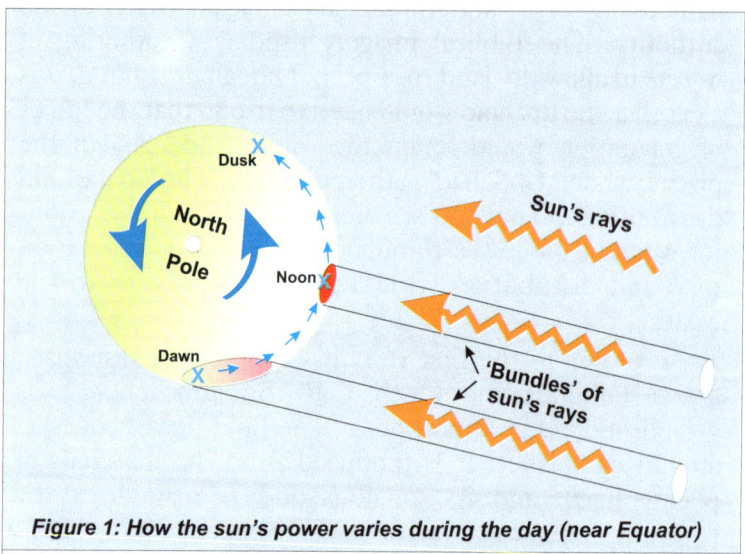

Figure 1: How the sun's power varies during the day (near Equator)

Figure 1 shows a rotating Earth lit by rays from a distant sun. As the Earth turns , Point X (blue) near the Equator comes into the morning sunlight at dawn. Because of the very small angle of incidence, the sun's energy from a 'standard bundle' of rays is spread over a large surface area (shaded green-pink). This area receives only modest heat input. As X rotates around to the noon position, the angle of incidence increases until the surface is presented squarely to the sun's rays. The input of energy at this point is at a maximum (shaded red); each unit area of the surface is now receiving much more energy than it did at first light. Then, as the rotation of X continues, the angle of incidence decreases and the energy per unit area falls accordingly. When X reaches the dusk position, there will be only a small input of energy per unit area, just as there was at dawn. Thereafter, X rotates around into darkness and zero heat input.

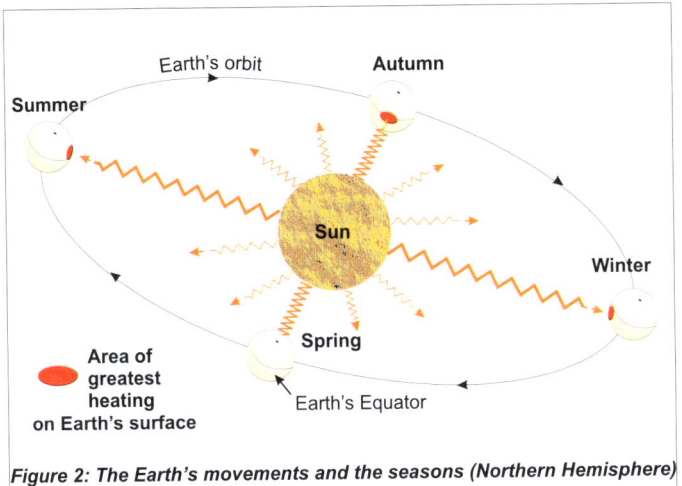

Figure 2: The Earth's movements and the seasons (Northern Hemisphere)

daily rotation of the Earth has already been discussed but this is not the only movement which the Earth makes with reference to the sun; the Earth makes an annual pirouette around the sun.

The combined effect of annual rotation and daily spin is further complicated by an axis of daily rotation that is inclined 23½ degrees from the vertical relative to the plane of movement around the sun. This inclination of axis

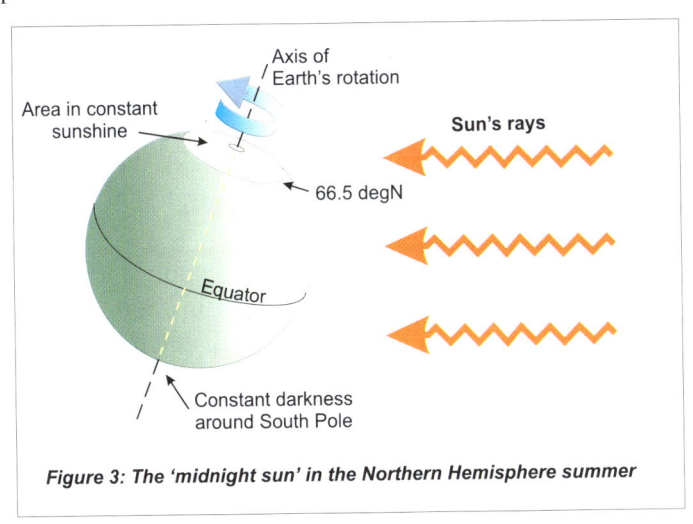

Figure 3: The 'midnight sun' in the Northern Hemisphere summer

Divine Weather / 37

means that the greatest heating from the sun will not remain at the Equator but will cycle back and forth from 23½ degrees North (23½ DegN) and 23½ degrees South (23½ DegS). Figure 2 page 37 shows how the area of greatest heat input (the red shaded area) achieves this cycling effect and produces the annual schedule of seasons.

In summer, it can been seen that the projection of the red maximum heating area is located entirely in the Northern Hemisphere; in fact the centre point is over the Tropic of Cancer (23½ DegN) and it is Midsummer's Day (21st June). On this day, all Northern Hemisphere areas will receive their highest annual daytime heat input, a combination of maximum heating per unit area (sun at its highest point) and length of day (sun is visible for the longest time).

Conversely, the Northern Hemisphere winter situation shows the heating maximum at 23½ DegS (the Tropic of Capricorn). Then, it is mid-summer in the Southern Hemisphere and mid-winter in the Northern Hemisphere. On Midwinter Day (21st December), the least daytime solar heating is available in the Northern Hemisphere, a combination of shortest day and lowest heat energy (sun at lowest point). Mid-autumn and mid-spring (the Equinoxes) occur when the maximum heating area is directly over the Equator. On these days, (21st March and 21st September) the length of day and night all over the world are equal (12 hours). These cyclic changes in heating affect the weather considerably in most areas of the Earth.

The tilt of the Earth's axis is also responsible for the high-latitude phenomena of constant sun and constant darkness. At high latitudes in both hemispheres, summer includes a period of constant sunlight, day and night, while winter has a corresponding period of day and night darkness. Figure 3 on page 37 shows the 'midnight sun' situation for the Northern Hemisphere summer.

Simultaneously, the Southern Hemisphere region will be experiencing constant darkness.

The lights of the night

In v16, God created two 'great lights' for the World. The greater of these lights, the sun, has already been established as the source of our daylight and heat. The introduction of the 'lesser light' is a significant addition to the 'light' and 'darkness' conclusions reached earlier. In this part of Creation, God is providing some light for the night, partly by the stars but mainly by the moon. Darkness, that force linked with fear, the unknown and evil, is not to be allowed to rule unchecked. In fact, total darkness is not to be allowed to exist anywhere on the Earth's surface!

The moon is a small planet which is a satellite to Earth. Like the Earth circles the sun, so the moon circles the Earth but it completes its rotation in a period of 4 weeks instead of taking a full year. Furthermore, it has a very slow axial rotation that keeps the same side of the moon forever turned towards Earth.

The moon is lighted by the sun, exactly as the Earth is and it is the reflected light from its pale surface that Earth receives. However its 4-week orbit means that only part of its lighted surface may be seen for much of the time. When the moon is located directly between the Earth and the sun, its lighted surface faces away from Earth and so cannot be seen at all; thus there is 'no moon'. Figure 4 (page 40) shows the 4-week sequence and indicates how our view of the moon (when visible) changes from a slim crescent to a full disk and back again to a sliver.

The moon is not just a variable light in the sky at night. It plays a very large part in producing the oceanic tides that affect seas and coasts everywhere in the world. We have all been to the seaside and have seen the tide coming in and out. Where the beach is gently sloping, this effect is dramatic; in the morning the sea may be lapping against

Figure 4: The phases of the moon

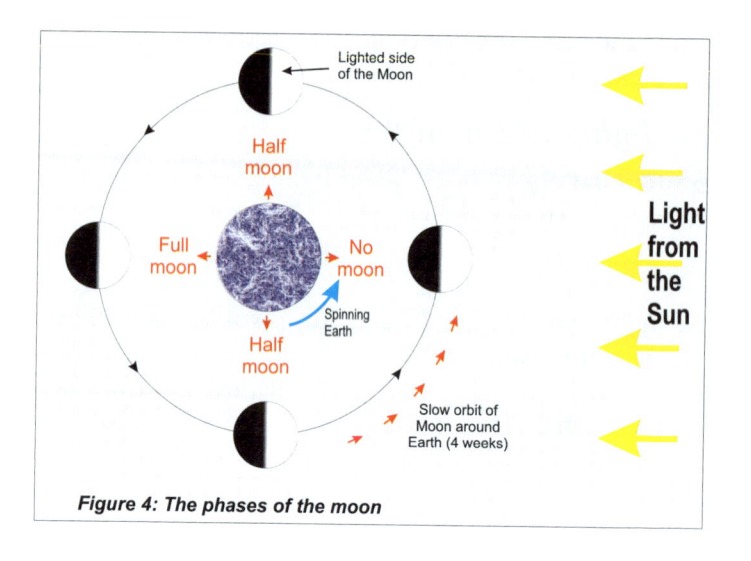

the sea wall, with every part of the beach under water. By the end of the afternoon, there are vast stretches of wet sand and a sea so far distant it can hardly be seen. The tide has been 'in' and now it is 'out'. Morning has been the time for 'high tide' and late afternoon the time for 'low tide'. Tidal times can be calculated accurately and are often published at seaside resorts. The time between each high

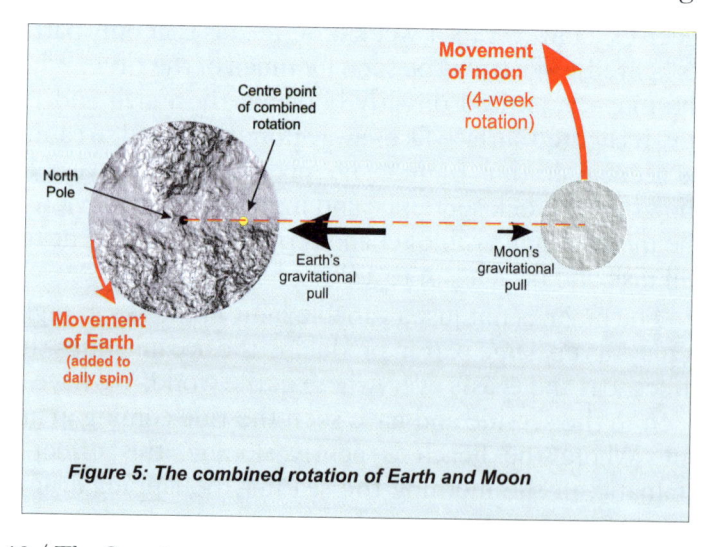

Figure 5: The combined rotation of Earth and Moon

40 / *The Creation*

tide and the following low tide is around 6 hours 25 minutes.

The moon is kept in orbit in exactly the same way as the Earth. Gravitation pulls it towards the Earth and is balanced by the centrifugal force of its motion. However, the existence of an orbiting moon creates a third element of movement to the Earth. Figure 5 (page 40) shows this effect..

Effectively, the Earth and the Moon are one rotating unit. Think of an Olympic hammer thrower; as he/she spins around to impart momentum to the heavy hammer, the axis of rotation is at a point between them; the hammer describes a circle but so does the thrower! For the Earth, this linked rotation with the Moon is added to its daily spin and its annual movement around the sun. The effect is quite complex. The Earth's elegant annual pirouette around the sun is actually a slightly wobbly dance with a small partner!

The generation of world tides lies within the combined effects of gravitation and rotation and it too is a rather complex model. The fluid nature of water means that it will respond to small changes in these forces. As already

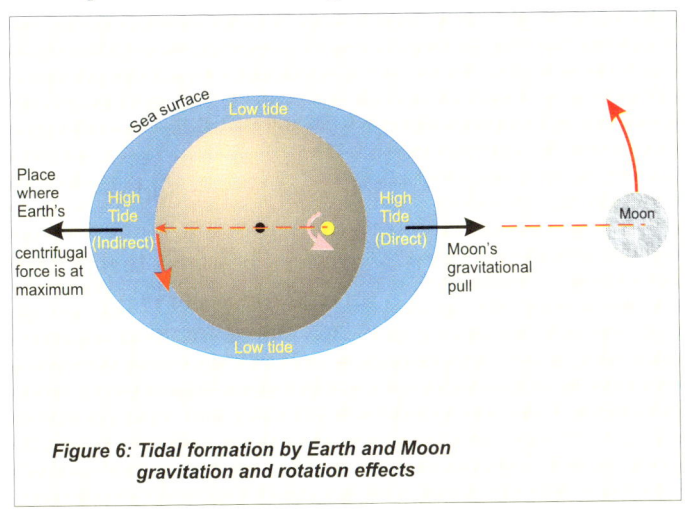

Figure 6: Tidal formation by Earth and Moon gravitation and rotation effects

discussed, the major gravitational effect on the water comes from Earth itself and that force holds the water to the planet's surface. But the seas (and everything else) are also affected by the gravitational effects of both sun and moon.

Of these, the moon's gravitational pull is the stronger (because it is much closer) and so the moon's presence above any point on the sea will actually oppose and effectively reduce the Earth's gravitation. Figure 6 on page 41 shows how the water is heaped up into a dome over a large area to create the 'direct tide'. The extra water required is supplied from those areas unaffected by the moon's gravity, that is, from the areas at the sides of the dome (shown as 'low tide' in Figure 6).

On the other side of the Earth, a similar dome of water (the indirect tide) is formed by the effect of the Earth's off-centre axis of spin. In this case, the mechanism involves the maximum of the centrifugal force – a consequence of the greatest distance from axis of rotation – and this too reduces the effect of the Earth's gravitation. As with the direct tide, the extra water required is supplied from the sides. So the combined effect is the simultaneous generation of high tides on opposing sides of the Earth.

As the Earth turns, the tidal effects flow around the globe so that each point receives a sequence of high and low tides.

A final complication is imposed by the addition of the sun's gravitational effects. When the sun comes in line with the moon, there is a stronger pull and higher tides called 'spring tides'. When sun and moon are in opposition, the tides are smaller; these are called 'neap tides'. The cycle of spring and neap tides is linked with one rotation of the moon, that is, four weeks.

Tides do not affect the weather directly but sometimes combine with particular weather situations in such a way as to exacerbate weather effects, usually flooding.

And so to life, mankind and stewardship

The rest of Genesis 1 concerns the creation of life in all its abundance, culminating in the creation of Mankind. Weather imagery is not used in these processes but it is of the greatest significance that Man was created in God's own image (Ge 1:26-27). Furthermore, the fact that humanity was given stewardship of the Earth and all its creatures is of great importance. Nowadays, it is known that some of the activities of humankind have resulted in changes to weather patterns and this raises queries on people's stewardship actions, or lack of them.

There are some well-known examples. There is the effect of 'global warming', in which urban and industrial pollution have enhanced the natural 'greenhouse effect' and caused mean temperatures to rise. The widespread occurrence of chemical pollutants has caused acid rain that has killed or altered plant and animal life. Man-made ozone destroying pollutants have been carried up to the high atmosphere and ozone depletion at these levels has reduced our natural protection from dangerous ultra-violet radiation.

The effects of all these interventions are extremely complicated and the outcome is still a matter for debate among the atmospheric scientists of the world. However for some time, one effect of raised temperatures has been clear evidence of melting ice-caps. In consequence, global sea temperatures are being altered and this in turn has a significant effect on world weather patterns.

Such man-made changes are imposed upon the natural weather variations caused for instance by volcanic eruptions (natural pollution, tidal waves) and *El Niño*, which is a cyclical alteration in powerful sea currents. The combined effects of the natural and man-made variations have the potential to be much more catastrophic for the planet.

The solution to these and all other man-made interventions that affect weather are very much a matter of stewardship of the Earth. The first Creation story makes it crystal clear that humanity is responsible for what happens to planet Earth. There is an increasing awareness of danger throughout the world community but co-ordinated action appears to be in its infancy as yet. Humankind would do well to read Ge 1:27-28 and consider their full implications.

The weather creation stage is set

The first three verses of Genesis 2 complete the poetic six-day Creation by designating the seventh day as a day of rest (Ge 2:3). Thereafter, there is a second poetic story with a more detailed version of the creation of Man. This describes how Adam and Eve were brought into being and placed in the Garden of Eden (Ge 2:7-25). In these verses, there is no mention of weather but the importance of water is once again emphasised by the description of the river structure in the garden of Eden, to provide life-giving water (Ge 2:10-14).

Weather is mentioned specifically at the beginning of this section, however. In Ge 2:5, there is that mention of rain, the very first time a specific weather word is used in the Bible. Without rain (water), the verse says, there can be no life. This situation is then corrected by God. 'But there went up a mist from the Earth and watered the whole face of the ground' (Ge 2:6).

Mist forming near the surface of the Earth is a common phenomenon. The start of the process is a wet ground surface, either pre-existing or resulting from condensation by cooling. Then if minor low-level atmospheric turbulence occurs, the water is evaporated into the air but re-condenses as atmospheric lifting and overturning occurs. This type of situation can often be seen after a cold, clear night when dew has formed. In the early morning, the sun provides enough energy to increase the ground temperature and slight low-level turbulence is generated. A layer of mist or fog then forms as an evaporation/condensation cycle is created.

In the Biblical setting of Ge 2:4 onwards, the created situation as described specifically excludes the presence of water from any source (v5). Therefore the mist referred to in v6 must be judged a mysterious intervention, a mist created by God to add that most essential of substances, water, to the dry land areas of the Earth, so that the plant and animal life already created could be sustained.

This verse is a wonderful and economical piece of poetry, creating a vivid picture of that most gentle form of watering; here, the writer is emphasising that the mighty power of God can be very gentle, caring and loving.

The range and mastery of the first two chapters of Genesis are truly astonishing, especially the first 19 verses of Genesis 1 which provide us with awesome images of the basic physical Creation events. It is striking that the imagery used is related to the natural processes of the weather. Water and light (heat) are the basic elements of weather generation. Day, night, seasons, land and sea all have important contributions to make. The writers of Genesis had the incredible task of communicating God's Word to the people of the time, specifically to make it possible for them to grasp the vastness, power and majesty of God's Creation.

Despite all our technological advances, the primary elements of human communication and learning are the same today as they were then; learning processes have to make connection with comprehensible experience. As an ever-present natural phenomenon, considerably important to all, weather imagery and concepts were able to be employed for this purpose. This realisation provides us with an additional insight into the Creation stories of Genesis.

Thus, by Ge 2:6, the Universal stage had indeed been set. Life on Earth had been created and established. All

Divine Weather / 45

the necessary components for global weather development were now in place. These components are brought together in the next chapter.

4

Weather Creation

The universal stage is ready

The previous chapter concluded that the Universal stage had been made ready for a planetary weather performance. The major characters upon that vast stage were established as an incandescent star and a particular orbiting planet. These two stage principals are named in the programme as the sun and the Earth. The set includes other more distant stars and a number of other orbiting planets that are members of the chorus. However there is one small cold planet which is seen to be orbiting around the Earth; this small planet (the moon) has a part to play.

The dynamic which holds these stage characters together and interactively in balance is a range of various fundamental forces, particularly those involved with radiant energy, molecular attraction and physical movement. The focus of the play is upon planet Earth and the story describes how the Universal forces affect the planet. The resultant action is seen to be determined by the reactive and contributory roles of the Earth's land, water and air. The stage play starts; planetary weather begins.

This chapter gathers together all the information from Chapters 2 and 3 and extends it to present an overview of the basic workings of our planet's weather. The chapter ends by focusing that knowledge upon those geographical areas in which the Bible events are set.

A weather overview

Weather generation starts with the sun, an active star approximately 150 million km (93 million mi) distant, which constantly transmits heat energy towards Earth in the form of short-wave electro-magnetic radiation. The expanse of Space is transparent to this radiation, as are the cloudless areas of the Earth's atmosphere (almost). The sun's radiation impinges on the Earth and heats its surface.

Our atmosphere was formed by chemical and dynamical interactions with the Earth's surface. It is constantly maintained by these interactions and is held in place by the force of gravitation (a molecular attraction which affects all bodies, including our own). The atmosphere consists largely of nitrogen and oxygen but also contains a small and variable amount of water vapour (hydrogen and oxygen). It is this atmosphere which sustains all plant and animal life on Earth.

The sun's heat provides the energy to stir up the fluid (air) of the atmosphere. It is spread by conduction (transfer by contact), convection and radiation from the heated Earth's surface. The resulting atmospheric motion, along with the role and involvement of water, is largely responsible for the weather that occurs across the whole world.

Unequal heating

There are a number of important factors that combine to ensure that the Earth's surface will always be heated unequally. The effect of this is to complicate air movement considerably. These complex air movements then generate the weather processes that affect the Earth.

Day and night variations

We have already discussed the day and night sequence in Chapter 3. The rotation of the Earth not only provides the light of day and the darkness of night but also is a cause of variable temperatures during the day. In Figure 1 (page

36) we have seen that only weak solar heating is available just after dawn and before dusk with the strongest heating available in the middle of the day.

However you will have noted that the highest daytime temperatures are not usually reported at midday, the time of strongest heating. It usually becomes hotter in the afternoon. The explanation is simple. The sun's radiation heats whatever it impinges upon and that body (or surface) heats the air in contact with it by conduction; then convection and turbulence spreads the heating away from the surface. Because air temperatures are measured away from the ground surface (normally around 1.2m, 4ft), it takes time for these effects to work.

A similar lag effect happens at night. The surfaces heated during the day are warm at the beginning of the night. When the sun's radiation stops, the Earth starts to radiate heat and cools down as a result. So air temperatures drop throughout the night and continue to fall for a short period after dawn until the sun's rays become strong enough to overcome the Earth's outgoing radiation.

Because the Earth is always very much cooler than the sun, its radiation has a much longer wavelength – radiation wavelength depends on the temperature of the transmitting body. This factor is the basis of the 'greenhouse effect', whose name is based on the analogy that your greenhouse happily lets the sun's heat in though its glass, traps it inside and restricts it from leaving.

The atmospheric 'greenhouse effect' produces a similar outcome but without panes of glass! Water vapour and carbon dioxide, both always present in the atmosphere, absorb long-wave radiation. When the sun's short-wave radiation passes through a cloudless atmosphere, almost all of it reaches the Earth's surface and heats it. By contrast, the long-wave radiation transmitted from the heated Earth is readily absorbed by water vapour and carbon dioxide. This means a significant reduction in night-time heat loss from the Earth and so our planet stays warmer than it would otherwise.

Without the greenhouse effect, the Earth would in fact become extremely cold. It has been calculated that temperatures would be in the order of 100 DegC colder if there were no greenhouse effect, so everything, including the seas, would be frozen solid!

Latitude and climate

We are all aware that tropical areas have a very hot climate while Polar regions are extremely cold. Climate is the general weather which affects an area and is often described by long-term statistics of weather measurements. The word climate is derived from the Greek *'klima'* which means 'inclined', referring to the effect of the different inclinations of the sun.

The explanation for the basic climatic temperature effect is very straightforward – see Figure 7 on page 52.

Seasonal effects

Unequal heating is also related to seasonal variations as we saw in Chapter 3 (Figure 2). We have seasons because the Earth spins on an axis which is tilted at 23½ degrees from the vertical, relative to the plane of rotation around the sun. At any location on Earth, this causes the amount of heating from the sun to vary throughout the year. These seasonal changes are added to the basic latitude variations discussed above. Everything in meteorology is cumulative!

Effect of cloud

The degree of cloudiness contributes to unequal heating. When clouds shield the Earth from the sun they reflect some of the sun's energy back into space and also absorb a little of the heat. So the presence of cloud invariably reduces the amount of heating reaching the Earth's surface. How much it will be reduced depends upon cloud type, particularly how thick it is. A thick continuous sheet of cloud will have a big effect while wispy or scattered clouds will have virtually none. Dense fog on the surface of the Earth has the same effect as thick cloud.

The presence of cloud at night has the opposite effect. The Earth's long-wave radiation is greatly reflected by cloud (as well as absorbed), so heat is retained in the atmosphere and much of it returns to Earth. This is why a clear, cloudless night becomes cold (relatively little heat reflected back) while a cloudy night shows only modest temperature falls, if any. Cloud acts as an insulating blanket at night.

Surface factors

A final range of factors is associated with the Earth's surface; yet another cumulation! Bodies of water (the oceans, lakes, etc.) are translucent to incoming radiation and the heat penetrates more deeply than it does on land. So although sea water does not become hot like land surfaces do, the oceans become vast stores of heat energy retained within the water volumes.

Land tends to heat up (and cool down) much more quickly than water, although the actual type of surface determines how this occurs; bare rock or sand will heat and cool very quickly while a forested area will be much more conservative in its range of temperature. Every single land surface has its own thermal characteristics and at any time there will always be temperature variations across any area of land.

The wetness or dryness of the land will also determine how the energy of the sun is received and stored. Wind and humidity will also contribute, in the same way they affect that personal climate of ours (as discussed in Chapter 2). The question of reflectivity also arises; all surfaces reflect to some degree and reduce the effect of incoming solar energy. Where surfaces are highly reflective, little of the sun's energy is received. For instance, a snow or ice surface reflects most of the radiation that impinges upon it, so

Divine Weather / 51

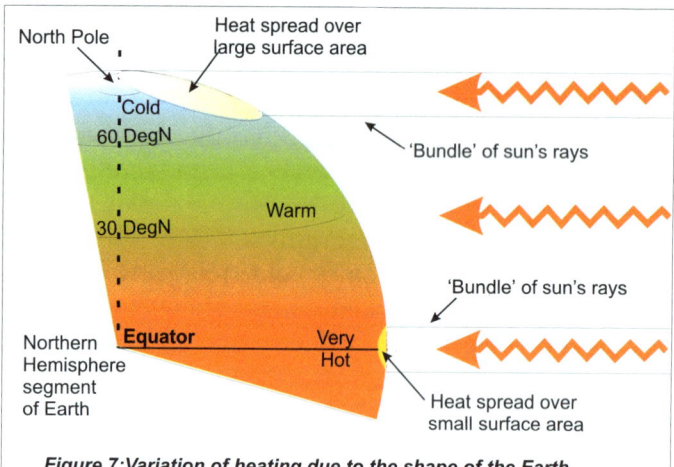

Figure 7: Variation of heating due to the shape of the Earth

The heat energy from a 'standard bundle' of rays from the sun is given to a relatively small ground area near the Equator. Travelling north to higher latitudes, the angle of incidence becomes increasingly oblique and heating per unit area decreases. The same amount of heat has to be spread over a much larger ground area further north. Basically, this explains why it is very hot in the tropics, very cold at the Poles and generally temperate in mid-latitudes.

maintaining its extreme coldness. Figure 8 (page 53) gives an idea of some air-surface temperature and humidity interactions that commonly occur in the lower atmosphere.

As these surface/atmosphere exchanges take place, a factor of great importance for weather comes into play. Evaporation and condensation of water are part of weather exchange processes and each of these is involved with a special sort of heat energy, latent heat. This is the energy involved in the change of state of a substance. In water, the changes are from ice (solid state) to water (liquid state) to water vapour (gaseous state) and vice versa.

Evaporation requires energy – this is easily noticed when liquid on our skin feels cold as it dries. Conversely condensation releases energy; this is why a steam burn can be more injurious than a liquid burn – the release of heat is much greater. It is the release of latent heat in atmospheric condensation processes that can enhance already powerful weather systems to become severe storms.

Broad-scale weather processes

All the components of unequal heating discussed above cumulate to produce what the meteorologist defines as 'broad-scale weather processes'. This refers basically to the behaviour of our atmosphere all around the globe, specifically to the very complex horizontal and vertical airflows which develop, and to the resultant changes in temperature and humidity. These processes determine what weather conditions will exist at any point in space and time, not only at the Earth's surface but also throughout the atmosphere to great height.

It is the task of the meteorologist to define the global weather of the moment and forecast what will happen in the future, using knowledge of the dynamics and thermodynamics of the atmosphere. There is a great deal

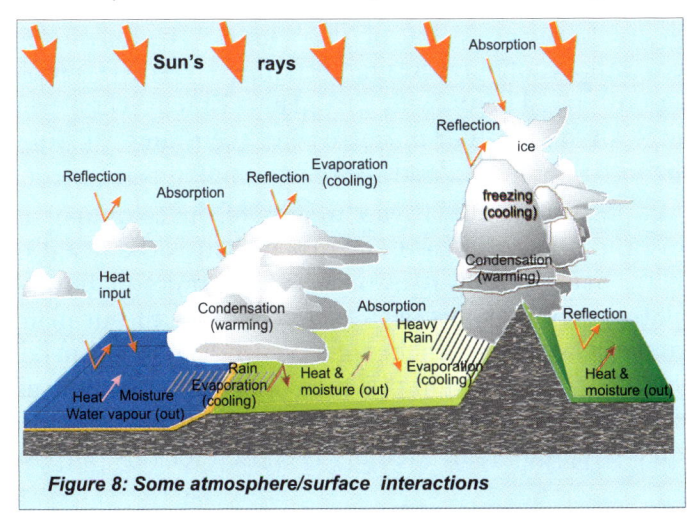

Figure 8: Some atmosphere/surface interactions

of information to be assimilated. Weather maps similar to those shown on television are examples of the tools used by the meteorologist to analyse and forecast the weather.

A more detailed explanation of broad-scale weather processes is given at Appendix 2.

Pressure, isobars and fronts

Pressure

You may be surprised that atmospheric pressure has not been mentioned before now. It is true that air pressure is an important parameter in meteorology but it does not have the personal relevance of the other weather measurements already discussed. While changes in temperature, humidity and wind can be registered directly by the human body, small changes in air pressure are not noticeable, although some people claim that air pressure changes may affect certain aspects of physiology.

It has long been known that air pressure can be a crude indicator of general weather types in mid-latitudes and this is the basis of the words found on the domestic barometer which many people hang traditionally in their hallways. Low pressure is equated with 'stormy' and 'rain'; high pressure with 'fine' and 'very dry' while middle values indicate 'Change' – a sort of 'don't know'! Unfortunately the weather cannot be accurately defined by such a simple relationship. There will be many times when the complexity of weather processes and their range of scales will cause a barometer's advice to be completely incorrect.

Air pressure is merely the 'weight' of the column of air above the point of measurement – weight is the result of gravity. Scientifically it is measured in units of force – 'millibars' (1000 dynes per square centimetre) but many barometers still show 'inches of mercury'. Literally, 'inches of mercury' is the height of a mercury column that the air pressure will be able to drive up a closed tube that has been evacuated of air. Mercury is chosen for this purpose because of its great density – water could be used but the column of water would be of the order of 10 metres tall!

The barometer was invented in the mid 17th Century. Early 'stick' barometers consist of mercury in a glass tube; the air pressure is read directly from the level of mercury. An early development from this was the 'wheel' barometer (about 1760) where the level of the mercury was transferred to a calibrated dial to give a more visible reading. These barometers are large and are usually in the traditional 'banjo' shape. More modern barometers often retain the 'banjo' shape but the pressure is measured by amplifying the movement of a small partially evacuated vacuum capsule.

The actual pressure value at any point is determined by two simple factors – how tall the 'column' of air is and how dense it is. The former will be increased by air heaping up at very high levels – in meteorology this is called 'upper convergence'. The latter is increased by reducing the mean temperature of the column – colder air weighs more. High pressure readings may result from either, or a combination of both.

The lowest pressure measured in a geographical area is called a 'depression' or simply a 'low', while the highest pressure is an 'anticyclone' or 'high'. Air near the surface of the Earth always flows into a low, rises, and eventually there is outflow in the high atmosphere. A low will 'deepen' (decrease its value) if the upper-level outflow exceeds the lower-level inflow. It will 'fill' (increase its value) if the upper outflow is less than the lower-level inflow.

The opposite happens with a high. Air flows in at high levels, sinks and eventually flows out at lower levels. A high will 'intensify' if the high-level inflow exceeds the lower-level outflow and 'weaken' if the lower-level outflow is the stronger. Pressure values always decrease with height because the higher you are when you measure pressure, the less weight of atmosphere there will be above you.

Isobars

When pressure values over an area are all corrected to be readings at the same level they can be plotted on an area map or chart. Meteorology usually uses Mean Sea Level Pressure (MSLP). If all pressure values are corrected to MSLP, lines of equal value can be drawn to construct a chart of pressure contours. These lines are called isobars and appear on some of the charts shown on television weather broadcasts. In addition to showing the position and intensity of lows and highs, the spacing and orientation of isobars may be used to give an indication of the low-level wind speed and direction at any point on the chart.

In the Northern Hemisphere, the low-level wind spirals into a low pressure area with an anti-clockwise rotation; conversely, the wind rotates gently clockwise out of a high pressure area. Rotations associated with Southern Hemisphere lows and highs are opposite; the spiral into the low is clockwise, the spiral from the high is anti-clockwise. The reason for the spiralling motion is the effect of the Earth's rotation. The norm is for stronger winds near lows and light winds near highs. Central pressures of intense lows may drop to 920 Millibars (27.17 inches) or occasionally even lower; highs may reach or exceed 1050 Millibars (31.00 inches).

Fronts

The other features that appear on television charts are 'fronts'. Fronts are important mid-latitude features because they mark the surface boundary zones of air masses of different types. Meteorologists identify three basic kinds of fronts, but the weather associated with each individual part of a front is determined by a complex range of atmospheric factors.

'Warm' fronts are drawn where warm air is replacing colder air; in its movement, some of the warm air flows over the top of the denser cold air. 'Cold' fronts are marked where cold air is replacing warm air; in this case, the cold air undercuts the warm air and lifts it mechanically. Occluded fronts occur when cold and warm fronts have become combined – i.e. in their movements, one (normally the cold front) has actually caught up with the other. Map 1 shows a typical North Atlantic weather chart analysed with isobars and fronts.

All types of fronts are zones of rising air (the areas of 'mass uplift' referred to in Chapter 2) and so are linked with the formation of cloud and precipitation. So where fronts are marked on a chart, unsettled weather with precipitation is likely. However the type of precipitation (e.g. rain, snow), its intensity (e.g. light, heavy) and duration (e.g. brief, prolonged) is determined by dynamical and thermodynamical processes which take place throughout the depth of the atmosphere.

In a simple sense, the movement of a front is controlled by the pressure field but this in turn is actually determined by the broad-scale processes discussed in Appendix 2, especially by the behaviour of waves in the upper airflow.

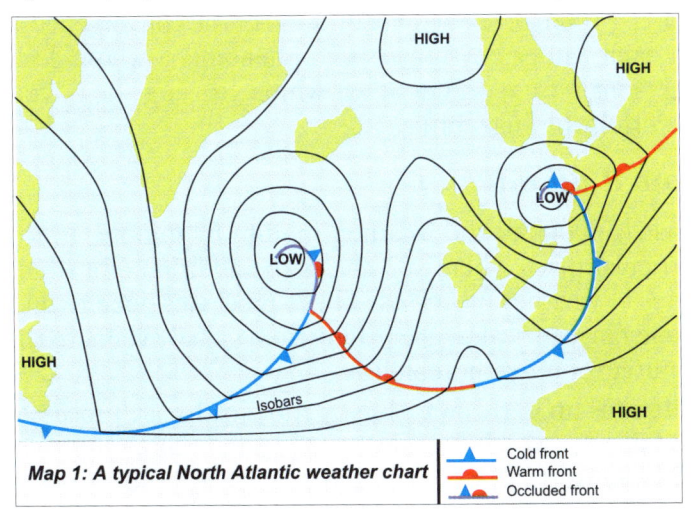

Map 1: A typical North Atlantic weather chart

Divine Weather / 57

Most fronts appear in the zones between troughs and ridges, which are the areas in the atmosphere where the greatest temperature contrasts occur.

In the lower latitude areas, away from the effects of high-level atmospheric waves, there are no fronts. Instead, the very large solar energy input enhances unequal heating and generates strong upward airflow that in turn causes strong low-level convergence. The main convergence zone which oscillates around the Equatorial region is called the Inter-tropical Convergence Zone and meteorologists mark this as a line on their charts. The strong upward motion (another region of mass uplift) is further enhanced by the role of latent heat (condensation) and violent weather is common.

Even in the 20-30 DegN/S zones, where the norm is for generally sinking air, little cloud and high pressure, the large energy input can cause smaller scale but very active 'convergence lines'. In desert regions, such convergence lines may result in thunderstorm activity if there is sufficient moisture available at medium and high levels.

Without moisture, the extreme turbulence associated with convergence line activity may still produce sandstorms and duststorms that can reduce visibility to a choking 100m or less. Concentration of the convergence at one spot can cause tornado-like phenomena whose scale may range from minor 'dust-whirls' to large and very powerful whirling storms.

How it all adds up

What happens to the weather, minute by minute, in the particular place where you are, is the addition of a whole series of weather processes. These processes operate on a whole range of scales, everything from global events to the minutiae of micrometeorology.

It adds up in this way. Firstly the broad-scale processes provide a working canvas of potentially hot/cold, settled/unsettled weather. Upon this will be imposed medium-scale variations. These will determine (for instance) general temperature, humidity, wind values and the intensity of unsettled activity across large areas (e.g. whole countries).

Then area geography will add its effect by bringing the effect of mountain ranges, major valleys, coasts, etc. into play. Local topography effects will then be added, items like small hills, valleys, large buildings etc. Finally, the contribution of the smallest scale features will play their part – local ground type, vegetation, areas of water, road surfaces, small wind-flow barriers and even the effect of moving vehicles.

This is why adjacent areas can experience quite different weather conditions at the same time. For instance, one side of a hill may be bright dry and sunny, the other side dull and drizzly; night frost destroys the plants of one garden while a nearby garden stays frost-free. This is why weather forecasting is so very complex.

Weather in the Biblical Lands

The Biblical Lands cover a much larger area than many people appreciate. In terms of Latitude they extend from 45 DegN southwards to 25 DegN; in Longitude from 10 DegE to 50 DegE. The total area is of the order of 6.25 million square km, 2.44 million square mi.

The geographical areas covered by the Old and New Testaments are not identical, although they overlap substantially. Map 2 on page 60 shows the areas concerned.

It is possible to say that the vast area of the Biblical lands is affected by one of four basic types of weather, although there are many variations within each. The determinants are latitudinal position, height of land areas and the influence of the Mediterranean Sea.

1. The north-west.

This area includes Central and Northern Italy, Northern Greece and the west and north of Turkey. Here there is a

Map 2: The biblical lands

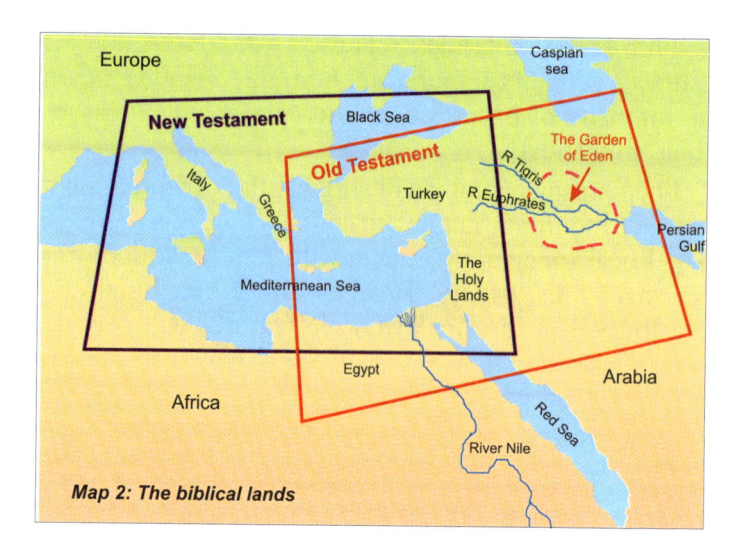

Southern European type of climate involving hot and generally dry summers and unsettled mainly temperate winters. However this area is also affected by powerful weather systems from the Atlantic or Northern Europe and these can bring extreme weather conditions. Natural vegetation ranges from Mediterranean grass and scrubland to mountain vegetation on high ground areas. There is some afforestation in the northern parts.

2. The north-east.

This includes much of inland Turkey (a high plateau, increasingly mountainous in the east), along with northern parts of Iraq and Iran. The general climate in this area is harsh; hot and dry in the summer, cold or very cold in the winter, with some rain or snow especially in the more hilly regions. Snow is common in the high mountains of eastern Turkey and the adjacent lands; snow lies all year round on the highest ground. With this semi-arid type of climate, natural vegetation is that of steppe country (coarse grass and few trees) or mountain scrub.

3. The coasts and islands of the Mediterranean.

The Mediterranean Sea (like all seas) has a large effect on the climate and the 'Mediterranean' type is pleasantly hot in summer, with little rain. Mediterranean winters are generally mild and unsettled at times. There are significant variations in climate from north to south and from west to east.

The west can be much more unsettled with some severe weather from mid-latitude depressions (from the Atlantic or continental Europe) which often become re-energised over the warm waters of the Mediterranean. North African coasts are affected by inland desert disturbances at times – dust and sandstorms, thunderstorm activity, as well as the effects from Mediterranean low pressure systems. Bad weather is less common in the east – but it does occur. In the Eastern Mediterranean countries, coastal strips experience the mainly pleasant Mediterranean type of weather but this soon gives way to other more extreme conditions inland. Here, latitude and height of ground determines whether the weather is steppe, mountain or desert types.

4. The inland areas of the south.

This area includes inland North Africa, northern Arabia and some central and southern parts of Iraq and Iran. This is a 'desert' type of climate, with vegetation of desert scrub and bare sand. Desert summers are extremely hot and dry. Winters are also dry, hot by day and cold at night. Sub-zero temperatures occur. However the weather is more temperate near large rivers (the Nile, Tigris, Euphrates) and also in the coastal strips adjacent to the Red Sea and the Persian Gulf. All these climates include severe weather events. Central and northern parts of the area may be subjected to the effects of mid-latitude storms, either from developed low pressure areas or from thunderstorm activity, produced by very strong atmospheric instability and consequent deep convection. Only the desert areas escape the effects of mid-latitude weather systems but thermally driven disturbances are common (e.g. sandstorms, dust-whirls) and isolated violent thunderstorms can occur.

The desert regions are the hottest places on the Earth; Azzizia, in northern Libya is reputed to have recorded the highest shade temperature, 58 DegC, 136 DegF, in September 1922. The highest annual mean temperature is attributed to Dallol, Ethiopia, 34 DegC, 93 DegF.

By contrast, winter temperatures in the northern plains routinely fall below freezing. Ankara, situated at 862 m, (2,825 ft) on the Turkish plateau, has recorded winter minimum temperatures as low as minus 25 DecC (minus 13 DegF). Tehran, in northern Iran, has recorded winter temperatures almost as low. Even lower values have no doubt been attained in the high mountains.

Weather variations in history

The last few paragraphs have described variations in the general weather of a large area of the Earth, in effect, what amounts to its current climate. A relevant question is: 'Was the weather in Biblical times the same as it is today?' Climatologists have studied (and continue to study) the weather of the past and have concluded that there have been significant climatic fluctuations in the past.

A useful approach has been through the science of dendroclimatology that looks at the growth rings of very old trees. This provides a climatic sketch back into history; the oldest trees on Earth can be 3,000 years of age. Of course this will only suggest something about the weather in the immediate area where the tree has grown. Also, it is well to remember that good weather in one area inevitably means bad weather in another, as atmospheric processes work to keep the Earth's energy in balance.

Other approaches have involved geology, glaciology and the study of Arctic sea-ice. Broadly, it has been suggested the last 'Ice Age' ended around 10,000BC and then there was a warm period between 5,000 and 2,000BC. In the Middle Ages, when there are more information sources available, it is reported that the period 1550 to 1850 was significantly cold. From these conclusions, it appears that the period 2,000BC to AD400 may have had general climatic patterns not dissimilar to those of today. Therefore, it is valid to apply current meteorological analysis to the weather situations that appear in the Bible, apart from the Creation and Flood stories, which take place outside that period.

So a wide range of weather types undoubtedly affects the vast 'Biblical Lands' area. In addition, there is the potential for considerable variability in the day to day weather for a variety of reasons. This introduces a good deal of interesting complexity into biblical weather considerations. In this study, it will be necessary to examine each weather-related event against its background of geographical position, details of topography, season, time of day, etc., where these can be determined.

A focus on Israel

Of course the land of Israel is an important focus for the Christian religion, because this is the area where Jesus Christ was born, worked and ministered. Furthermore, this same land (then called Canaan) became the home of the Israelites of the Old Testament – the land of Canaan was divided up into 12 areas for the 12 Tribes of Israel. This was the 'land flowing with milk and honey' first promised to them by God (at Ex 3:8) as the end of the Exodus from slavery in Egypt.

This description 'a land flowing with milk and honey' is repeated 19 more times in the Old Testament, in various books ranging from Exodus to Ezekiel. It is a beautiful and tremendously emotive phrase, which conjures up images of widespread fertility, lushness and pleasurable living. This is probably not the Middle Eastern countryside images conjured up by most people today; most would picture scenes which were rather barren and arid; hot sun blazing down upon rock and scrub. This raises the question – was the climate for the Israelites really the same as today's? Was there any variation in the climate at the time of Jesus?

Today's Middle Eastern climate

The first thing to establish is a true picture of today's climate in the part of the Middle East which contains Israel. Unlike areas in higher latitude regions, The Mediterranean area has only two real weather seasons – summer and winter, with rather brief transition zones in between. It has already been stated that there is a marked difference between the weather of coastal strip areas and inland in the more mountainous regions. In fact the climate of this region is rather more complex and divides into five climatic types, the first four bounded by north-south divisions and the fifth located in the south. There is the coastal strip, the Palestinian mountain range, the rift valley region, the Transjordan mountains to the east and the Negev Desert to the south.

The coastal strip has typical 'Mediterranean' weather. Sunny, hot (32 DegC) and rainless in summer (though it can be somewhat humid near the sea); mild (18 DegC) in winter with rain which tends to be heavy when it occurs. Frost and snow, though not unheard of, are rare. A similar sort of climate is experienced by the coastal areas of Southern California or sub-tropical Western Australia. Israel has significant agriculture in the plains and foothills area, with fruit, vegetables and grain grown widely as well as areas stocked with livestock of various kinds. Today, these activities require careful husbandry of the land, with special attention to irrigation.

The Palestinian mountains are a broad mountain range rising to over 1000m in places. The city of Jerusalem is within this area at a height of 557m. Summer temperatures are not dissimilar to those of the plain (the effect of the drier heat is offset by height) but winter temperatures are significantly cooler (13 DegC). The higher mountain areas are colder still, with winter frosts and snowfall permitting some winter sports. Sufficient rain provides pasture land especially on the lower slopes. Strong and gusty winds, especially those blowing from the east, can be unpleasant. This sort of climate will be found in higher ground areas not far from the Californian or Western Australian coasts.

The rift valley is a dramatic region which contains the River Jordan, flowing through the Sea of Galilee in the north and terminating in the Dead Sea in the south. The land around the Dead Sea is the lowest point on Earth, nearly 400m below Mean Sea Level. At one end, the Dead Sea has a depth of 400m! Highly sheltered, this area is extremely hot and dry, (summer over 40 DegC) especially at its southern end. In some ways, this area may be likened to Death Valley in California (54m below Sea Level), to Phoenix in the Arizona desert or Alice Springs in Australia's Northern Territory, though temperature values in Israel will be rather lower. By contrast, the rift valley's protected position makes it a warm winter resort.

The Transjordan mountains lie to the east of the rift valley and are significantly higher than the Palestinian range. The high ground helps to generate rainfall and this is the wettest part of Jordan. There is pasture-land, as indeed there was for the flocks attended by Jacob (Genesis Chapter 31). The climate here is generally similar to that of the Palestinian mountains but winter frost and snow is common (minimum temperatures zero or below) and the highest mountains are snow-covered in winter.

The Negev presents typical desert conditions, very hot and dry with little or no rain, typical of all hot desert areas of the world. Night-time temperatures plummet in the dry, clear conditions and frost can occur.

Was the climate of ancient Israel different?

None of the above descriptions would imply 'a land of milk and honey' though it has been suggested that a comparison between Sinai and Canaan could have encouraged the Israelites to believe such a fulsome description! The other possibility is that there was a rather different climate at the time, one more conducive to a 'land of milk and honey'.

It is notoriously difficult to identify small or subtle changes when assessing ancient climate information. With the information available from dendroclimatology, geology, etc., it has already been suggested that average temperature and rainfall in the region were likely to be similar to those of today. However, ancient writings identify places where there would appear to have been significant agriculture in areas which are now largely desert. In addition to the 'land of milk and honey' which Israel was, there is evidence that Egypt and Cyrene (now Libya) later provided the Roman Empire with considerable grain – in fact the Southern Mediterranean was regarded as the 'breadbasket' of the Roman Empire. Is this a pointer to the fact that the past climate was more clement? Perhaps.

It is possible that small changes in temperature and rainfall were just sufficient to produce an appropriate climate for all this agricultural activity. However other factors may also come into play and one of these is desertification, a process which has affected many semi-arid farming areas. Such major failures of grain crops have been recorded within the last century. In the 1950s, the major grain producing areas of Russia became barren. In the 1930s, desertification happened in the American mid-west plains (an area referred to as the breadbasket of America). Both these catastrophes occurred because of inappropriate or excessive cultivation which resulted in poisoned soils and/or topsoil layers blown away by the wind. Similar tragedies have occurred more recently in central Africa. In the past, it is known that the northern edge of the Sahara Desert was forested. When this was cut down (for firewood or to use the land for agriculture) the desert spread rapidly north. It is very likely that similar actions took place in ancient times and this could explain the change across the region. In semi-arid regions, a productive agricultural balance is difficult to maintain; once desertification takes hold, it is extremely difficult to reverse. It is therefore possible that the 'land of milk and honey' which was ancient Israel, was subject to desertification processes over a period of time; the same may well apply to the areas defined as the 'breadbaskets of the Roman Empire'.

The Israel of 2,000 years ago

New Testament texts make no mention of a 'land of milk and honey' and this would not be an apt description if desertification had taken place earlier. However there are a number of references to 1st Century farmers who produced cereal or fruit crops while others farmed animals of various types. There are also references to barns and storehouses as well as to the various processes of farming, ploughing, threshing, milling, slaughtering, etc. Clearly there was significant agriculture taking place in Israel 2000 years ago, as indeed there is today. There are a number of weather descriptions (e.g. references to rain, showers, dew) which do not disagree with today's conditions for the Middle Eastern farmer. Therefore it is reasonable to assume that the Israel climate of 2,000 years ago was broadly similar to that of today.

5

The Flood

The story of the Flood, starring Noah and the Ark, illustrates a fundamental point of dispute long present in theological study. It is a point of contention which ranges across all the earlier books of the Bible (and, to a lesser extent, beyond). It is generally agreed by Bible-based religions that the Bible is a work inspired by God; but within this inspiration, how much is literal truth and how much is fabrication to illustrate truth? At one end of the scale there are biblical scholars who are 'literalists'; they believe and argue that every word of the Bible is the literal truth. Such scholars believe that in the Bible we are reading history – though not just history; the biblical accounts all reveal something of God and his activity. At the other end of the scale we have those who propose that much which is presented in the Bible is illustration to communicate truth – God revealed through stories, allegories, parables, legends and myths. Of course there is every opinion in between these opposites, often fiercely argued.

It is beyond the scope of this book to enter this arena of dispute, which is already the subject of many learned texts. Here, as in all other biblical texts presented throughout the book, the story of the Flood will be taken as printed in the AV and examined to illustrate how weather in its widest sense is involved in the written account. The results may then inform new insights or provide confirmation and comment upon previous opinions.

An overview of the Flood

The Flood is a widely known account of destruction and re-creation that appears in an early part of the Bible. It demonstrates the powerful link between Scripture and weather concepts because the mechanisms used by God to achieve his awesome purposes appear to be those of the natural weather forces of the world. The Flood is recorded in the Bible where it may be understood as an unique act of *almost* total destruction by God the Creator. The word 'almost' gives us the clue that the destruction was also the precursor of a new beginning.

In Ge 6:5, God recognised that man, His greatest creation and the one made in His own image, had become filled with absolute evil. God saw that this evil had pervaded other living creatures as well. After an agonising review, God judged that the situation was hopeless so He determined to wipe out this totality of evil by destroying the life He had created (vv6-7).

However God found that there was one notable exception, one man who had not fallen into the terrible pit of evil but had maintained a life of goodness and righteousness both personally and within his family. This man was Noah and v9 describes him as a 'just' man, a man who 'walked with God'. It was no wonder that Noah 'found grace in the eyes of God' (v8) among that morass of evil which the Earth had become! So Noah was chosen to carry forward not only the human race but the lives of all the other animals which God had made for the Earth during the Creation.

Forces of destruction

In Ge 6:13-22 God told Noah that He would destroy the vile and corrupt life on Earth by sending a vast flood. So that a new beginning could occur, God made a covenant with Noah that he would be saved, along with his family. Noah was instructed to build a very large floating vessel (the Ark) and, on God's subsequent command, fill it with perfect male and female pairs of all God's creatures, so that each species could continue after the new beginning. The Ark was to be filled with sufficient provisions to sustain life for all on board until it was possible for them to return to dry land. This was God's first divine command and Noah did as he was bid. Precise measurements had been given and the result was a very large completely closed craft with several decks whose overall length was an impressive 137m (450ft). This is a large vessel, even by today's standards. It is certain that it would have been absolutely enormous in comparison to any floating craft of these ancient times.

It is in v17 that weather is first mentioned – indirectly. God would bring a 'flood of waters upon the Earth', although this text does not suggest how the flood would be delivered. The Hebrew word used here is interesting. Apart from Psalm 29 v10, *mabbul* is used only in Genesis 6 to 11 and so really becomes the Hebrew name for the Flood, that is, the name for this particular devastating event. It is also noted that the word may be translated as 'deluge', which might suggest torrential rain. In the subsequent reference in Ps 29:10, *mabbul* appears in the phrase 'The Lord sitteth upon the flood *(mabbul)*'. This is taken to be a reference to the very first Creation event, when God's Spirit tamed the chaotic waters (Ge 1:2). We will see that this idea is in accordance with the more mysterious generation of floodwater discussed later in this chapter.

In Genesis 7, Noah is instructed to establish himself, his family and the animals of the world on board the Ark. This is God's second divine command. It is immediately noticeable here (vv2-3) that the instructions for animal numbers are different. The required number of certain animal species (those defined as clean beasts) has been increased to 'seven pairs'.

Biblical scholars explain this anomaly by revealing that the book of Genesis is not the work of one man (traditionally it had been attributed to Moses) but the work of many writers, working within several 'schools of thought'. Their writings expressed 'traditions' which may well have developed over many years. It is possible to attempt identification of these discrete schools of thought by the content and style of their writing. Studies usually refer to the various 'schools' by single letters – in this case P and J. In fact it can be seen that the structure of the Flood account is repetitive, confirming the work of more than one input.

In Ge 7:4, weather elements are introduced directly when God reveals that He will cause it to rain continuously for 'forty days and forty nights'. Seven days later, the rain starts and the waters begin to rise (vv6-7). In the repeated section that follows, although rain is mentioned in v12, the description of the flood mechanism is widened considerably. V11 refers to much more mysterious mechanisms; the 'fountains of the great deep (were) broken up' and 'the windows of Heaven were opened'. So the waters deepened rapidly, the Ark floated and, as the waters 'prevailed.....150 days' (v24), all living creatures on Earth except those on board the Ark were destroyed.

Genesis 8 concerns the ending of the Flood, the abating of the waters and the eventual rehabilitation of Noah, his family and his charges. The rain stopped. The 'fountains of the deep' stopped flowing. The 'windows of Heaven' were closed. The water level fell and the Ark grounded on 'the mountains of Ararat' (Ge 8:4). This suggests a landfall in the extreme eastern parts of modern day Turkey.

About one year after they had entered the Ark, Noah, his family and all the animals were able to return to dry land and begin to rebuild a normal life. We read that the cessation mechanism used by God was a wind which 'passed over the Earth' (Ge 8:1), yet another reference to weather elements. So God's purpose was fulfilled and there was a fresh beginning on Earth.

Divine Weather

Weather and flooding

It is obvious that heavy and prolonged rain can cause flooding. We have all experienced this to some degree during our lives, even if it is only to the extent of some very deep puddles outside our door! Of course there are certain areas in the world where very serious flooding is a regular event and it is common knowledge this can cause great devastation and loss of life. Sometimes, the media reports describe these catastrophic events as 'floods of biblical proportions'. That raises a pertinent question for this discussion: 'What were the proportions of the Flood?' Two basic views emerge. The Flood was either a whole world happening or it was confined to a limited (but large) area.

The answers to these questions really determine what sort of mechanisms God may have used to fulfil his purposes. Did he use extremes of weather or other physical phenomena potentially understandable to us, or mysterious powers we can only wonder at? A range of possibilities are discussed below.

Limited flooding by rainfall

Looking first at the question of limited flooding by rainfall (the mechanism specified by the biblical text), it seems likely that the Earth's population at the time of the Flood would be numerically small and confined to the area surrounding their creation. The Creation account is thought to focus upon the fertile valleys of ancient Mesopotamia. Traditionally, this is suggested to be the location of the Garden of Eden, the area where mankind and all other living creatures were created. Map 2 shows the general geographical area. Of course the areas now watered by the Rivers Tigris and Euphrates are currently in eastern Iraq and western Iran. The story suggests that it was somewhere in this area the Ark was constructed by Noah. Therefore an extreme flood delivered to that area and extending to the north and west (where the Ark came to rest) would have the effect God wanted. It would destroy the limited amount of life that had spread out slowly from the region of the Garden of Eden.

Ge 7:19-20 specifies that 'all the high hills' were covered to a depth of 15 cubits (7m, 24ft). Using today's topography, general flooding to a depth of 5,130m, 16,832ft above sea level would be required to cover Mount Ararat (the highest mountain in the region) with water.

Taking the text literally, this implies 40 days of rainfall accumulating at a depth of 128m per day – an intensity of rain equivalent to over five metres of water depth per hour. One-hundredth of this, 5cm of rain per hour is an absolute torrential downpour! Also, to sustain the Flood, there would need to be little or no water drainage from the area. Looking at existing topography, there is no way that such a depth of water could be confined within this geographical area, even if it were possible to generate rainfall of such cataclysmic intensity. On these terms of understanding, a rainfall produced limited-area Flood in this specific region seems impossible.

However, two mitigating factors may be argued. The term 'forty days' is one which is used a number of times throughout Scripture – for instance Moses was with God on Mount Sinai for 'forty days' when he received the Ten Commandments (Ex 34:28) and Jesus was tempted in the desert for 'forty days' (Mk 1:13). It is generally agreed that the term 'forty days' represents 'a long time' rather than a specified and finite period. Therefore, the period of rain at the time of the Flood could have been considerably longer than 40 x 24 hours.

The other factor concerns land configuration at the time of the Flood. The Ararat region is known to be an area subject to earthquakes (there was a major earthquake as recently as the year 1840) and so the whole region could have been topographically very different. It is possible that it could have been much flatter and surrounded with sufficient high ground to retain rainwater without significant loss. Only with a greatly extended time period

Divine Weather / 73

and a totally different land configuration can this Flood model be envisaged..

Finally, the fate of humanity (and animals) needs to be considered realistically. In this model of limited area flooding, the water has to be contained by surrounding topography. Unless the Flood occurred with devastating rapidity (this is not suggested by the Biblical text), surely it should have been possible for at least some people and animals to climb above the water level on to the containing slopes or cliffs? Mankind has shown how possible it is to climb up even vertical and smooth rock faces and some animals are even more skilled. Therefore a further element of divine intervention would be required to prevent this happening and guarantee death for all. A filled bathtub-type model would be needed – with completely smooth vertical sides impossible to climb. Also flying creatures would need to be disabled. As we can see, this model requires considerable speculation plus divine intervention.

Limited flooding achieved by other physical means

The enquiring and inventive mind of humanity has long sought other plausible explanations for the delivery of the Flood. The following sections investigates several.

Ice Age involvement

There are propositions which link the Flood with the ending of an Ice Age. The theories propose a dramatic rise in sea levels caused by the melting of many millions of tons of ice. This would cause many land areas – including that populated by mankind – to become inundated with very deep water. Some propose an extremely rapid ice melt; the Flood would occur very quickly and all life would be extinguished by catastrophic water torrents. To provide physical support for this, some theorists locate mankind in large enclosed valleys – the huge basin which is now the Black Sea is one choice. This theory starts with a very large enclosed dry land basin populated by mankind and then has huge volumes of sea water pouring in through the Dardanelles from the Mediterranean. The image is again of a gigantic bath but this time with the taps turned full on – all life swept away and drowned! Makers of epic action films have shown us such effects many times!

Ice Ages are now well-documented features of our past climate. They are variable periods of time (millions of years) when the temperature on Earth becomes very much lower than normal; this causes very extensive volumes of ice to form across sea and land areas which are normally ice-free. By means of palaeoclimatolgy studies, particularly by examining where layers of glacial drift rocks are to be found, it has been shown that Ice Ages have occurred periodically.

The last Ice Age probably started about 2.5 million years ago and lasted until about 10,000BC when continental ice sheets withdrew from mid-latitude regions of the Northern Hemisphere. There is evidence for further Ice Ages back into pre-history. A very extended Ice Age began around 300 million years ago and lasted for at least 50 million years. Earlier Ice Ages have been suggested around 425, 600, 800, 950 and 2,500 million years ago. Ice Ages affect different parts of the world; the last Ice Age affected North America and Northern Europe while the previous one was located in the Southern Hemisphere. The Ice Age of 425 million years ago appeared to affect more Equatorial regions, extending from Brazil to North Africa.

The reasons for the occurrence of Ice Ages continue to be speculative. Modern theories suggest an essential link with the rotation of our galaxy. Astronomical observation has established that the Milky Way galaxy which contains our solar system completes a rotation every 300 million years or so. Because of this movement, our solar system is carried through areas of changing gravity, magnetism and interstellar dust. These variations, combined with other Earth changes (e.g. continental drift in accordance with the Plate Tectonics theory) are sufficient to set in motion periodic planetary cooling which alters world climate and is the start of an Ice Age across a large area of our planet. Conversely, it is argued that those same galactic variations will signal the end of an Ice Age. It has been calculated that Ice Ages occupy about 10% of the total time Earth has existed, with normal temperatures at other times.

It has also been speculated that known changes in the axis of rotation of the Earth may determine which areas of the Earth will be affected by each Ice Age. These same axis changes may also explain climate variations within each Ice Age – periods when it becomes colder or less cold. These variations appear to be cyclic, occurring every 100,000 years or so.

It is certain, therefore, that the ending of an Ice Age would indeed cause a significant rise in sea levels on Earth and that many land areas would become flooded. The problem for those who support 'end-of-Ice-Age' Flood theories is speed of occurrence. Ice Ages end gradually and the sea level rises would be slow. Even flooding 'break-throughs' (e.g. a 'Black Sea' type of event) would occur quite slowly; only narrow ravines would experience the type of powerful flooding rapids which characterise, for instance, the collapse of a major dam across a narrow channel.

Of course the Bible text does not suggest flooding by torrent but a progressive water level rise caused by 'rain'. The text describes steadily rising water which eventually covers 'all the high hills' (Ge 7:19). Again, as discussed previously, one can envisage at least a proportion of humanity climbing the containing walls to stay above the rising water levels, unless divine intervention had made it impossible for them to do so.

Meteorites, volcanoes and tsunamis

The above realisation about the survival actions of humanity has made some theorists turn to possible mechanisms which would dramatically accelerate the onset of the Flood.

Meteorites

A popular theory explaining the demise of the dinosaurs is linked to the impact of a large meteorite on the Earth. This caused a cataclysmic explosion which destroyed much life. The after-effects of climate alteration and atmospheric pollution then killed many more living things, including all species of dinosaurs. Some have suggested that a large incandescent meteorite arriving at the end of an Ice Age would cause a much more rapid flood to occur. The Flood would then subject humanity to a drowning torrent from which escape was impossible. However it is suggested here that the heat input from even a large meteorite could only have a minor and very local effect on the melting of a truly vast ice-field. This scenario could not produce the widespread and rapid ice melting required.

An alternative suggestion, uninvolved with Ice Ages, produces a large 'tidal' wave from the impact of a large meteorite falling into deep sea. Such an impact could indeed generate a large tidal wave which may temporarily flood oceanic coastal areas sufficiently close to the event. A temporary tidal wave of this type would not produce the sustained biblical Flood situation described by the Noah story.

Volcanoes

Volcanic action occurs regularly in many areas of the Earth, caused by the incandescent core breaking through a weakness the Earth's crust. An awesome amount of heat energy is involved in these events which can be prolonged. If volcanic action occurred under the ice field at the end of an Ice Age, there must be some effect on the ice melting rate in the area of volcanic activity. However, even the largest areas of volcanic activity are tiny in comparison to the area affected by an Ice Age, so the overall effect on the vast ice field will still be small.

Tsunamis

The Japanese word 'tsunami' describes a form of 'tidal wave' (again, nothing to do with daily tides) which is generated by an undersea earthquake. These waves can travel at very high speeds over great distances and grow in shallower water to become terrifying walls of water. Coastal areas may be suddenly and temporarily flooded to great depth, with much destruction and loss of life. Again, a tidal wave of this type is not a description of the biblical Flood.

Global flooding

The second basic view suggests that the Flood covered the whole Earth. This view cannot find any explanation within the meteorology of the world as we know it. The atmosphere keeps itself in balance, world-wide. Practically, this means that what goes up somewhere must come down somewhere else. You will remember the explanation of convection given in Chapter 2; this is a small-scale example of what happens in much larger-scale weather systems. Mass uplift over one large area must be balanced by atmospheric sinking elsewhere.

The atmospheric balance over the whole world is very complex but an idea of the motion involved may be visualised from the complicated turbulence that can be seen in a fast-flowing river. If such turbulence is imagined in a much less dense fluid (e.g. like steam) and visualised in world dimensions, you have a sketch of what atmospheric air movement is like. Air moves in all three dimensions and the combination of air currents, areas of stagnation, whorls and spirals keeps the atmosphere and its energy in balance throughout the world.

As already discussed in Chapter 4, prolonged and heavy rain over a large area requires rising warm and moist air over that area. This happens frequently in our world, especially in tropical regions where the air is hot and thus able to contain a great deal of water vapour. This in turn releases a great deal of latent heat as it cools and condenses; this energy fuels even greater vertical motion.

Serious flooding is normally a consequence of rainfall and groundwater inflow from higher adjacent ground. This inflow adds considerably to the overall volume of water. Rivers burst their banks, the ground becomes saturated, natural drainage is inadequate and flooding occurs. However, as previously indicated, global physics demand that this huge area of rising air has to be balanced somewhere else in the world. Thus it is impossible for the air to rise everywhere in the world at the same time; the Earth's energy balance could not be maintained.

Consequently it is necessary to turn to a more mysterious explanation and there is Biblical evidence to allow this to be done. The 'fountains of the great deep' and the 'windows of Heaven' have already been mentioned. The 'fountains' were 'broken up' (Ge 7:11) implies that water stored under the Earth was brought to the surface. This could be interpreted as a reversal of the separation of land and sea which was described in the Creation process (Ge 1:9).

Also, the 'windows of Heaven were opened' (Ge 7:11). In Ge 1:6-7 God made a firmament (see Creation, Chapter 3) to divide the waters which covered the Earth. He named the firmament Heaven and beyond this boundary the chaotic waters would continue to rage. If the firmament were breached ('windows opened') then the mighty and chaotic waters would again descend upon the Earth, returning it to its original state (Ge 1.1-2). It would seem that God's specific design of Noah's Ark would allow this vessel exist *within* these waters. In fact, the Ark would contain the only living remnant of God's previously created life on Earth. In the case of global flooding, there would be no question that all other living creatures would perish, since all land would be flooded to great depth.

When the task of the Flood was done, God then re-created the Earth. A 'wind' was passed over the Earth, that same wind *(ruach)* we read about in Ge 1:2, to impose order on the chaotic waters. The firmament of Heaven would be reintroduced; this time the imagery is 'closing the windows of Heaven' (Ge 8:2). The sea would be divided from the land – the imagery here is 'stopping the fountains of the deep' (Ge 8:2). The continuation of the wind would dry out the land by increasing evaporation. The Ark would then float on the surface of the receding waters and finally come to rest on dry land. Effectively, what can be argued here is a complete reversal of the Creation story discussed in Chapter 3 and its re-imposition when God's will had been done.

The landing of the Ark

Traditionally it has been suggested that the Ark grounded on the top of Mount Ararat, the highest mountain in that region at 5123m, 16,808ft high. Today the mountaintop is perpetually snow-covered (above 4,300m approx.) and it is bitterly cold at such heights.

If the Flood was area-limited (the first view), then normal air pressure considerations would apply and so the air at that height would be very thin, that is lacking in oxygen. At that height, the air is much expanded (less dense) and just over 50% of the normal low-level oxygen would be available. While it is possible for animals (and humans) to exist at these heights, it requires a great deal of acclimatisation and most creatures who live at such heights have specially adapted body systems. It would also be very cold. Normal atmospheric decrease of temperature with height would apply. Of course these same considerations would have applied to all within the Ark during the time they rode on top of a limited area Flood of that depth.

By contrast, if the Flood were global (the second view) then the atmospheric situations discussed above would not apply. Those within the Ark would need to be protected within the deluge that would submerge the vessel completely. In this case, God would need to supply a sustaining atmosphere within the Ark itself. Thus this universal Flood view would bring the Ark into a domain of mystery where normal meteorological considerations do not apply.

However the traditional mention of 'Mount Ararat' is actually an interpretation of Ge 8:4 which does not mention the peak but only the 'mountains of Ararat'. Taking the words of Scripture as they were written, it would seem that the grounding could have taken place at a lower level. Even today, there are many ridges in this area with heights around 2,000-2,500m, (6,500-8,000ft). The foothills and plains are generally at a height of 750-1350m (2,500-4,500ft) below.

In any event, it is unlikely that Noah, his family and their menagerie would wish to establish their lives in the freezing cold and rarefied air of the mountains! In fact Ge 8:4-19 shows a five month period between the initial grounding and disembarkation during which time the Ark must have sunk towards low ground. God's third divine command released Noah and his companions from the Ark into a fertile and pleasant land.

Conclusions on the biblical Flood story

If Earth science principles are strictly adhered to, it is unlikely that the Flood area implied by the biblical account (Mesopotamia, Turkey) could have been confined to this limited area. It requires much speculation to make this model work. Topography would need to be vastly different from today. 'Forty days' must be expanded into a very much longer time, perhaps up to a period 100 times longer.

Divine Weather

Normal drainage principles suggest that the huge body of water would be extremely difficult to maintain throughout such a large area.

Even if the arena of action is moved to a place which looks much more viable (e.g. the Black Sea basin), there remains the problem of human/animal action in the face of rising flood water. Unless disabled in some way (by divine intervention), many would surely save themselves by somehow climbing the walls containing the flood water. Regarding the alternative question of very rapid onset, none of the schemes discussed in previous sections could scientifically support the cataclysmic water inundation which would imply instant destruction of all life.

With global flooding, total destruction is assured and completely mysterious principles must apply. Although these cannot be explained scientifically, the Flood account can be interpreted as a reversal of the initial Creation, followed by a re-Creation. Although different imagery is used in the re-Creation, it is compatible with Genesis 1 in every way. This is an interesting insight. Belief in this theory requires the acceptance of God's mystery.

It is relevant to mention that this type of destruction/new beginning story appears in many other cultures in a very similar form. There are flood/ark stories in the literature and mythology of other ancient Near East cultures. There are also flood motifs in the cultures of India, Greece, China and the Aboriginal religion of Australia.

It is therefore concluded here that the biblical writers of this part of Scripture chose to use weather imagery within a Flood story as a comprehensible and succinct way of expressing the mysterious events of the destruction and re-Creation of life. In the Bible, the Creation imagery used in Genesis 1 and 8 are both very powerful and remain eminently comprehensible down the centuries as an illustration of God's power.

The real ending of the Flood story

Before the Flood, in Ge 6:18, God made a covenant with Noah. This is the very first time a covenant is mentioned in the Bible and the concept of covenant is of great importance in biblical religions. A covenant is a solemn and binding agreement between two parties. In ancient times such agreements were often made orally and sworn before gods. The Hebrew word for covenant is *berit* and the meaning of this word is wide. A *berit* could be anything from a simple business agreement to a constitution for a country or a treaty between nations.

So God chose to use the *berit* to emphasise the solemnity of the agreement He was making with Noah. Noah was to carry out God's plans for a new Earthly beginning and, in return, it seemed that God would save him and his family from destruction. In fact this was only the starting-point of the covenant that God was offering.

When Noah finally left the Ark, he built an altar to the Lord God and, in the tradition of the day, made offerings upon it (Ge 8:20). God's reaction was impressive. He promised in His heart never again to impose punishment universally as He had just done. Also, (Ge 8:21) God now recognised the inevitability of evil within Man but promised to remain faithful despite it.

In v22, weather imagery is used to communicate this solemn vow in a poetical sense. God says He will be faithful through 'seedtime and harvest' (a reference to the seasons of agriculture), 'cold and heat, summer and winter, day and night'. This is an all-inclusive and comprehensive promise couched in the weather-associated terms that everyone could understand.

The expansion of the covenant promise that God made to Noah is detailed in Genesis 9. This is God's fourth and final divine command within the Flood story. The covenant promises great blessings and lasting peace. Noah and his sons are blessed and made fruitful (v1); this ensures the continuation of the human race. Reference to Ge 1:28 will reveal this to be a repeat of the blessings given at the Creation to Adam and Eve and all the other life God had made. Note that stewardship of the land is again emphasised in the words 'replenish the land', a message for which much of the humanity of today continues to have insufficient regard.

Ge 9:2 then gives Noah command over everything, an echo of same responsibility given to Adam and Eve (Ge 1:28). Most importantly, there is a repeat of the blessing of Man recognised as God's image (v6). Finally God promised that He would never again bring universal destruction upon the Earth (vv11-12), in confirmation of the vow made in Ge 8:21-22.

The demonstration of God's covenant with His people (all the descendants of Noah, including all mankind today) was to be the rainbow, that beautiful and strange bow of colour which is a miracle of our own skies. Once again, the culmination of the story is expressed in yet another feature of weather.

The rainbow

The rainbow is indeed a beautiful sight. The sky has been dark. The rain has poured down. Then the rain stops and sunshine breaks through. You look towards the black cloud that has passed over and there it is, a vivid rainbow set against the dark contrast of the sky. A glowing arc of banded colour containing – guess what? – 'All the colours of the rainbow'! It comes as no surprise that generations of mankind have looked at the rainbow in wonder and awe and remembered God's covenant from ancient times.

So what is it and how does it appear? It is an optical illusion. Every time each one of us sees a rainbow, we are seeing our own personal optical illusion! Scientifically, it is easy to discover that white light can be split into a complete colour spectrum. You may recall the physics experiment that you did at school when investigating the science of light. White light would be projected through a simple glass prism and the reflected light would emerge in 'all the colours of the rainbow'.

Even if you have not actually done that school experiment, you will have seen the same effect in your home when sunlight is impinges upon the edge of a mirror; the result is a display of the complete spectrum of colours. Outside, 'local' rainbows may be created by your garden sprinkler. Similar rainbow effects can often be seen in waterfalls or even in the spray thrown up by sea waves.

The dividing of a beam of white light into the spectrum of colours happens because each colour corresponds to a small range of wavelength within the visible spectrum of electromagnetic radiation. It is these very small differences in wavelength which result in a slightly different angle of refraction (bending). So when a beam of white light is shone through a glass prism, it is refracted and emanates as a fan of colour, starting with red light, which bends least and finishing with violet, which bends most. The complete colour spectrum starts with red, merging to orange, then yellow, green, blue, indigo and finally to violet.

All those colours come to our eyes as part of the electromagnetic radiation that we receive from any light source. If the wavelength of the radiation is within the visible spectrum of 0.4 to 0.7 microns (a micron is one-millionth of a metre) then our eyes recognise it as light. If the radiation is received in all wavelengths then we see white light. Otherwise we will see the colour or colours which correspond to the particular discrete wavelengths being transmitted or reflected.

If the wavelength is longer than 0.7 microns then the radiation is infrared and we may feel it as heat. If the wavelength is shorter than 0.4 microns then it is ultra-violet and it may burn our skin (sunburn). As the wavelength shortens further, they eventually become

Divine Weather / 85

X-rays and other forms of radiation that can be injurious to living cells.

The formation of a rainbow in the sky requires three elements to be present. Water droplets, the sun and you! The water droplets act as the prism to refract and split the light. The sun provides the light source. You are the receptor. Simply, the sun's rays shine on a raindrop, the light is refracted within it and split into the colour spectrum described previously. The colour spectrum is then reflected from the rear surface of the raindrop back towards the sun and the eyes of the observer.

The reflected light is transmitted from the raindrop in a cone shape that presents an angle of around 42 degrees to the sun. The most intense part of this light is concentrated at the edges of the cone. Thus an observer on the ground looking towards the raindrop and away from the sun will see a series of colour arcs with red as the outer arc and violet as the inner arc. The arc will be complete from horizon to horizon but may well be very faint if it is seen with a bright sky behind. The most intense arcs are seen against a dark sky. This 42-degree arc is known as the 'primary bow'.

Often, there will be a fainter 'secondary bow' outside the primary, with the colour sequence reversed. This describes an arc of 50 degrees approximately and is caused by a double reflection within the raindrop. The light spectrum does not emerge until it has been reflected twice within the raindrop. The secondary bow is also a complete arc but, because it is much fainter, it is often invisible against a bright sky.

The height of the arc that can be seen depends upon the angle of elevation that the sun presents to the observer. If the sun is very low in the sky it is possible to see an almost semicircular bow. If the sun is higher in the sky, less of the bow will be visible. Towards an elevation of 42 degrees, only a very small part of the arc can be seen. When the sun is elevated above 42 degrees, a primary rainbow cannot be seen at all. At ground level, it is never possible to see more than half an arc but it is possible to see a whole rainbow circle from a high-flying aircraft, if other conditions allow.

The intensity of each colour in a rainbow depends upon the size of the raindrops and the brightness of the light source. The largest raindrops produce the most brilliant bows with a distinct emphasis on red. As the drop size decreases, the brightest colour changes from red to orange and finally to white with tinges of colour at the edges. As the light source becomes weaker the colour spectrum becomes paler. It is possible for rainbows to be generated in moonlight but the human eye is incapable of distinguishing colour at low light levels. A moonlight rainbow is very faint and seen as a pale white arc.

The Rainbow Covenant

The establishment of the rainbow as a token and reminder of God's covenant with his people is an inspirational one. The rainbow is not only beautiful but it is to act as a reminder. Its presence signals that all rainstorms in the future will be brought to an end before they destroy the Earth. This is in accordance with God's promise to his people through the covenant, to be ever faithful despite all that happens. In addition, the ephemeral beauty of that weather phenomenon is an appropriate reminder to Mankind of the existence of God the Creator.

In Ge 9:13 the imagery is of God 'setting His bow in the cloud'. This is a new creation. Before this time, the implication is that the rainbow did not exist. God the Creator made the rainbow and arranged it to appear in the sky, set against the clouds, so that its full beauty could be seen. He wished to make use of the rainbow as a periodic reminder of the covenant He had made with 'the Earth' (v13). This is an especially significant promise, because it extends the covenant to all people. This promise is positively reinforced in v15, when God says 'And I will remember my covenant, which is between me and you *and every living creature of all flesh*'. Thus the covenant made initially with Noah has now been extended to all life.

It is important to remember that covenants are solemn agreements between two parties. God's position has been made abundantly clear in the writings of Genesis 9 and the rainbow has been established for His use. However, mankind (through Noah) has also agreed to the covenant and therefore the rainbow reminder has also been established for man. The sight of the rainbow should always remind mankind of the existence and beneficence of God the Creator. In addition, the responsibilities of mankind should be remembered, particularly those relating to Earth stewardship in the broadest sense.

6

Moses: from Birth to Red Sea

Moses is a renowned Biblical character from the Old Testament, famous for what happened to him as a baby and then as a great leader of the Israelite people. He makes his appearance in Exodus, the second book of the Old Testament, and then proceeds to dominate the following three books, Leviticus, Numbers and Deuteronomy. Although there is weather imagery to be found in every one of these books, the major stories involving weather are found in Exodus.

The book of Exodus

Essentially, Exodus is the story of the birth of the Israelite people. At the beginning of Exodus, the Hebrew tribes had been settled in Egypt for some time in an area just to the east of the Nile delta (Goshen). The tribes had a long and good relationship with the king of Egypt (the pharaoh) and they had prospered greatly, becoming numerous, successful and well off. Then the political climate changed abruptly!

Egypt acquired a new pharaoh whose attitude to the Hebrews was completely different from that of his predecessor. He regarded them as a serious threat to his own power base and determined to remove this danger as quickly as possible. He sent his army to capture all the Hebrews and make them his slaves. All their possessions were confiscated. However, even as slaves, the Hebrew numbers continued to increase and when this was brought to Pharaoh's attention, he issued a terrible decree. He ordered that all male babies born to the tribe were to be killed at birth by throwing them into the River Nile (Exodus 1).

Moses: Birth, boyhood and exile

It was into this climate that the baby Moses was born. After a hazardous three-month period of concealment, his mother knew she could not keep her secret any longer. To give her beloved son a fair chance of survival, she made his basket crib waterproof – the AV Bible describes this modified crib as an 'ark' (Ex 2:3). He was placed in the crib (the very first Moses basket!) and it was floated carefully among the reeds on the bank of the River Nile. By good fortune, the basket was found by Pharaoh's daughter who was filled with compassion and wished to save the child. With the help of Moses' sister, who had kept watch to see what would happen, Moses' mother was employed secretly as a royal maidservant. So the child was looked after by his own mother in safety and security.

When Moses grew up, even although he became the adopted son of Pharaoh's daughter, his sympathies were always with his own people. As a young man, when he came upon an Egyptian overseer mistreating a Hebrew slave, he killed the Egyptian. His crime was discovered and, as a result, he had to flee into exile. Moses fled eastwards to the land inhabited by the Midianite people and settled there for many years. However God had not forgotten him. Eventually, God appeared to Moses and directed him to return to Egypt to lead the Children of Israel out of slavery (Exodus 3-4).

The return of Moses and the Ten Plagues

As instructed, Moses returned to Egypt and became the leader of the Israelites. He tried very hard to obey God's command to lead his people out of slavery but, for a long time, this proved impossible. Despite Moses' eloquent pleas to 'let my people go', Pharaoh proved to be extremely intransigent! He refused on every occasion. Moses sought God's help and the Lord arranged a series of 'persuasions' for Pharaoh. These took the form of various catastrophic disasters (plagues) which were imposed upon the land, the animals and the people of Egypt.

The story of the disasters is a repeating sequence of events. Each time, Pharaoh is told by Moses what will happen and is given the chance to release the Israelites from slavery to save the country from a particular disaster. Each time Pharaoh refuses and the plague is delivered. In the midst of the suffering that results, Pharaoh capitulates and calls for the plague to be removed. When this is done Pharaoh changes his mind and refuses to release the Israelites!

As this sequence continues, a subtle difference is introduced into Pharaoh's changes of mind. On the first seven occasions, we read that Pharaoh *hardened his heart* and so went back on his promise. Thereafter, we read *God hardened Pharaoh's heart;* the last three plagues were an additional punishment from God for Pharaoh's continuing dishonesty. This emphasised that God was totally in control. It may be that the control was not a positive intervention to *harden* Pharaoh's heart but an act of non-intervention; that is, God did not act to *soften* Pharaoh's heart.

Several of the plague stories introduce significant weather imagery. The first six disasters, turning the Nile to blood, (Exodus 7), plagues of frogs, gnats, flies, pestilence (fatal epidemic diseases) and fever boils (Exodus 8,9) are apparently not associated with weather. However, closer examination reveals some contributing connections.

Several Biblical studies have suggested that the waters of the Nile were red because of sand in suspension. Heavy and prolonged rainfall upstream would result in flooding of the plains and delta, with a swollen and sand-polluted river flowing rapidly towards the sea. Such an explanation is possible but sand does not poison the water. Filtering or leaving it to stand would remove a good deal of the sand and render it fit to drink.

Another suggestion has the water poisoned by red algae. This would imply a different sort of weather involvement, since calm, hot and humid conditions would be required for the growth of the algae. Likewise, the following plagues of insects (the gnats and flies) are usually associated with a similar type of hot and humid weather, providing conditions suitable for explosive insect population growth.

A third suggestion has the fish of the Nile killed by a flesh-eating micro-organism. This made the fish bleed and turn the water red – literally to blood. It seems unlikely that the quantities of blood released from the dying fish would be sufficient to pollute the running waters of the Nile to the degree suggested.

Of these three propositions, the second seems the most likely and these conditions could also be responsible for the plagues involving insects and disease. In north-eastern Egypt, the persistence of such humid conditions for an extended period is highly unlikely but they could occur periodically; the biblical account could accord with this since there is a time gap (unspecified) between each plague.

The seventh to the ninth disasters are directly associated with weather. The seventh was hail, a severe weather phenomenon. The eighth was a plague of locusts, brought in and later removed by the action of wind. The ninth was total darkness throughout the day the night for three days.

Plague Number 7: The very grievous hail

Hail is one of the more extreme manifestations of the weather and we have already touched on the subject in an explanation of 'rain' and 'showers' in Chapter 2. The fierce rattle of hailstones against your windowpane is invariably a startling event. A look outside at solid pellets of ice

92 / Moses: from Birth to Red Sea

bouncing high from the ground makes you glad you are not outside. Most of us have had the experience of stinging hail lashing against our hands and faces – enough to make us run for the nearest cover as fast as we could!

But hail can of course be much worse than a period of minor inconvenience. Plant life frequently suffers from the effect of an ice pellet bombardment and those fragile spring plants, just at that tender budding stage, can be totally destroyed. Larger hailstones can not only destroy tender plants but will leave their mark upon more mature plants, small and large. Other fragile materials can suffer too; roof tiles, panes of glass or even the bodywork of your favourite car that you wish you had parked in the garage!

Extreme hailstorms can leave you with seriously shredded and broken plant life, shattered glass and heavily pockmarked surfaces. For those in weather sensitive industries, perhaps especially those involved with commercial growing, a short period of heavy hail can mean the total destruction of a crop with heavy financial loss.

In addition to growing large as individual pseudo-spheres of ice, hailstones can clump together into irregular chunks; these have been reported as large as 13cm, 5in in diameter! Such missiles falling from the sky can be extremely frightening as well as highly damaging. The layers of ice left upon the ground bring an additional hazard.

The storms of hail, lightning and thunder

If we feel grateful to be indoors when we see hail, we are probably doubly grateful when the hail is part of a heavy thunderstorm! It is then that the weather seems exceptionally fierce. Dark, dense clouds, strong turbulent gusting winds, lashing hail and, periodically, those terrifying flashes of high intensity electricity, following by deafening thunder claps. Our fear of these elements is justified, because we know that it is possible to be struck by lightning; unfortunately, many people have been injured or killed in this way.

From the biblical description in Ex 9:23-35, it is certain that the hailstorms were very heavy ones indeed. V24 designates it as an exceptional 'never-seen-before' type of weather event. It was reported to affect all the cultivated land of the Egyptians; this would be concentrated mainly in the Nile delta, the coastal areas to the west and, to a lesser degree, along the River Nile to the south. There would be few attempts at cultivation in areas away from a plentiful source of water, although some inland oases may have allowed limited crop growing. From the description of the crops, the time of year was within the spring. Transition months. Significantly, the hailstorm did not affect the land of Goshen, the area occupied by the Israelites.

Ex 9:23-24 links the hail with thunder and 'fire'. It is certain that the fire is a reference to lightning, since it is impossible to have thunder without lightning. It is unsurprising that severe hailstorms should also be accompanied by lightning and thunder since these phenomena are always produced in association with cumulonimbus clouds. The existence of lightning brings additional dangers of fire and electrocution to the situation.

Firstly, (v25) the hail destroyed all 'herbs' and broke bushes and trees. The word 'herbs' is translated in most Bible versions as 'all plants' or 'all growing things'; in the AV, a whole range of small food plants are often described as herbs. The Bible texts state that animals and people were also affected and there is the implication of injury, although this is not stated explicitly. As the storms continue, the early crops of flax and barley were destroyed (v31) since they were at the tender budding stage. Of course these are significant crops for food and clothing materials and their loss would be serious for the Egyptians. However, the main summer harvest crops of wheat and rye (many translations call this 'smelt') were unaffected because they had not yet sprouted.

Spring-time weather in Egypt

Egypt normally experiences some bursts of precipitation in the spring transition months, usually of a heavy and convective nature. Statistically, the Mediterranean coast receives significantly more rainfall than areas away from a narrow coastal strip. Current coastal statistics suggest that up to 25mm (1.0in) of heavy rain may fall in these months while adjacent inland areas may only have one third or a quarter of that. However, the inland rainfall will almost always be received as heavy precipitation, delivered from clouds well capable of generating hail.

The heaviest of these hailstorms needs to be associated with very large convective clouds, generated in an atmosphere of considerable instability. Such large clouds can produce an extensive period of precipitation. Ex 9:25 states that the hail was 'throughout the Land of Egypt'; this is likely to refer to the main cultivated areas already defined. It is possible for a large area of cumulonimbus clouds to move slowly over these areas, depositing very heavy precipitation everywhere.

Hail formation

Hail is a type of precipitation that forms in freezing clouds where there are very strong upcurrents; such currents are invariably convective in nature – that is, they are thermally driven. Scientifically, the development of convective precipitation requires an 'unstable' atmosphere and a very unstable atmosphere is a prerequisite for hail. Meteorologists are able to define the atmosphere as 'stable' or 'unstable' by sampling the vertical temperature and humidity environment at a particular time and area.

This information is often acquired by releasing a large buoyant balloon with a radio-equipped instrument package attached to it. The instruments return readings of temperature, pressure and humidity as they are carried to high levels through the atmosphere. Meteorological satellites can also provide similar information by downward-sampling techniques, though this information is rather less precise. The profiles that may be constructed from this information allow the meteorologist to judge the degree of stability or instability of particular atmospheric samples.

We have already discussed the fact that the atmosphere cools with height due to decreasing air pressure. However there are variations in the actual temperature structure of each sample of atmosphere as a result of a previous cumulation of processes. When a new sample of air rises, either by heating or mechanical lifting (by a frontal surface or a mountain), it cools because of pressure decrease; then, if the lifted air is still warmer (less dense) than the surrounding environment, it will continue to rise spontaneously. If the difference in temperature is significant, the air will rise rapidly. This process will continue at least until the rising air reaches the same temperature as its environment, by which time it may well have risen rapidly to very high levels.

At some point, the rising air may become 'saturated' (unable to hold its water vapour invisibly) and condensation will occur, forming cloud. This process will release latent heat (the energy involved in change of state) and this in turn helps to keep the rising air warmer than the surrounding environment. Precipitation formation processes then come into play. This is a simple description of convection taking place but the condensation and precipitation processes are rather more complex than the above would imply.

For condensation to occur, it is necessary for 'condensation nuclei' to be present in sufficient quantities. These are minute suspended particles in the atmosphere, often originating from dust-storms, sandstorms, volcanic eruptions and sea salt. As the air continues to rise, it will cool below freezing point at some level. For ice crystals to form, 'freezing nuclei' need to be present and they are much less plentiful than condensation nuclei. Because of this, sub-zero temperature clouds often contain large amounts of 'supercooled' water droplets; these are droplets whose temperature is well below freezing but they remain in the liquid state.

When supercooled water droplets and ice crystals collide as a result of the air currents within the clouds, the supercooled water freezes on to the ice and so the ice crystals grow larger. In the active convective clouds where hail forms, there are large amounts of supercooled water droplets, so the ice crystals grow rapidly and form hailstones. For a time the upcurrents within the cloud are strong enough to keep forming hailstones suspended. Finally, they either become too heavy to be supported by the upcurrents or are transported to an area of the cloud where the upcurrents are weaker. One way or another, the hailstones fall from the cloud. Cumulonimbus clouds often develop strong downcurrents of air adjacent to the cloud. Hail falling into these areas will be driven to the ground with additional violence.

As previously stated, hailstorm processes normally take place within cumulonimbus clouds which are the largest and most active of the convective clouds, often extending from a few thousand feet to forty or even fifty thousand feet high. If they have been formed from simple convection, they are very large but separate clouds, with areas of clear sky in between. This is when you can see them most clearly as a huge puffy cloud often with a striated anvil shape protruding from the top. The anvil is the part of the cloud that consists entirely of ice crystals.

Cumulonimbus clouds can also form in association with other weather features. Sometimes they are embedded in the structure of an active cold front or in an area where mass uplift is taking place. This may be within a line (a convergence trough) or in a large area of strong ascent in which a number of cumulonimbus clouds are embedded (a supercell). These situations can cause the most severe weather since the upcurrents will be augmented and the activity prolonged.

Lightning and thunder

It is surprising that we talk about 'thunder and lightning' when in fact the correct chronological order is as shown in the sub-title! Although lightning is not mentioned in the biblical text we are examining, it is certain that it had to be present, since thunder cannot exist without lightning. The sequence of events comprises a huge electrical discharge that causes an explosive expansion of the air along its path. The path may be within the cloud or between cloud and atmosphere or ground. This explosive expansion generates a strong sound wave which travels through the atmosphere in all directions, weakening rapidly as it does so. The speed of light (electromagnetic radiation) is very much faster than that of sound, so invariably we see the flash and then hear the thunder afterwards.

A rough idea of the distance you are from the lightning discharge can be gained if you count the time between the lightning flash and the thunderclap. The number of seconds divided by three gives the distance in kilometres; divide by five to obtain the measurement in miles. A discharge that occurs nearby will produce a very loud and almost instantaneous thunderclap; thunder from more distant discharges becomes progressively fainter and those that occur over 20km (12.5mi) away are likely to be inaudible. This is why we see lightning flashes and hear no thunderclap, especially in the darkness of night.

There is always electrical activity in the atmosphere. It is part of nature and it is part of life itself. The combination of turbulent motions within cumulonimbus clouds and the physical processes involving water and ice are responsible for increasing atmospheric electrical activity. The outcome is a concentration of atmospheric electrical potential of opposite polarity within and around the cumulonimbus cloud.

Because there are considerable variations in the makeup of thunderstorms, it has not been possible to formulate a single model that explains every lightning generation event. It is known that most thunderstorm clouds build a negative charge near the cloud base and a positive charge at the top. The surrounding atmosphere builds a charge of opposite polarity; the ground beneath becomes positively charged. When the potential difference becomes sufficiently large (many millions of volts) it eventually discharges along an ionised atmospheric path. This forms the lightning we see within the cloud, between the cloud and the atmosphere or between the cloud and the ground.

People have defined many types of lightning, of which 'sheet' and 'forked' are probably the most common. Sheet lightning is a discharge within the cloud or one that is obscured by a cloud, so it appears as a very bright but diffuse light. Forked lightning is from the cloud to the atmosphere or to the ground and the path of the discharge is clearly seen. References are also made to 'chain, ribbon, streak, pearl necklace or ball' lightning; each of these is a description of their appearance. Ball lightning is particularly interesting because this could be what is described in Ex 9:23 '...and fire ran along the ground'.

Ball lightning is a rare phenomenon that nevertheless is reported periodically. It is a form of lightning in which the discharge somehow produces a slowly moving luminous ball of electrical energy which moves with a floating motion, often quite close to the ground. The ball usually decays and disappears after a time but sometimes it explodes. There are many theories about the formation of this type of lightning but its formation and maintenance remains a mystery.

In Ex 9:23, the presence of ball lightning (if indeed that is what it was) would be extremely frightening and potentially very dangerous. Lightning, thunder and hail are certainly several of the most violent and frightening manifestations of our planet's weather. There have been many occasions when lightning strikes (cloud to ground) have caused considerable damage, injury and loss of life by fire and electrocution.

Pharaoh's seventh promise broken

This account of the seventh plague is an extremely powerful description of very severe weather conditions affecting Egypt. The writers of Exodus had no doubt experienced the power of the hail and thunderstorms that occasionally affected this area and so could envisage such an event as a punishment of God. Their readers would have had the same experience of the power of the weather and are likely to have seen crop destruction by hail. Doubtless, people or animals had been struck by lightning; it is certain this would be regarded as the hand of God. A combination of danger, destruction and possible death is indeed a most powerful messenger.

As the biblical storms continue, there is yet another dialogue between Moses and Pharaoh, who once again promised to let the Israelites go in return for relief from this particular 'plague' (Ex 9:27-30). Moses agreed and carried out his part of the bargain by praying to the Lord outside the city (v33). Once Pharaoh saw that the storms had gone, he went back on his word, just as he had done six times before and this then leads on to the imposition of the next plague.

Plague Number 8: The locusts

Anyone with a garden knows the havoc which insect pests can wreak on flowers and vegetables. Where insect numbers are high, serious plant destruction can take place. This is what happens with the locust, though this large and destructive insect is in a class of its own! The Bible uses the locust many times to indicate total plant destruction and desolation of the land.

Locusts are large voracious insects from the grasshopper family. They are migratory in behaviour and band together in huge swarms. As they cross the land, they strip all plant life bare. This is done at devastating speed. As they continue on their path of destruction, they breed and leave eggs. When the grubs hatch, they ensure that any remaining plant life is destroyed. Thus an area visited by a swarm of locusts becomes totally stripped and barren. The arrival of locusts is indeed a devastating event for the people of the area because it means the total loss of all crops and vegetation.

The arrival of the locusts

Exodus 10 begins by Pharaoh being warned of the impending plague of locusts. Ex 10:1-11 is unequivocal! God will bring swarms of locusts and they will eat the crops that had earlier escaped the hail, namely the wheat and rye, along with any other plant life and vegetation that remains. Although Pharaoh's servants tried to persuade him to acquiesce, he was his usual intransigent self once again!

As promised, the swarms of locusts duly arrive, carried upon the east wind (Ex 10:13). Without this wind, it is unlikely that the insects would have arrived; entomologists recognise that migratory insects fly in the first few thousand feet of the atmosphere and depend on wind currents to make significant progress. So the imposition of the east wind was an essential for the insect swarm to arrive.

The east wind means that the air in the lower atmosphere flowed across northern parts of Arabia and the Red Sea. Locusts live in hot dry lands but true desert regions would not provide sufficient food for the survival of a large population. The eastern shores of the Red Sea would be able to support some locust colonies but it is likely that very large concentrations of the insects would need to be located in the more fertile areas further east. This may suggest the areas to the west and north of the Persian Gulf.

Such areas are a considerable distance away (around 1200km, 750mi) and therefore the east wind would need to be consistently strong enough to carry the flying insects a considerable distance in one day. Assuming that the insect swarm would only fly for a total of 12 hours in the day, a wind of 60kph (38mph) in the low atmosphere would carry the insect swarm a distance of 720km. This could be increased to 800km by a personal contribution from the insects themselves. So it is clear that locust swarms could travel a considerable distance in a short period of time, with the assistance of the wind. With very strong winds, it is possible that a swarm could travel from fertile Tigris/Euphrates basin to the Nile within a day.

Easterly winds of 60kph at two or three thousand feet are most certainly possible in this area. Early summer brings weak low pressure areas to the desert regions while high pressure can often be a feature of areas further north. This generates an easterly wind flow over northern Arabia and northeast Egypt. Additionally, smaller scale weather disturbances generated by extreme temperature differentials over desert areas can boost the wind significantly. These developments produce much stronger winds that can sometimes persist for extended periods.

The locusts are removed

When Pharaoh capitulated yet again (Ex 10:16-19) a 'strong west wind' was produced which bore the locusts away and 'cast them into the Red Sea'. The most likely meteorological situation that would produce this sort of wind is an active low pressure area over the eastern Mediterranean, close to the Egyptian coast. This is possible in the early summer season although the likelihood decreases as high summer approaches. The situation is usually engendered by a plunge of cold air southwards over Europe at medium and high levels. This results in a low pressure development at low levels and, when the plunge of cold air extends to the Mediterranean, the contribution of the relatively warm waters deepens the low, sometimes dramatically.

In Ex 10:19, it is implied that the west wind was swiftly imposed. Meteorologically, it may be assumed that the strong east winds had decreased and the situation over Egypt was relatively quiescent as the locusts went about their business of destruction. In this situation, there is no reason why the west wind should not arrive quite suddenly. As the locust swarms rose from the destroyed and barren land, they would be carried away to the east and their removal from Egypt would be complete.

God uses the natural forces of nature

In his direct use of insects and wind, God enlisted the natural forces of nature that he had created. Both elements of this plague would be familiar to the readers of Exodus and the punishment would be fully understood. The suggestion that the locust swarms were 'cast into the Red Sea' is an added dramatisation that emphasises the positiveness of God's action and his power over all life.

The use of wind as a part of weather has an additional meaning. It links to that concept of *ruach*, that mysterious Hebrew word which means wind, air, breath, spirit, life force and which was linked positively to God the Creator in Ge 1:2 (discussion in Chapter 3).

Plague Number 9: The thick darkness

The disobedience of Pharaoh is repeated. Once again he goes back on his word and so the ninth plague was imposed upon that unfortunate land. The 'thick darkness' covered all the land (Ex 10:22). As described, this darkness was complete. We have already discussed the effect of total darkness upon Mankind (Chapter 3). In darkness, our principal information gathering sense is made useless and this lack of sight brings a primeval fear. Darkness is linked with the unknown and with evil. Darkness was the state of the world before the Creation (Ge 1:2).

The image here in Exodus 10 is one of total darkness for three whole days. During this time, the Egyptian people had no access to light of any type, either natural or artificial. This complete lack of light would have been absolutely terrifying for the people. They were paralysed where they were, afraid to move for fear of what may happen to them in the unknown void around them. Meanwhile, God protected the Israelites by giving them light inside their houses (v23).

Mechanisms for the 'thick darkness'

Some Bible commentaries suggest that God imposed the 'thick darkness which may even be felt' (v21) by means of a severe sandstorm. Severe sandstorms occur in northeast Egypt when a weather development generates very strong surface winds that blow from the desert. Large quantities of sand are picked up and spread through the atmosphere to a depth of many thousands of feet. Areas affected by such sandstorms experience extremely dry heat, strong turbulent winds and stinging, choking sand that penetrates everywhere. Visibility can be reduced to a few metres in the most severe cases. The thickly polluted atmosphere makes breathing difficult for man and beast.

Although such conditions are extremely unpleasant and potentially damaging to structure and health, daytime conditions would not be completely dark. Even if a thick layer of cloud overlaid the sand-polluted lower atmosphere, very weak light from the sun would still penetrate through, providing dim daylight. It is reasoned therefore, that the 'thick darkness' could not have been caused by natural weather conditions. The same comments apply to other forms of pollution – smoke, volcanic dust; these would not obscure daylight totally.

The only other natural phenomenon that can cause day darkness is a total solar eclipse but this can be quickly rejected. Solar eclipses occur when the moon is interposed between Earth and sun. At such times an area of shadow is cast on the Earth's surface. Anyone within this area will have the disc of the sun totally obscured by the physical presence of the moon. However such darkness is far from complete because the sun's corona still provides reflected light, albeit weak. Continued planetary movements mean that total solar eclipses last for a maximum of 7½ minutes.

Therefore it is proposed that the total darkness of the ninth plague cannot be explained by any natural occurrence and so it must be judged as an inexplicable event, one in which the Lord God withdrew the light of day from the land of Egypt for three days. However, there is more. The passage clearly states that the Egyptians did not have light within their houses (unlike the Israelites). In other words, the Egyptian people were struck physically blind; lighting their house lamps or fires produced no light. The writers of this account emphasised the horror of the situation for the people of Egypt, totally paralysed with fear. Filled with terror and dread, they remained immovable, not daring to investigate the unknown and unseen space around them.

The 'thick darkness' as described was actually a double imposition. There was a total absence of normal daylight; this affected the Israelites as well as the Egyptians. The Israelites were saved from the terror of the situation by being given light – but only inside their houses. Outside remained totally and absolutely dark.

The emphasis here is once again the total control that God has over His world and all life upon it. The components of this double imposition showed God's control over the elements of the physical world and also over the senses of every person in it.

Divine Weather / 105

The Tenth Plague and the release from slavery

The final disaster (which did not involve weather concepts) was the death of all firstborns, a 'plague' to be imposed on all of Egypt, human and animal. This is the origin of the Jewish 'Passover'; God instructed Moses to prepare the Israelite people in a number of very special ways. On a certain night, they were to stay in their houses and partake of a ritual feast that included the killing, cooking and eating of an unblemished lamb. The blood of the lamb was to be smeared on the doorposts of their houses and this sign would be recognised by God when He came to kill all firstborn life in Egypt at the hour of midnight. Because of the blood signs, the Lord would recognise the Israelite households 'pass over' them, not harming anyone within. The Passover is of course a Jewish festival of thanksgiving that is celebrated today.

So the familiar sequence of events was repeated a tenth time as Pharaoh was warned about the forthcoming plague and invited to capitulate (Exodus 11). When he refused, the plague was duly delivered (Ex 12:29-30) and there was death in every Egyptian household. The people were immediately thrown into great grief and panic, for they feared that the cycle of death would be repeated. As predicted by God, Pharaoh now sent the Israelites away in great haste and the Egyptian people loaded them with gifts as expiation. The Israelites were free at last – apparently! The 'exodus' of an estimated 600,000 Israelites to the 'Promised Land' began.

In Ex 13:17, God directed that the Israelites should not attempt the direct route near the Mediterranean coast, but should travel to through 'the way of the wilderness of the Red sea (sic)' (Ex 13:18). So the Israelite people began their journey by travelling south to Succoth and then turned to encamp 'before Pihahiroth, between Migdol and the sea, over against Baalzephon' (Ex 14:2).

The Red Sea crossing

It will come as no surprise to learn that Pharaoh now changed his mind about releasing the Israelites! He called for his army and a great pursuit began, with many thousands of soldiers, horses and chariots. The mighty army soon caught up with the Israelites encamped 'beside Pihahiroth' (Ex 14:9). It was adjacent to this area that the famous 'Red Sea' crossing was made.

At the sight of Pharaoh's great army, the Israelites were greatly afraid and berated Moses for bringing them to die at this place (Ex 14:11-12). In reply, Moses assured them that God would look after them and save them; he then prayed to God for guidance (vv13-15). God's guidance resulted in the very famous story of the division of the waters of the Red Sea (vv16-31). The Israelites walked across the dry seabed to safety. The following Egyptian soldiers were all drowned when the divided waters were released and crashed back into place. It is a story of great drama, presenting us with a saving, powerful yet loving image of the Lord God towards His chosen people. Equally, it presents an awesome image of the destroying power of God, applied to those who plan harm to His people.

Weather and the Red Sea crossing

Weather imagery is much involved with the saving miracle of the Red Sea crossing. Firstly, the view of the Egyptian army was obscured by a 'pillar of cloud' (Ex 14:19). This pillar of cloud was associated with 'the angel of God' who had accompanied the Israelites on their journey. The cloud was darkness to the Egyptian army but provided light for the Israelites. Cloud imagery is used a great deal throughout the Bible for a great many purposes. God then empowered Moses to divide the sea and we read that the division mechanism was 'a strong east wind'.

The use of the east wind is significant here. Throughout Scripture, the east wind is associated with negative power. In north-east Egypt and in the eastern Mediterranean lands as a whole, the east wind comes from desert or mountain regions. Therefore it will be dry, very hot in summer and very cold in winter; an arid withering wind whatever the season. As we will see from other texts, the east wind is often associated with crop destruction. Even though west winds can be strong, they are inevitably more balmy as a result of their association with the Mediterranean Sea.

Turning now to the division of the water as described, it is true that a flow of atmospheric wind over a water surface interacts with it and there are energy exchanges. Some of the wind energy is transferred to the water and this sets up wave motions there. However a low level atmospheric wind, even one of hurricane force, could not divide water and maintain the division as described in Ex 15:21. It is possible to create this effect in a very small way by pointing a very powerful and concentrated jet of air (like that from a compressed air hose) obliquely at a shallow water surface. The resulting water division is minor, unreliable and unsustainable.

The biblical image is of walls of water to the left and to the right (v22) as the Israelites walked through; a jet of air powerful enough to create and maintain such a water division could certainly not have been walked through! Once again, acceptance of the division of the waters as it is written in the AV could only be explained by the involvement of the inexplicable power of God. However, there is another explanation.

The location of the crossing

Throughout Scripture, there are many occasions when science and theology fail to explain the events described. Despite painstaking examination from various points of view, explanations remain theories and these are often at

Map 3: Possible routes of the Exodus

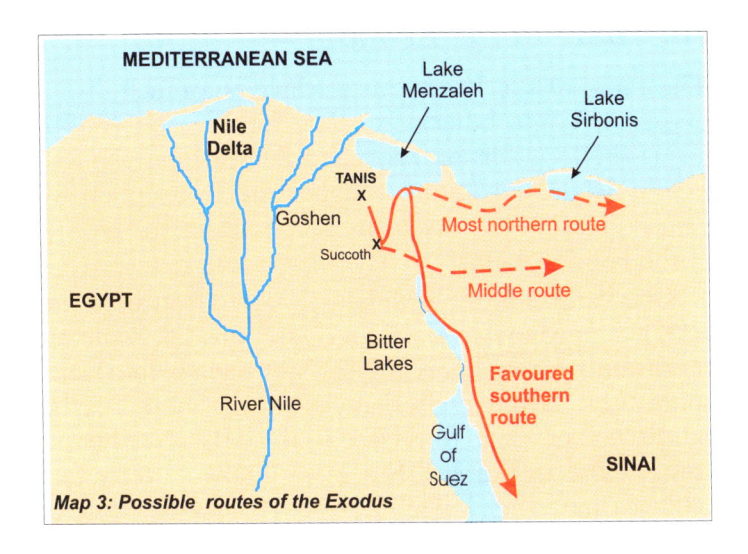

variance with each other. The Red Sea crossing is something of an exception, because biblical scholars generally accept that there has been a mistranslation of the Hebrew texts.

Some time ago, it was noted that the Hebrew words *Yam Suph* had been translated by the writers of the Septuagint (the Greek translation of the Old Testament) as the 'Red Sea'. In fact the literal meaning of *Yam Suph* is 'Sea of Reeds'. Most studies into this part of Scripture now accept that the 'Red Sea' of Ex 13:18, 15:4 and 15:22 is actually the 'Reed Sea'. This alters earlier perceptions of the route of the Exodus, which clearly involved a dramatic 'Red Sea' crossing.

The long-standing tradition that the Exodus was across the Red Sea may then be mistaken – this anomaly is explained in all modern Bible commentaries. Some Bible versions either explain the error in a footnote (e.g. Good News Bible) or correct the text from 'Red Sea' to 'Sea of Reeds' (e.g. Jerusalem Bible). The crossing of the 'Reed Sea' presents a series of different factors that require new consideration.

Divine Weather / 109

The route of the Exodus

The route of the Exodus as a whole is a much-disputed question. While biblical scholars seem to be confident about the locations of Tanis and Succoth, no one knows exactly where Pihahiroth, Migdol and Baalzephon were. Consequently there are many proposals for the early part of the Exodus route.

One version of the generally favoured 'southern' route is shown in Map 3 as a solid red line; this takes the route northwards to the shores of Lake Menzaleh before heading south. Less favoured alternatives are the more 'northern' routes, one of which runs close to the coast. Neither route comes close to the Red Sea as we know it today but in biblical times, the Gulf of Suez was probably referred to as the Red Sea. It is notable that none of the proposed routes actually involves a crossing of the Red Sea. Indeed it would hardly be logical for the Israelites to place themselves on the western side of the Gulf of Suez. The logistics of transporting an estimated 600,000 people and their animals across several kilometres of water would be enormous.

Some studies have suggested that the Sea of Reeds was the marshy southern part of Lake Menzaleh; others have suggested a location near the Bitter Lakes. A third proposition accepts an alternative translation of *Yam Suph* as 'Sea of Termination'. This may locate the Sea of Reeds in the marshes of Lake Sirbonis; in this case the Exodus would be following the most northern route.

In any event, a change from the Red Sea to the Sea of Reeds implies a different sort of crossing. The Red Sea (as described) consisted of deep water. By definition, a sea of reeds is a marshy area with shallow water. With God's help, the Israelites were able to cross dry-shod and safely across the Sea of Reeds while the pursuing Egyptian army were drowned.

It is easy to envisage that the Egyptian army would be physically much heavier than the Israelites. There would be heavy war-horses, chariots, soldiers laden with equipment, cumbersome supply wagons and all the weighty paraphernalia of a fighting army on the move. With the help of the Lord God, the Israelites would be guided across the solid parts of the marshes; this may be the meaning of Ex 14:16. The pillar of cloud obscured the view of the Egyptians (v19) and so they could not take note of the safe route. When the Egyptians followed, God made sure that they were guided into the most dangerous parts and so they sank into the waters and drowned.

This explanation is not totally satisfactory, however. It ignores the imagery of the dividing of the waters by the east wind. It ignores the 'walls of water' (Ex 14:22). Although the previous analysis of these matters must remain, there is one other weather fact that should be considered. If the crossing were on Lake Menzaleh (or Lake Sirbonis), the Sea of Reeds would be affected by Mediterranean tidal variations.

Although the tidal range in the Mediterranean Sea is small (because the Sea is almost sealed by the narrow and shallow Straits of Gibraltar), it is still significant. On the Egyptian Mediterranean coast, a tidal range of 0.3 to 0.5m currently occurs and so the very flat area of coastal marshland would experience water level changes on a tidal schedule (approximately 6½ hours from low to high tide). Furthermore, the tidal flow across the very flat area would be rapid and this would be further enhanced if there had been a strong north or northwest surface wind across the Eastern Mediterranean; the wind would have generated significant waves that would roll quickly across the marsh area.

Thus a journey across a southern Mediterranean sea of reeds at low tide may be relatively dry underfoot whereas the same journey six hours later near the time of high tide would present a flooded and stormy area with a significant

Divine Weather / 111

depth of water. Additionally, at the time of maximum tidal influx, the rapid inland flow combined with the waves could well have been observed as a 'wall of water'. This would certainly occur if there was a flow into a narrowing inlet, producing a tidal 'bore' of nearly vertical water. This is a common phenomenon in many parts of the world.

The addition of these tidal and sea wave considerations may provide an explanation that is more aligned with the biblical text. The explanation supports the location of the Sea of Reeds on the southern coastal area of the Mediterranean Sea; the tidal argument would not apply if the Sea of Reeds were in the Bitter Lakes area where there would be no tidal flow.

Whatever the truth, the Sea of Reeds realisation does not alter the saving and loving image of God for His chosen people. However it does alter the details of the drama. Instead of the walls of water, much beloved of the special effects departments of epic film productions, there is the image of God guiding His people lovingly through a very dangerous part of their journey, placing their feet on the safe and solid paths of the Sea of Reeds area. When their enemies attempted to follow, the physical conditions had changed and God's guidance led the army and their equipment to the deepest and rapidly flooding parts of the marshes, where they perished.

The message remains clear. God nurtures and protects His people through all adversity, using His control of both natural and unknown forces. Likewise, those who are His enemies and the enemies of His chosen people are destroyed by those same forces.

7

Elijah, Ezekiel and Jonah

Many of the prophets found in the Old Testament have links with weather accounts or imagery. The three prophets who are the subject of this chapter have been chosen because they are associated with some well-known events which include weather; this continues the theme of the previous chapters. The sections below will not present an exhaustive examination of all the weather imagery that is to be found in the words and lives of these prophets but concentrate on a few major events. All the other weather references involving these three prophets will be recognised in later chapters.

Elijah

Elijah was an important Old Testament prophet whose major activities were linked to highly dramatic weather events, not least his eventual departure in the middle of a whirlwind! His story appears in a rather brief section of the Bible, in only 8 chapters from 1Ki 17:1 to his dramatic departure in 2Ki 2:11. He is generally thought to have been the most important prophet in the Northern Kingdom around the mid-9th century BC. Elijah is one of a handful of significant prophets whose life is not described in a Biblical book named after him.

At the time of Elijah, the country was ruled by the evil and very powerful King Ahab. His wife, the infamous Jezebel, had influenced the king to reject the God of Israel and adopt Baal worship, based on pagan gods of fertility and nature. It was believed that worship and sacrifice to the god Baal would, *inter alia*, ensure essential rains for the area, a crucial factor for the health and economic prosperity of the country.

The name Elijah is very much a description of the prophet's personal position – a sort of constant advertisement! A Hebrew translation of the name Elijah is 'my God is Yahweh'. Yahweh is a pronounceable version of the personal name of the God of Israel 'YHWH'. Elijah was a devout and active servant of the Lord God who was surrounded by what he regarded as the abomination of Baal worship. Thus he came to be in a fierce religious struggle with King Ahab.

The prophecy of drought

This story focuses upon that essential rain. In 1Ki 17:1, Elijah speaks to King Ahab and prophesies that there will be a total drought across the land for several years. Scripture suggests that this conversation took place in the city of Samaria, a lavish royal city built on the plain about 30km inland from the sea.

Two direct weather words were used by the prophet – '…there shall not be *dew* or *rain*'. The complete lack of both these sources of atmospheric water means that the land would dry up very quickly; food crops would not survive and natural vegetation would also wither and die. Drinking water for animals and people would decrease as water holes and then wells dried up as a consequence of falling ground-water levels.

This area of the Middle East receives virtually no rainfall in the summer months, so it is totally dependent on rain falling at other times of the year. Although inland areas of Israel are desert or tundra, the proximity of the Mediterranean Sea and the contribution of active weather systems which penetrate to the Eastern Mediterranean usually mean that sufficient rainfall is received. For instance Haifa (on the coast of this region – near Mount

Carmel) would expect around 350mm (about 14in) of rain in the first four months of the year, then becoming totally dry during June, July and August. Areas well inland would replicate this general pattern but rainfall amounts would drop to one-third of the Haifa values, or even less, although west-facing mountainous areas become wetter again.

Mount Carmel (which becomes significant later in the story) is around 10km south-east of Haifa and the ground rises to 628m (2060ft). The peak is the highest part of a hill ridge that runs southeast. High ground, especially if part of a ridge, will always enhance the potential for precipitation, especially when the wind has a component of movement across the ridge axis. The air is forced to rise (lifted mechanically) and the physical effects of cooling and possible condensation will be added to whatever other meteorological processes are in progress (e.g. convection, coastal effects). So in a moist westerly wind situation, whatever rain may be generated at the coast is likely to become heavier and more persistent on the upslope parts of the mountain ridge inland; in a showery situation, the showers will be enhanced on the upslopes of the ridge.

Elijah's inclusion of dew is interesting, because this form of ground watering comes from a different mechanism. Unlike rain, whose larger drops can cause damage to plant life, watering by dew is extremely gentle; the water just forms imperceptibly upon the ground surfaces.

Dew formation is straightforward. Every sample of atmospheric air contains some water vapour. When the air is cooled, eventually some of the water vapour will condense into visible water droplets. This happens when air rises due to convection or mechanical lifting (as explained in Chapter 2) but it also happens when air is cooled by conduction – by touching a cold surface. This effect is commonly seen when the glass containing your chilled drink becomes covered with condensation.

Divine Weather / 115

The surface of the earth cools at night and the air in contact with it also cools. As the air is cooled below its dew-point (the temperature at which it can no longer hold all its moisture as water vapour) condensation forms on the ground as dew. The coverage of the dew will be dependent upon the nature and temperature of the variable ground surface; this is why grass may become very wet but a warmer road surface remains mostly dry.

The nature of dew is also very variable. Some dews are a mere light moistening while others drench everything. The amount of water vapour that air can hold depends upon its temperature, so warm air can hold a lot more invisible water vapour. Cold air can hold much less. Therefore warm moist air has the potential to deposit much more condensed water upon cold surfaces. By contrast, warm dry air will produce little or no dew even when cooled markedly; its dew-point temperature will be very low and is much less likely to be reached.

Like all other areas in the world, the eastern Mediterranean and its adjacent lands have periodic variability in their weather and the establishment of particular broad-scale weather patterns will cause some years to be drier than others. In physical terms, there is no inconsistency between Elijah's prophecy of no rain and no dew; with severe drought conditions, dew formation becomes very unlikely.

In a meteorological sense (taking the story as written), a continuous drought persisting in this area right through the winter and spring transition months would be extremely rare. It is noted that any extended drought would be certain to affect a very large area, much larger than the area of Israel and quite possibly the whole of the Eastern Mediterranean and all adjacent lands. The physical possibility of this situation persisting without respite for two or more years is remote.

It seems more likely that the country was affected by a very prolonged dry spell with vastly reduced and insufficient rain in the winter months. Such a scenario would lead slowly and inevitably towards great hardship as progressive failures in all types of farming production steadily reduced all the available essentials for life – a creeping towards famine conditions. This may explain how the people were able to survive for several years. If the drought occurred precisely as reported in 1Kings 17, that is, a total and continuous drought, it is questioned whether life could have been sustained for such a long period. Also, a normal meteorological explanation could not be proposed for such an extended circumstance.

Whichever explanation is chosen, this may be interpreted as another demonstration of the power of God over the elements and His supremacy in the situation. The chapter also shows God's care for His prophet. In this time of great hardship, God directed Elijah to places where he could be sustained, protected and looked after. This again emphasises the nurturing aspect of God's love for His own people.

The contest for supremacy

Finally, God speaks to Elijah (1Ki 18:1) and informs him that He now intends to restore the rains. By then it was '… the third year' of the drought and there was a great famine across the land. Elijah was ordered to return to King Ahab and when he did so he found him unchanged. The prophets (priests) of Baal were still deceiving the diseased and starving people of Israel. What ensued was a very dramatic competition!

Fundamentally, the competition was between God and the pagan god Baal but the Earthly combatants were to be 450 Baal prophets on the one side and the lone figure of Elijah on the other. On God's instructions, Elijah asked for all Baal prophets to be assembled at Mount Carmel, 850 in total. These comprised King Ahab's Baal priests from around the country and 400 priest chaplains who lived at

Queen Jezebel's court. In the event, it seems that only Ahab's priests attended (1Ki 18:22).

In front of the people of Israel, Elijah issued a challenge (1Ki 18:21-24). The combatants were to prepare identical bullocks as burnt sacrifices but no fire was to be lit. First, by their prayers and rituals, the Baal priests were to exhort the god Baal to send fire to burn their sacrifice. Then Elijah would call upon God to send fire to burn his sacrifice. Whichever prayer worked would establish absolute supremacy and the people would turn to that god.

The Baal priests failed to elicit a response from their god, despite lengthy prayer and extremes of ritual (vv 25-29). Elijah then prepared his sacrifice and called upon the Lord God. God responded immediately and '…the fire of the Lord fell and consumed the sacrifice…' (v38). The pagan god Baal was defeated and the people returned to God (v39).

This dramatic story is typical of many in the Old Testament books. The use of fire from Heaven as an awesome instrument of destruction can clearly be compared with the physical phenomenon of lightning. Chapter 6 has already discussed the weather phenomena of lightning, thunder and hail, three of the physical weather products associated with the awesome cumulonimbus cloud.

The eastern Mediterranean area experiences heavy thunderstorms mostly in the winter months because of the penetration of European or Atlantic weather systems. In the earlier winter months, the mechanism is usually convective – triggered by the temperature energy and plentiful moisture from a warm Mediterranean Sea. So the people of the area would have experienced lightning many times. For them it would be a terrifying and completely incomprehensible bolt of light and heat that flashed dramatically from the sky, causing fire, devastation and, at times, death to animals and man. The deafening crack of thunder which followed would enhance the terror further.

It is small wonder that they would link this with their all-powerful and sometimes angry God.

However, in this case there is no suggestion of the presence of cumulonimbus cloud. The 'fire from the Lord' occurred before the drought had been ended and the biblical picture is that of a 'bolt from the blue', a phrase which we use to describe a totally unexpected event. In this case it was literally a bolt from the blue! It was a blinding flash of light, high temperature and energy which streaked down from the sky and consumed the offering prepared by Elijah, including the altar and its surrounding moat of water. Could such an event occur physically from a cloudless sky? The answer is 'no'.

Although atmospheric electricity is present around us at all times (we often refer to it as 'static'), electrical distributions can only reach the required potential differences of several million volts within active cumulonimbus clouds; the roles of water, ice and violent air motion within such clouds provide the necessary mechanisms. This 'bolt from the blue' was a miracle sent by God. It is possible (but not stated) that thunder would also occur. If the mysterious 'bolt' was physically a path of incandescent heat, then the sudden expansion of the air (fully described in Chapter 6) would produce thunder in the normal way.

So the supremacy of God over the pagan god Baal is characterised by a miracle and reported in the most dramatic way possible. However the miracle is made more understandable by its close similarity to a violent physical weather entity well known to the people of the time. As today's readers, we too have experience of lightning and it is easy for us to visualise and understand the scene at Mount Carmel. Thus the power and mystery of God is obvious to all through this story.

The end of the drought

The final part of the drama is played out at the summit of Mount Carmel. God had promised the end of the drought. Elijah sends Ahab to eat and drink, promising him abundant rain. He actually 'hears' this rain by faith (1Ki 18:41); of course God had already promised it (1Ki 18:1). Elijah then retreats to pray at the top of Mount Carmel, a fine vantage point for the actions to come. He is accompanied by a single servant.

He prostrates himself to pray and orders his servant to ascend to the summit and look west across the Mediterranean Sea. As Elijah continues to pray with great humility ('his face between his knees'), the servant returns six times to report that the sky remains cloudless. However, the seventh report is of a distant cloud '…like a man's hand' (v44). This cloud develops, extends, moves east and envelops the whole land with heavy rain. God's promise is fulfilled.

Obviously, a cloud viewed from afar is seen as a small object just above the horizon. A number of Bible versions describe the cloud as '…as small as a man's hand'. However the Hebrew word used here is *'kakap-iysh'*, this literally means 'a man's hand', more specifically 'the hollow of the palm' *(kakap)*. Other meanings of this word part are connected with hollow items like a bowl or a spoon.

This suggests that the cloud had a particular shape – hollow, like a partially cupped hand. The topmost part of a developed cumulonimbus cloud, (the 'anvil') would be the first part of a storm cloud to be seen above the horizon. As Figure 9 shows, a distant cumulonimbus cloud top seen on the horizon of the Mediterranean Sea could present that concave shape to the observer. The stormy conditions that arrived subsequently would accord with highly developed cumulonimbus clouds. Thus a careful examination of the Hebrew text suggests that the popular translation of

Figure 9: A cumulonimbus cloud seen from afar

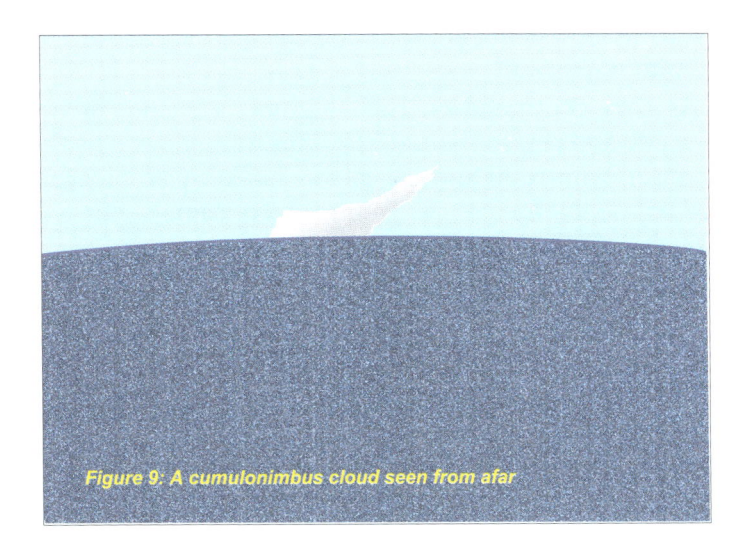

'*kakap-iysh*' – '…as small as a man's hand' may actually miss an important piece of evidence.

God's promise had been delivered (1Ki 18:45) but, this time, it is notable that the natural forces of nature, normal weather processes, are being used. God controls everything, whether natural or miraculous. Again, the power of nurturing is strong; God's people have deserted their false gods and returned to Him. He transformed their situation from one of dire hardship to one of abundance. This is God's teaching to those who are His children. Hardship when parted from God. Abundance when with Him.

Elijah's ascension to Heaven

This is Elijah's final drama on Earth. In 2Kings 2, we read that '… the Lord would take Elijah into Heaven by a whirlwind' (v1). In this part of the story, he is joined by the prophet Elisha, who succeeds him after his departure. As instructed by the Lord God, the two prophets go to the city of Jericho (about 80km inland) and onwards across the

River Jordan – a crossing achieved by another 'parting of the waters' account.

As they continued on their journey, a chariot of fire appeared and parted them (v11). This was followed by the promised whirlwind and Elijah was taken up to Heaven. His mantle fell back to the ground and became a source of Elisha's power and authority.

Dust-whirls

The region in which this event took place suggests that that the 'whirlwind' may have been the desert weather feature which is called a 'dust-whirl' in meteorology. However, a small tornado from the base of a cumulonimbus cloud is also a possibility. Dust-whirls are very common in the hotter parts of the year in the countries of the Middle East, especially in desert or semi-arid areas. They are caused by intense differential heating at the surface; for instance a sheltered sand or rocky area may become much hotter than the surrounding land surface. Figure 10 page 124 shows the structure of a developed dust-whirl.

Dust whirls occur in many parts of the world. Scales range from small, short-lived features (perhaps only 10m in vertical extent and in existence for a few moments) to circulations that extend to 700m and persist for hours. The largest dust whirls occur in the hottest desert regions. Because the circulation will become filled with dust and sand, they are unpleasant but, more importantly, the strong and turbulent wind flow can result in damage. Also, the very rapid pressure fall that occurs at the centre of the circulation can cause damage by the explosion of air trapped within buildings. The vortex may lift up items from the ground and carry them away for some distance.

Small tornadoes associated with cumulonimbus clouds

The alternative to the dust-whirl would be a small tornado extending downwards from the base of a cumulonimbus cloud. Such circulations form as a result of the vast convection currents which develop within such clouds. Similar forces of convergence and rotation apply to tornadoes and their effect is like that of a well-developed dust-whirl – damage by extreme wind and pressure fall. Material from the ground is lifted and carried up into the cloud to be ejected elsewhere.

The imagery of the Elijah story

In the story of Elijah's 'taking up' into Heaven, the writers once again used weather imagery which would be familiar to the people of Israel. They would have seen the effects of powerful whirling storms many times and would be familiar with their power of destruction. It may be that they would have seen injury and death as a result of lifted items falling upon animals and people. However it is unlikely that a heavy item, such as a human being, would be lifted by either a dust whirl circulation or a small tornado. The more powerful manifestations of cyclones (tropical storms) are capable of this because there is vastly more energy involved.

The choice of dust-whirl or small tornado would be determined largely by the time of year. Dust-whirls occur in the hot summer months; small tornadoes and cumulonimbus clouds develop mainly in the winter. The biblical text gives no indication of the time of year but there is no mention of bad weather during the journey of the two prophets.

The purpose of the story of Elijah's departure from Earth is to emphasise that he did not die but was taken by God directly from life into Heaven. This is an indication of Elijah's great service to the Lord God. There is an earlier parallel in Ge 5:24 when Enoch, a man who 'walked with God', was taken directly to Heaven without passing through death. However, the mechanism for Enoch's departure is not revealed. In the Elijah account, God's love for His prophet is emphasised by the glorious imagery which describes the way in which the prophet was swept

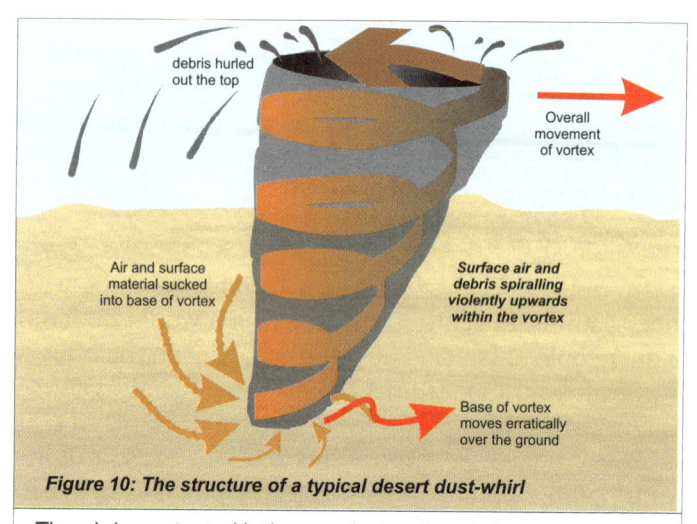

Figure 10: The structure of a typical desert dust-whirl

The air in contact with the very hot surface is heated and rises rapidly, producing strong convergence near the surface. Inevitably, this air movement acquires rotation and the conservation of angular momentum (as described in Appendix 2 – 'office chair' demonstration) accelerates the air into a rapidly spinning and rising air mass, usually assuming an inverted cone shape. Because the air is very dry, rising and cooling does not cause cloud formation. Once formed, the dust-whirl normally moves with the prevailing wind flow at the top of its circulation; the narrow base will move much more erratically.

up to Heaven to be with God. God is emphasising His love and care for those who serve Him well and granting this special passage to heaven without intervening death.

Ezekiel

Towards the end of the sixth century BC, the southern kingdom of Judah had come under the control of the Babylonians. Many inhabitants had been taken to Babylonia as captives and one of these was a young priest named Ezekiel. In captivity, he became a prophet and issued many prophetic warnings to his fellow captives. In particular he warned of the impending destruction of Jerusalem that finally took place in 587BC. Ezekiel's later prophesies change to ones of hope. There is a considerable amount of weather imagery in the book of Ezekiel.

The commissioning of Ezekiel

'Weather words' occur early in Ezekiel 1. This chapter records the commissioning of Ezekiel as a prophet of the Lord God and the imagery is awesome. Ezekiel describes (v4) the arrival of a whirlwind and a great cloud with 'fire infolding it'. This was the method of arrival of the power of God and there is then a rich and detailed description of the glory of God and His servants. In v13, the description of blazing fire is further enhanced by the imagery of associated lightning.

The focus of the description was the appearance of a magnificent throne, upon which was seated 'the glory of the Lord'. (vv25-28) Part of the description of the throne included a bow of rainbow colours, like that 'in the cloud in the day of rain'. In this case, the beautiful and mysterious appearance of a rainbow is used as a figure of speech. The scene glowed brightly with iridescent fire. It was this iridescent fire which the prophet Ezekiel likened to a rainbow. In these verses, the appearance of God to Ezekiel is described with the richest of imagery. Awesome and mythical creatures, fantastic shapes, vivid colours, heat, light and … weather.

Here again is the powerful and damaging whirlwind, capable of lifting items (and prophets!) into the sky – a common sight in this land. In fact if this whirling circulation was associated with the cumulonimbus thunder cloud also described, it is more likely to be a small tornado rather than a dry dust whirl. So we are given an approaching image of a dark and brooding cumulonimbus cloud, with flickering lightning within and an associated tornado circulation reaching towards the ground – extreme weather indeed!

It is significant that the description of the approach and the details of the Lord's attendants are linked to violent weather. By contrast the image linked to the person of God is a gentle one – the absolute beauty of that optical illusion, the rainbow. This is a powerful and meaningful contrast; God's power is infinite and full of glory but He is gentle with His own people.

The fate of the false prophets

Ezekiel 13 reports that some prophets of Israel are making false and selfish prophecies. Ezekiel is to issue a prophecy of reproof and a dire warning. The false prophets are full of vanity; they claim the gift of prophecy from God but in fact their prophecies are fabrications. They are deceiving the people with their lies. They tell the people there is peace when there is not; they say all is well when in fact there is dangerous sickness in the land.

God is angry with them. In Ez 13:10-15 He likens their false words to the building of a weak and defective wall which is then deliberately covered over with whitewash so that its dangerous faults are concealed. The Lord then warns how He will knock this wall down to reveal its weakness and defects to all the people. He uses weather imagery to describe the destruction process. Heavy rain will batter down upon it. Large hailstones will be driven like missiles against it by strong and turbulent winds. Furthermore the false prophets will be crushed beneath the falling stones and meet their death.

Here again weather imagery communicates the meaning effectively. All may understand the wrath of the Lord God, who has the power to send destruction. Hearing this prophesy from Ezekiel, the people will realise that they have been hearing falsehoods from people with no prophetic gift from God. They will turn away from these false prophets and reject them. God's truth will be established; God's purpose will have been achieved.

The valley of the dry bones

The book of Ezekiel cannot be left without visiting the valley of the dry bones. This is another well-known story, not least because it is the subject of a popular spiritual song. The story is told in Ez 37:1-14. Ezekiel has a vision in which he is placed in a valley where there are many human bones scattered around. The Lord instructs Ezekiel to prophesy to the bones 'Hear the Word of the Lord'. After he has done this, in a series of scenes of great mystery, the bones are reassembled, reconnected with ligaments and clothed with flesh. The fully reconstructed bodies are then brought to life. A 'great army' stands before Ezekiel.

In v9, Ezekiel is instructed to call for breath, for life to be put into the reconstructed bodies. He is to 'prophesy unto the wind', to 'say to the wind', to call 'from the four winds', for the breath of life. The call is addressed by name to 'O breath'. These instances of 'wind' do not refer to the meteorological movement of air.

In the Hebrew text, each instance of 'wind' is a form of the word '*ruach*'. This word is encountered at the very beginning of the Bible (Ge 1:2) and was discussed in Chapter 3 (The Creation). It is a wonderful and mysterious word with a range of meanings, including wind, air, breath, spirit, soul, life force. In addition, the words 'O breath' in v9 are also translated from a form of the same Hebrew word. Ezekiel was addressing his request to the *ruach*, making a request for the souls of those who had died there in the valley, asking for the restoration of their own personal breath, minds and spirits. 'Come and restore them to life – breathe upon them'. The Hebrew text suggests 'puff breath into' at that point. The following verse records that the '*ruach*' was received by all of the bodies and 'they lived'.

God explained to Ezekiel that this vision was a message about the nation of Israel. He would never abandon them. When they were lost, broken and destroyed, when all hope was gone, when death was a reality, they should know that the Lord God would always reconstruct them and give them back their life. God's love, care and mercy are infinite.

So this story is of great importance for God's people. It is a resurrection story and all Christians know how the death and resurrection of their own saviour Jesus Christ bestows upon them that same resurrection after death. In time, all God's people will know that resurrecting force of wind, air, breath, soul, and life spirit, that 'ruach'.

Jonah

The book of Jonah is one of a number of 'minor prophetic books' – that is to say, it is short in length but not in importance. The story of Jonah and the 'whale' is likely to be encountered in childhood and retained in adulthood. Poor Jonah certainly had a hard time! Almost drowned at sea, swallowed by a huge fish but eventually saved to carry out God's instructions.

Jonah was a prophet in Israel in the 8th Century BC. He is identified in 2Ki 14:25. The trouble started when Jonah disobeyed the Lord. The Lord instructed him to go to the city of Nineveh in Mesopotamia (a considerable distance away) to give prophetic warnings to the people about their wickedness. Jonah did not want to go and decided to run away from the Lord in completely the other direction! He went to the port of Joppa and there boarded a ship due to sail for Tarshish. Although it is not known for certain where Tarshish was, it was certainly a long way to the west, most probably on the Spanish coast; it may even have been the name for the whole Iberian peninsula. No doubt Jonah thought God would not be able to reach him once the boat had sailed. God would then choose someone else. This proved to be a vain thought!

In Jonah 1:4, God sent a great storm, sufficient to damage the ship and place it in danger of sinking. The sailors did everything they could to ride the storm, throwing cargo overboard to lighten the ship. It seems that the crew were a devout group, for they also prayed to their own gods for deliverance. When the battle was sure to be lost, Jonah revealed to the crew that it was his fault and directed them to throw him overboard. This action would save them. Finally, in desperation, they did so and he 'sank below the waves'. The sea became calm and the ship was saved. Then Jonah was swallowed by a 'great fish', lived in its belly for three days and finally was disgorged back on dry land – presumably near where he started. Then God said to him 'Arise, go to Nineveh...' – and, not surprisingly, Jonah went!

The account does not give any indication where the storm occurred but provided it was not high summer, such a storm is entirely possible anywhere in the Mediterranean. The most likely meteorological situation to produce an intense area of low pressure over the Mediterranean is a high-level incursion of cold air from the north. This broad-scale situation, coupled with the contribution of warm Mediterranean waters (warmest in October/November) often intensifies low pressure areas that have moved south or south-east from Europe. The resulting weather is very stormy, with turbulent gale force winds and much precipitation. Driven by the eastward movement of the upper air cold trough, the surface low would move steadily east across the Mediterranean, meeting the ship with Jonah aboard.

Additionally, it is wind that causes sea waves to form. Some of the energy from the wind is transferred to the sea, setting up a wave motion in the water. The stronger the wind and the longer it blows, the higher the waves. A severe and prolonged storm could easily produce waves 3-4m high within 24 hours. Such conditions would certainly be very dangerous even for the larger sailing ships of the day; sails, masts and other essential equipment could be seriously damaged and, once control of the ship was lost, there would be a very real danger of foundering.

Of course the obvious point of the story is obedience to the Lord God. If, like Jonah, you have become a true servant of the Lord, then you must be prepared to obey. However, this was not a punishment for Jonah but merely God's way of bringing him to his senses, so that His will could be carried out. The details of the story are presented so powerfully that you are not likely to forget it! The account shows how merciful and forgiving God is to His people.

A deeper realisation is God's concern for the Gentiles of Nineveh. In order that they should be saved, it was essential that Jonah carried out bidding. In the event, the people of Nineveh heeded Jonah's words, turned from their evil ways and repented. Thus the will of God was achieved and the clarity of God's love for all mankind is demonstrated.

8

Galilee and Judea

This chapter looks at several important weather-related events in the life and teaching of Jesus Christ, the central figure in the Christian religion. The main accounts of the life of Jesus are found in the first four books of the New Testament, the Gospels of St. Matthew, St. Mark, St. Luke and St. John. The first three are designated 'synoptic', that is, they tell the story of Jesus chronologically (in a general sense). The earliest of the three is Mark, probably written around AD65. The other two synoptic gospels are considered to be have written in AD80-90. In these gospels, it is common to find reports of what are clearly recognisable as the same events. The fourth gospel, John, was written some 10 to 20 years later. John does not write a chronological history of Jesus. Instead, his purpose in reporting the deeds, teachings and miracles of Jesus Christ was to engender and strengthen the faith of those in the early Christian Church.

By the time Jesus Christ was born, the homeland of the Jewish people had at long last known peace for a generation. With support from Rome, King Herod the Great had achieved stability in the area. The country was divided into three regions, (Map 4 next page) Galilee in the north, Judea in the south and Samaria between them.

When Jesus' ministry began (reputedly when he was around 30 years old) much of his teaching took place in Galilee, especially in the area around the Sea of Galilee, which was in these days a thriving and well-populated part of the country. Several of the most powerful accounts of

Jesus' life and ministry occurred actually on the Sea of Galilee, with weather playing an important role.

The city of Jerusalem was the religious and administrative centre for the country. It was located in the southern province of Judea. The city contained the Temple and the king's palace within its walls. Jerusalem was also a very important place for the later ministry of Jesus. It was there that his followers received his final teachings before he was put to death. Weather elements and imagery appear in some of the gospel accounts of events at Jerusalem.

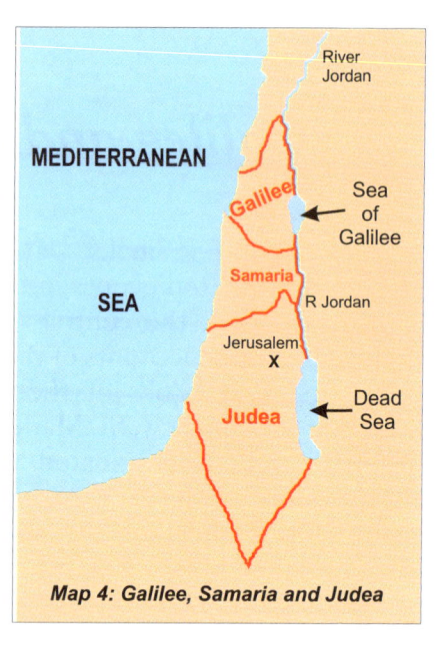

Map 4: Galilee, Samaria and Judea

Galilee

The Sea of Galilee (alternative names, Lake Tiberius, Sea of Chinnereth, Lake of Gennesaret) was an important fishing centre in these early New Testament times (commercial fishing continues today). This beautiful inland sea is around 23km long, 13km wide and up to 45m deep. The waters are encircled by a beach. Beyond that, much of the area is surrounded by escarpments but there are sloping plains extending to the north and north-west. The fresh waters of the River Jordan flow through the Sea from north to south.

The Sermon on the Mount

The Sermon on the Mount was the first extended teaching discourse of Jesus. Matthew 5-7 gives a full account of Jesus' words; details of the Sermon are also found in Lk 6:20-49. The Sermon covers a comprehensive range of ethical and religious matters. The dominant theme is the Kingdom of God and justice. There is much teaching on the fundamentals of the Christian life, on a Christian's relationship with God and on the role of God's Kingdom on Earth. The teaching was aimed specifically and personally at the people listening but it is as relevant today as it was then. There are many familiar sayings; three examples are the Lord's Prayer (Mt 6:9-13), the Beatitudes (Mt 5:3-12) and the exhortation to love one another (Mt 5:43-48).

At the end of the Sermon, Jesus makes a very effective use of weather imagery to drive home the teachings. He tells his listeners about the wise and foolish builders. Today, the meaning of this parable is well-known not only as a Bible story but because very similar concepts appear in at least one popular children's story.

In Mt 7:24-27, Jesus exhorted his listeners to be wise – to be like the wise man who builds his house upon solid rock. The house withstands subsequent wind, rain and storm. Such a man would assimilate and act upon the teachings of Jesus. On the other hand, a foolish man would build his house on sand; this pitiful house would collapse and be swept away when the storm and flood came. Such a man would ignore the teachings of Jesus through stupidity. The version of this parable in Luke 6:48-49 is very similar except that the destruction mechanism is stated to be by flood alone.

This was an excellent way for Jesus to commend his teachings, for who would want to be judged foolish? The physical situation Jesus described could be envisaged easily by everyone (including us). We can all see the inappropriately built house being destroyed by the violence of the weather while the finely built house stands proud and solid above the storm. The people in the crowd would want to associate themselves with the wise man whose house was sensibly built – therefore as wise men they would accept and act upon the teachings of Jesus. In using the weather in this way, Jesus promoted his essential teaching with great skill.

There is an interesting parallel here with the story of the flimsy wall in the book of Ezekiel (Chapter 7). In that story, the weather was used to destroy the defective wall in a similar way. God used this earlier parable to illustrate His point effectively. This indicates how the Old and New Testaments of the Bible link together in a complementary way.

The calming of the storm

In the following chapter of Matthew's Gospel (Matthew 8), Jesus healed several people and, as a result, huge crowds of people now followed him. Jesus knew he had work to do in other places so he called for a boat to take him and the disciples to the other side of the Sea. As the boat made its way across, it was struck by 'a great tempest' (v24), the waves became dangerously high and the boat started to fill with water. Despite all the commotion, Jesus was asleep and had to be awaked by the disciples. 'Save us; we perish' they cried. Jesus rebuked them for being so fearful, for having so little faith; then he stood up and rebuked the wind and the sea. All become calm! This very famous story appears also in Mark's gospel (Mk 4:36-41) and in Luke 8:22-25 with some variations of detail.

It is reasonable to assume that the 'great tempest' would not be of the same intensity as those that affect the Mediterranean Sea (such as the storm experienced by Jonah). Likewise the waves which would be generated on a relatively small inland sea would certainly be much smaller. However there is no doubt that sudden squalls can affect areas like the Sea of Galilee where there is mountainous ground surrounding a stretch of water.

The wind at ground level is greatly affected by topography. An area of hills, valleys and mountains with variable vegetation cover will provide the environment for the most complex wind structure near the surface. Our own experience of hill walking will have shown us the extreme variability of the wind – calm at one moment and extremely gusty the next. The effect becomes even more marked in mountainous areas, especially where the ground is a combination of jagged peaks and deep valleys.

There are many reasons why these very marked variations of wind should occur. The variation of topography can present significant sheltering effects. Conversely, strong winds may be boosted significantly by funnelling along valleys and ravines. Powerful vertical wind currents can appear suddenly near steep slopes. Looking at the topography and at photographs of the area around the Sea of Galilee, it is likely that any of these effects could apply. A small shift in wind direction or a critical change in the vertical wind structure could change a calm or light wind near the Sea surface into a powerful, turbulent and chaotic flow within a few seconds.

The sudden blustery wind would soon interact with the water surface, transferring some of its energy, so that waves would be generated; these may not be very large but it is certain that the surface of the water would become very rough and chaotic. The cessation of this situation could be equally sudden when a smoother wind flow pattern was re-established at height. Then, with little wind near the sea surface, the waves would subside quite quickly.

It must also be remembered that the fishing boats on the Sea of Galilee were not sea-going ships but small open craft. Today's fishing boats on the Sea of Galilee are generally 6-10m (18-30ft) in length and it is very likely that those of Jesus' time would be similar or smaller. Their normal method of propulsion would have been by rowing;

Divine Weather / 135

perhaps occasionally it was possible to hoist a small sail, if the boat had been rigged for this. There is little doubt that the stormy weather described would be a great danger to such small open boats.

So in all three Gospel accounts, the boat is foundering. Jesus is awakened by the disciples who are in fear for their lives. Jesus rebukes them for their fear and lack of faith. He then commands the wind and the sea to be still and this happens immediately. A physical mechanism for the sudden cessation can be proposed (as above) but the atmosphere's obedience to the words of Jesus cannot be explained other than by coincidence or divine power. You may well think that coincidence is stretching credulity!

There are several other important teachings to be gleaned from this dramatic story. The fact that such a severe storm occurred at that precise time was an indication to the disciples that there will be storms to be coped with through life; such storms are the action of those who are opposed to God. The disciples' reaction to the storm was a test of their faith; Scripture teaches that 'faith can move mountains' but in this situation the faith of the disciples failed them. The rebuke of Jesus was a teaching to them to depend upon their faith in God. Faith will always dispel fear. Finally, the calming of the storm shows that a word from Jesus Christ can change nature, restore calm and bring peace.

Walking on the water

This is another powerful teaching story set upon the waters of the Sea of Galilee. Even for those with little knowledge of the Bible, the report of Jesus Christ walking on the water is extremely well-known. It is an account that is found in Matthew, Mark and John – but not in Luke. This omission from the third synoptic gospel has been used by some to question whether there were really two storm events associated with the Sea of Galilee.

It is true that there are some similarities of detail in the events surrounding the main action. Jesus had been with a 'great multitude' (in fact this is when the famous 'feeding of the 5000' took place). Afterwards, he had healed some people. He now detached himself from the multitude. He directed the disciples to obtain a boat to travel to the other side of the sea. The boat was caught in a storm and was in danger of sinking. The situation was saved by Jesus. These are the similarities.

However there are very important differences. On this occasion it was night-time; the previous sea crossing was during daylight. This time Jesus did not go into the boat; he directed his disciples to travel without him and wait on the other side. He then went alone to a mountain to pray. When the boat was caught in the storm, in danger and unable to make headway because of the strong and turbulent wind, Jesus came, walking on the water. The disciples were greatly afraid when they saw his figure appearing from the darkness (presumably lighted from a lantern on the boat); they thought it was a ghost. Jesus then spoke to them and they recognised his voice '…it is I; be not afraid' (Mt 14:27).

The disciple Peter, ever the bold man of the disciples, replied 'Lord, if it be thou, bid me come unto thee on the water'. 'Come' Jesus replied and Peter stepped from the boat and walked on the water towards Jesus but, as he walked, he became afraid and began to sink into the water. 'Save me' he cried in fear and Jesus stretched out his hand to rescue him, rebuking him for his loss of faith. Then they both stepped into the boat and the wind and sea were stilled. The report of the same event in Mark is shorter (Mk 6:47-51), mainly because it does not include the account of Peter walking on the water. John's account (Jn 6:18-21) is similar to that of Mark, with no mention of Peter's sea excursion.

The explanations for the sudden onset and cessation of the storm and its effect on a small open boat are exactly the same as for the previous event. The added drama on this occasion is Jesus walking on the water and, as always, there have been 'rational' explanations proposed for this. Here are four propositions which have been put forward:

(1) The disciples *imagined* that Jesus came to help them.

(2) In the darkness of night they saw something they *thought* was the figure of Jesus.

(3) Jesus did come but was *walking on a sand bar* just below the surface of the sea.

(4) Jesus came to help them but was actually walking *on the shore*. The disciples did not realise they were so close to land.

Regarding (1) and (2), it may be convenient to level allegations of 'imagination' or 'mistaken observation' at every happening that is not understood but this is hardly a scientific or even a rational approach. The suggestion that Jesus was walking along a sand bar (3) ignores the fact that some of the disciples in the boat were experienced sailors and fishermen who were familiar with the every part of the Sea of Galilee. It is simply not credible to suggest that they would not know the existence of such a shallow. The proposition that Jesus was in fact walking along the shore (4) is based on an alternative translation of a Greek word. The relevant phrase in Mt 14:25 is 'peripatōn epi tēn thalassan', literally 'walking on the sea'. The same Greek phrase is used in the Mark and John accounts. However 'epi' may also be translated as 'over, upon, at, by, against'. The selection of 'at' or 'by' for the translation is the justification for this suggestion. The proposition is that the boat had been blown close to the shore but none of the disciples knew this. Jesus had come to help them and was actually walking on dry land. They *thought* he was walking on the sea.

Again, this requires acceptance of a degree of incompetence on the part of the sailor disciples. Despite their knowledge and experience, it is alleged they did not know where they were on this small and very familiar sea. Even if this were so, the situation should have been obvious because there is a significant difference in the behaviour of waves in shallow and deep water. In deep water waves actually describe a rolling circular motion with the top part of the circle forming the smooth waves we see on the surface of the water. When the water becomes shallow, the circular motion is broken and the waves then present a 'breaking' pattern at the surface. This is why smooth waves roll towards the beach and then become breaking waves before crashing upon the beach. Thus in shallow water, there would be breaking waves around the boat and the sound of waves crashing on the beach would also be heard. These sights and sounds would alert any sailor to the proximity of land. It is thought, therefore, that this proposition is unlikely.

In fact the best explanation may be the one linked to the beliefs of the Christian faith. It is reasoned that Jesus Christ, the Son of God, God himself in human form, would be able to walk on the water if he wanted to; accounts of this event in the Gospels suggest that he did. Acceptance of this explanation requires belief in God and in his absolute power.

Did Peter also walk on the water? Matthew says 'yes' and the other Gospels are silent on this. If he did, then whatever mysterious mechanism allowed Jesus Christ to walk on the water also applied to Peter in these moments. While accepting the mystery, some Biblical commentators cannot resist making a 'scientific' comment in passing. It has been suggested that Jesus could walk on the water because 'the normal laws of gravity were suspended'. This is a striking thought, since if gravity were suspended in the Sea of Galilee area, the whole of the sea and its contents would be flung immediately into Space with great speed! Perhaps it is better to stick with 'truly mysterious'!

In actuality, the important knowledge to be gleaned from this account has nothing to do with the method of arrival of Jesus at the boat. Whether Jesus did or did not walk on the water is not an important component of the teaching. The important teachings are these:
- The fact that he withdrew to pray emphasises the importance of prayer and illustrates the humanity of Jesus. This is an important realisation for Christian understanding.
- As in the previous storm example, the Christian may expect storms in life but here Jesus' physical arrival at a time of danger emphasises that he will always come in times of need.
- The paramount role of faith is repeated twice, firstly in their fear of the storm and then in the story of Peter sinking. In fact, faith is the mechanism that achieves the mystery of walking on the water.
- As a reiteration of the previous storm story, Jesus showed again that he could control the forces of nature and restore peace and calm to any situation.

Some commentators have suggested that Jesus' act of walking on the water is a primary illustration of his divine status; therefore acceptance of this part of the story is essential. This is disputed here. The New Testament is full of accounts of the miraculous powers of Jesus; it is proposed that the evidence for his divine status does not depend upon this particular story.

Judea

The Second Coming foretold

The Second Coming is one of the fundamental beliefs of the Christian faith, although these actual words do not appear in the New Testament. There are about 300 references to the return of Jesus in the New Testament;

most use the Greek word **parousia** (e.g. Mt 24:3, 1Th 2:19) which means 'presence, being near, coming, arrival, advent', therefore by implication 'return'.

The Bible tells us that Jesus Christ, born a man but with the divine status Christians refer to as 'Son of God', lived on Earth to teach by word and example, heal and perform other miracles in his human lifetime. In the time of his ministry, his teachings and actions became dangerous in the eyes of the authorities and his downfall was plotted. He was arrested, falsely accused and executed. On the third day after his death he was resurrected and subsequently ascended to Heaven. Christian teaching says that Jesus will return 'at the end of this age'. The timing of this event is unknown, even to the human Jesus – 'no-one knows the day and hour' (Mt 24:36).

The Bible also presents evidence for the influence of Jesus on Earth. The Old Testament (Isaiah 53) tells of a 'suffering servant' who will establish justice on Earth. Ze 14:5-6 presents the picture of a returned saviour on the Mount of Olives. These Old Testament implications turn into positive teachings in the New Testament and weather imagery is used a number of times to describe the sequence of events.

The Second Coming of Jesus will not be a secret affair – it will be obvious to all. It will be 'as lightning cometh out of the east and shineth even unto the west' (Mt 24:27). A similar description is also presented in Lk 17:24. This is an excellent image since all are familiar with the experience of lightning at night. The high intensity flash of electrical discharge lights up the whole sky from horizon to horizon. Even in daylight, it is so bright that it still commands attention and recognition. So all who read this description can appreciate the awesome and all-pervading power that will be associated with the end of this age and the return of Jesus.

In Mt 24:29, it is stated that in the period immediately prior to the second coming the sun and moon will be darkened, the stars will fall from the sky and 'the powers of heaven will be shaken'. Similar words appear in Mk 13:24-25. Luke's version is more circumspect; 'there shall be signs in the sun, and in the moon, and in the stars' but here there is the addition of 'distress of nations, with perplexity; the sea and the waves roaring'. These are altogether very frightening images of uncompromising misery.

Throughout the Bible, darkness is presented as a symbol of spiritual blindness and ignorance. References to a 'time of darkness' often mean strife and calamity. In Chapter 3 the three sources of God's glorious light were identified as the sun, the moon and the stars. Here in the synoptic gospels it is made clear that all these sources of light will be dimmed. This is in accordance with Old Testament references (Is 13:9-10, Joel 3:15) which refer to a forthcoming time of judgement which will be preceded by a dimming of sun, moon and stars. There is no intention here to suggest any physical weather involvement; the image of all sources of light becoming dimmer is an indication of calamitous events coming to a climax.

The following verses in Matthew describe the Second Coming (Mt 24:30-31) and two weather words appear. The Son of Man will come '…in the clouds of heaven (v.30); his elect will be gathered 'from the four winds'. Similar words are used in Mk 13:26-27 and Lk 21:27.

The word cloud appears many times throughout the Bible, often linked to the presence of God. From Old to New Testament times, the writers of Scripture presented the image of clouds to illustrate events of great mystery. In this case, the Second Coming of the Lord Jesus will be associated with the appearance of a cloud in the sky, directly following on from many earlier references.

'The four winds' (Mt 24:31, Mk 13:26) is a reference to the four cardinal points, north, east, south and west. It is a literal translation of the Greek 'tessarōn anemōn' (The same is true of the Old Testament Hebrew translations). The 'four winds' is a rather poetic description of 'from every direction' and these words are found a number of times in both Old and New Testaments. The 'four winds' is a phrase still in use in today's language; many such phrases with maritime origins have found their way into the everyday English language. In this case, the poetic phrase emphasises the completeness of the gathering which Jesus Christ will call to him. Every single one of his people, 'the elect', will be called to his side.

In Mt 24:32, there is a reference to summer. Here Jesus is using a farming analogy to reinforce his teaching of the signs that will precede his coming. This little bit of farming logic appears also in the other synoptic gospels (Mk 13:28, Lk 21:29-30). Jesus emphasises that the terrible events he has warned about will be a precursor of the Second Coming just as the sight of a fig tree coming into leaf is a clear and inevitable precursor of summer. A very effective memory reinforcement for an agricultural community.

The crucifixion of Jesus

Jesus Christ was executed by crucifixion upon the Cross at Golgotha, just outside the walls of the city of Jerusalem. All four Gospels give detailed accounts of the Crucifixion and the important events of the days following. The death of Jesus is associated with two mysterious and dramatic happenings that have links with weather concepts.

The darkness all over the land

Mark's gospel states (Mk 15:25) that Jesus was crucified at 'the third hour'. This is 9.00 a.m., since the Jewish day begins at 6.00 a.m. The three synoptic gospels then report that from the sixth to the ninth hour (midday to 3.00 p.m.), there was 'darkness all over the land' (Mt 27:45).

Jesus died on the Cross at 'the ninth hour' and 'the veil of the temple was rent in twain' and 'the earth did quake'.

Bible commentators traditionally attributed the 'darkness' to a total eclipse of the sun, which probably affected the whole world. Such explanations are found consistently in older biblical commentaries. In the Bible, the Greek word used was '**skotos**' which may be translated as night darkness, shadiness, obscurity. The question of extent was contained in '**epi pasan tēn gēn**' – meaning 'over all the land'. However the word '**gēn**' may mean 'ground, soil, earth, region or world'. Choice of a translation other than 'world' would suggest a more limited extent.

However it has long been recognised that a physical eclipse of the sun (by the moon) is an inappropriate explanation. As explained previously (Chapter 6) an eclipse can only last for a maximum of 7½ minutes. In addition, the time is established as that of the Jewish Passover, which is a time of full moon. Reference to Figure 4 will show that the moon cannot possibly provide an eclipse of the sun at that time.

As an alternative, some commentators have suggested that the darkness was produced by atmospheric obscuration of some type. Thick clouds and sandstorms have been suggested, as has ash outfall from volcanic eruption. Certainly these physical phenomena would dim the sun but not in any mysterious way. An increase of convective cloud on a spring afternoon would be a normal event in that region; a sandstorm is not impossible but would need to be an event affecting a large area to produce significant reduction in sunlight. Regarding volcanic activity, there is no textual evidence for this.

In proposing a mysterious explanation, many commentators have linked the darkness to earlier Biblical events, particularly the 'thick darkness' which was one of the ten plagues of Egypt (Chapter 6). However it is reasoned that the description of the darkness at the Crucifixion is completely different. In the 'thick darkness' of the Egyptian plague, the people were effectively struck blind – their eyes could not see either natural or artificial light. They were paralysed, afraid to move. At the Crucifixion, there is no question of that. Although the sun was darkened, the people could still see clearly enough what was happening.

It is proposed that the darkness for three hours before the death of Jesus signifies his separation from God. So that evil could win, Jesus needed to be excluded from the light of God. The death of Jesus was the essential first part of the establishment of God's New Covenant with His people, a covenant which promised to transform them from within. The mechanism for the darkness could have been thick cloud, sand in suspension, or both; more likely it is the comprehensible symbolism chosen by those who recorded the event to communicate the separation of Jesus from God.

The curtain torn in the Temple

When Jesus died, the biblical text tells us the temple curtain was torn completely in two and the 'earth quaked'. The temple curtain would have been a large, thick richly woven tapestry that divided the 'Holy Place' from the 'Holy of Holies'. The temple was a very large area of nested courtyards of increasing importance, leading to a sacred building in the centre. The building was constructed in the same nested manner with its single door leading through a porch to the Holy Place and thence to the 'Holy of Holies' at its rear. The Holy of Holies' was the most sacred place in the temple, regarded as a type of heaven. The only person allowed to enter was the High Priest and this occurred only once per year when a general expiation of the sins of the people was made. No other person was ever allowed a glimpse of this sacred area.

The time of Jesus' death was a time of offering in the temple, so there would be priests officiating in the temple building. This implies there would be witnesses to the tearing of the curtain; such witnesses would be able to provide detailed accounts but none are given. Although there are many occasions when destruction was achieved by means of violent weather, this does not seem to be what happened in this case. A 'bolt from heaven' or a 'mighty wind' could have ripped the curtain apart but this is not reported. Although 'the earth did quake' it is unlikely that there was significant earthquake activity, since there is no report of damage to the structure of the building. There is therefore no conclusive physical explanation for the destruction of the curtain.

This raises the question of truth or myth. If the curtain was physically torn apart, then it would seem that the power of God was responsible – either manifested miraculously through the 'quake' or perhaps by means of the *ruach*. If the event is myth, then the writer is seeking to present the implications of Jesus' Crucifixion in a very dramatic and memorable way. Whether truth or myth, the meaning is clear. Before that moment, the people could not approach God directly – this could only be done through the High Priest. With the destruction of the curtain, God became accessible to all. There was no 'Holy of Holies' any more. It was revealed to everyone. A new way of living was brought into being; Jew and Gentile were united.

The last word

However the last word should come from the foot of the Cross, spoken reportedly by unbelievers. The Roman soldiers who were in charge of the Crucifixion were standing around the Cross when Jesus died. As they experienced the events described above it is written that they were awe-struck and very frightened. 'Truly this was the Son of God' they whispered to one another (Mt 27:54).

9

A Passage to Rome

The apostle Paul

The apostle Paul is a major New Testament figure. Following his introduction (Ac 7:58, but at this time named Saul), he becomes increasingly dominant as the book proceeds, especially after his dramatic conversion to Christianity (Acts 9) – the original 'Damascus Road experience'! Subsequently, he developed to become an active and well-travelled missionary, teacher and gifted letter-writer. The New Testament includes no less than 13 of his 'epistles'; these are letters addressed to the churches to which he made missionary visits or to individuals with whom he had a special relationship.

Paul was a highly educated Jew born in the city of Tarsus (in Asia Minor) and it is known that he also held Roman citizenship. This dual nationality explains why he had two names – Saul, his Hebrew name and Paul, his Roman name. As Saul, he is first identified as an enthusiastic and ruthless persecutor of Christians – his introduction (Ac 7:58) is as an official witness to the stoning of the first Christian martyr, Stephen. It is at Ac 13:9 that the name change to Paul is signalled: 'Then Saul (who is also called Paul)…' It seems he adopts his Roman name Paul as he starts the first of his three extensive Christian missionary journeys. Although each of these journeys involves sea passages at various points, there is no mention of weather; indeed there is very little description, merely a statement that the journey took place. We must assume that these sea journeys were uneventful.

All three missionary sea journeys took place in the north-eastern part of the Mediterranean Sea in the vicinity of the island of Cyprus, along the southern coasts of Asia Minor (now Turkey) and in the Aegean Sea. As already mentioned, the eastern Mediterranean Sea experiences less severe weather than central and western parts; although storms may occur, they are generally confined to the winter months. Also, such storms are unlikely to be as prolonged as those further west and so would involve only minor delays in sailing. In addition, the missionary routes themselves are relatively sheltered by the proximity of land. By contrast, Paul's sea journey to Rome was much longer and involved a much more exposed route (see Map 5 opposite).

Although the first part of the journey would be sheltered by the land mass of Asia Minor, it was then necessary to venture out into much more exposed waters. The route shows that the shelter of Crete was utilised but there then followed a long mid-sea journey to Malta. After a short northern leg across open sea, the final leg of the journey could seek the shelter of Sicily and Italy.

This journey was very different from those that had preceded it because on this occasion Paul made it as a Roman prisoner instead of a missionary. Paul's personal troubles begin to be reported in Acts 20. At the end of his third missionary tour he determines to go to Jerusalem, despite being warned several times that danger would await him there. Obviously, his reputation as a successful Christian missionary did not put him in favour with the Jewish authorities.

The story unfolds as a complex narrative tale. When Paul arrives in Jerusalem, his actions and words infuriate the Jewish authorities who several times stir up the crowds against him. Eventually, he has to be saved from a furious crowd by Roman soldiers who then arrest him for causing disorder. Once in custody, he is then accused of various other crimes. He spends several years in prison at Caesarea

Maritima, on the Mediterranean coast, and three times is called to appear before different Governors to answer his case. Although no case could ever be proven against him, he is not released and finally (as a Roman citizen) he decides to appeal to the Roman Emperor Nero for justice and freedom. This is why he is dispatched to Rome as a prisoner.

The journey to Rome

Acts 27 and 28 give a detailed chronological account of this journey, which started in the autumn of AD60 and was completed in spring of AD61. The journey was made in three sections, involving transportation by three different ships. Paul and a number of other prisoners were guarded by a detachment of Roman soldiers commanded by Julius, a centurion who fortunately was disposed kindly towards Paul. It is suggested that they were also accompanied by Luke, the writer of the book of Acts; this is why we now have such a complete account of the events.

The story of this sea journey is the most complete and detailed maritime account in the Bible and it provides us with a great deal of information about the sea-going activities of these times, as well as giving comprehensive

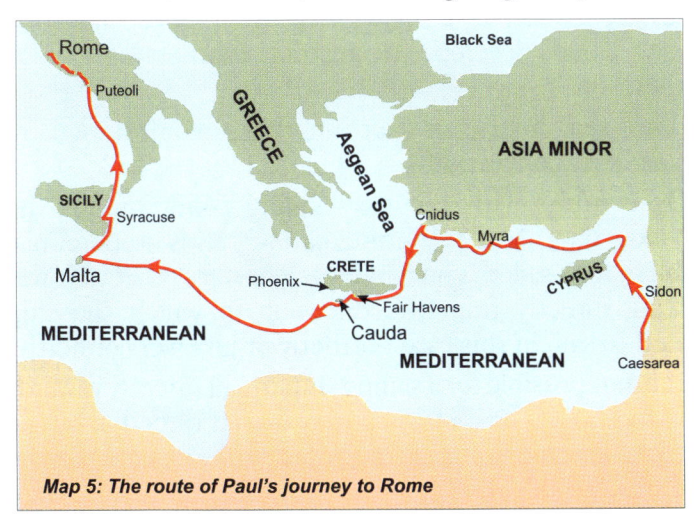

Map 5: The route of Paul's journey to Rome

Divine Weather / 149

weather descriptions which can be meteorologically evaluated.

Section 1: Caesarea to Myra

In all probability, the ship that carried Paul and his escorts from Caesarea to Myra was a coaster – that is a smallish cargo vessel designed to sail on inshore waters and call at many ports. Ac 27:2 states the intention of sailing 'by the coasts of Asia'. The cargo ships of the day were totally dependent on wind power and it is here that the skill of the sailing masters becomes evident.

On the first day, the ship makes a short journey from Caesarea to Sidon. Assuming this to be a daytime sailing, it is very likely that there would be a westerly sea breeze blowing towards the coast during the afternoon and early evening. Such a wind would enable the ship to sail north slowly but without problem.

Anyone who has been to the seaside is familiar with sea breezes. As we relax on the beach, the morning is fine, calm and sunny. The afternoon becomes increasingly hot and then suddenly, a strong cold wind blows in from the sea and continues well into the evening. The air temperature may drop by 10 DegC or more at the onset of a sea breeze and the strong wind makes it feel even colder. Often, cloud develops to restrict temperatures even further.

The sea breeze is yet another manifestation of atmospheric convection – see Figure 11, page 152.

By contrast with the easy sailing conditions of the previous day, Ac 27:4 immediately raises a perennial problem for a sailor. The wind was 'contrary', that is, it was blowing directly from the direction in which the ship wished to sail, in this case northerly or just west of north.

It is not possible for a sailing ship to sail directly towards the wind but it can make headway in that direction by the careful adjustment of sails to allow a series of zigzags to be made; as the ship sails to and fro, its mean direction is into the wind. In sailing parlance, this procedure is called 'tacking'. However, progress in the desired direction is slow and very labour-intensive since many changes have to be made to the sails. In such a case, it is often better to choose another route which, although more circuitous, will allow better progress to be made. This is what the master of this ship chose to do. Instead of north, he sailed north-west towards the south-eastern part of Cyprus. Although this direction was still against the wind to some extent, progress would be less impeded – that is, the angle of the 'tacks' (zigzags) could be increased. In addition, the landmass of Cyprus would modify the prevailing wind in the area, decreasing its speed and changing its direction. Sea captains would be familiar with the effects produced by the various landmasses under a range of conditions and could plan their route advantageously.

Again, Scripture describes the route succinctly. In v4, the route is identified as 'we sailed under Cyprus'. Other Bible versions present this as 'to the lee of', 'under the shelter of', 'close to' which are rather better translations of the Greek word '*hupepleusamen*' After the eastern tip of Cyprus was rounded, a prevailing northerly wind would permit a westward passage under sail. The effects of an onshore sea breeze may have assisted a daytime arrival at Myra.

The meteorological situation which would generate a prevailing northerly wind over the eastern Mediterranean would suggest high pressure to the west of Myra (See Map 6).

The surface wind circulation around the high would produce northerly winds on the route from Sidon to Myra. Wind decreases towards the centre of a high, so the stronger winds would be in the east; this confirms the situation where the ship had to re-route towards Cyprus to avoid these strong 'contrary' winds. The much lighter winds nearer Myra would allow onshore sea breezes to develop during the day.

Divine Weather / 151

Figure 11: Cross-section of a sea-breeze

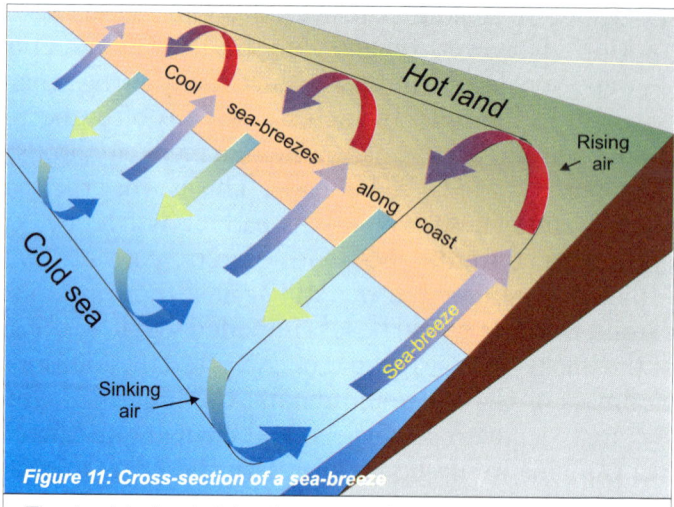

The land is heated by the sun and the air in contact with it becomes hot and less dense. This air rises and is replaced by much cooler air from over the sea. A convection circulation is formed when the lifted air flows out to sea (the green/yellow arrows show a flow around 5,000ft) and then sinks towards the sea surface. Since this happens along a stretch of coast, the model is that of a horizontally revolving tube of air.

The strength and dimension of the circulation is determined by the temperature contrast although other prevailing conditions (e.g. an existing strong wind) will also have an effect. The sea-breeze decays as the temperature contrast decreases. Sea breezes occur in all coastal areas but are strongest and most marked in hot climates. Powerful sea breezes are common on all Mediterranean coasts.

Section 2: Myra to Malta (Melita)

The journey to Fair Havens, Crete

The Roman prisoners and their guard disembarked at Myra and were put aboard an Alexandrian grain ship that was bound for Italy. Acts 27 suggests that this was a ship of considerable size, carrying a full load of grain and 276 'souls' (crew and passengers). It seemed that this ship

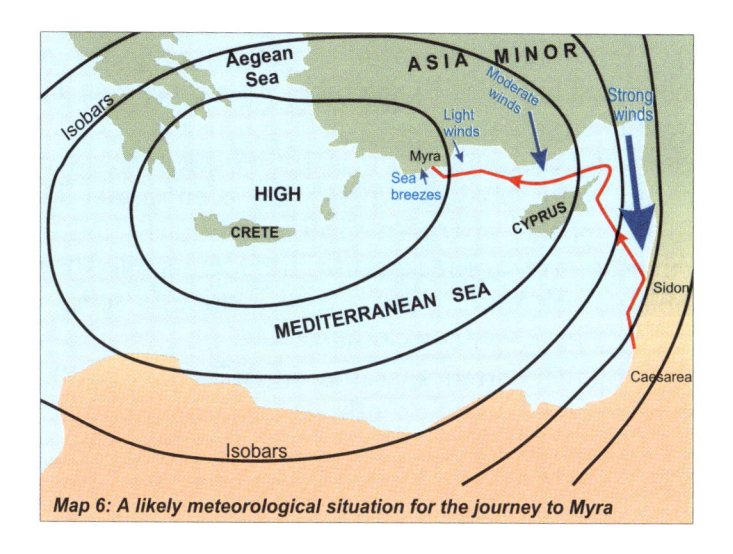

Map 6: A likely meteorological situation for the journey to Myra

intended to sail directly to Italy, passing between Greece and Crete; however it is clear the weather prevented this plan.

Ac 27:7 reveals that the westward journey from Myra to Cnidus was very slow, taking 'many days'. It is not apparent why this part of the journey took so long. It could

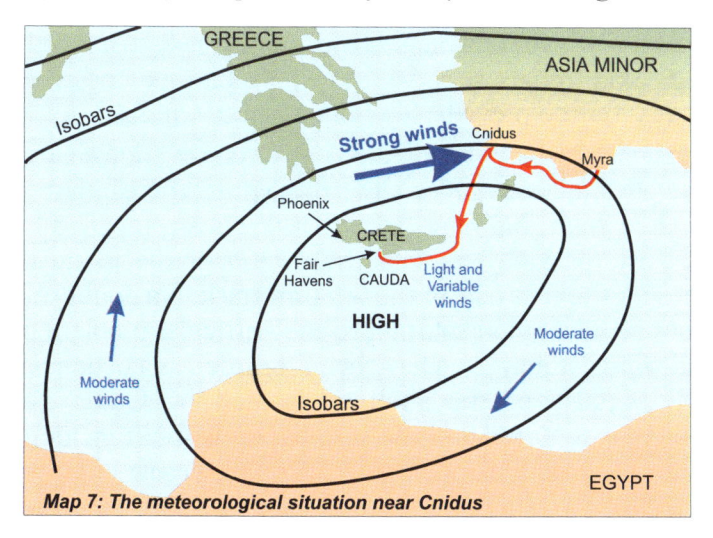

Map 7: The meteorological situation near Cnidus

Divine Weather / 153

(there is little wind near the centre of a high pressure area). Most Bible versions do not attempt to give any further detail but 'The Living Bible' is an exception. The Living Bible translates verse 7 as 'We had several days of rough sailing...' Examination of the Greek text reveals that the word 'braduploountes' has been used. The translation of this word is 'we had sailed slowly' and the only indication of rough seas is in a rather tenuous link with a similar Greek word 'plunō' which includes a sense of 'plunging' – as in washing clothing.

It is then reported that the situation for the ship deteriorated further at the south-western extremity of Asia Minor near Cnidus. There, we are informed that the wind was 'not suffering us' and the Greek word used means 'would not permit further progress'. Presumably, this was a direct headwind for the passage towards southern Greece; this would suggest a westerly wind of significant strength. This series of events implies that the high pressure centre was slipping south as a declining feature, so imposing westerly winds on its northern flank (See Map 7, page 153). In addition, the westerly winds may well have been further enhanced by the effect of the Greek mountains and islands. Meteorologically, this seems to be a reasonable sequence of events which would not suggest that strong winds and rough seas were responsible for the slow progress on the previous leg from Myra to Cnidus.

Just like the master of the coaster chose a longer but more advantageous route close to Cyprus, the captain of the large grain ship now chose to sail south (propelled by the westerly wind) to seek the shelter of the island of Crete for the first part of the western track. No doubt this would be a common solution to the particular problem of head winds; it may even have been regarded as a beneficial track because of the shelter provided by Crete. No problem is reported and the ship arrives without incident at Fair Havens, a harbour on the southern coast of Crete (Ac 27:8). With high pressure not too far south of Crete, prevailing winds would be very light near the south side of the island and southerly sea-breezes would develop during the day. A southerly wind would enable the ship to sail westwards to reach the Fair Havens harbour.

The following verse records that the ship spent 'much time' in Fair Havens and that 'sailing was now dangerous'. Reference to 'the fast' (the Jewish Day of Atonement in August) being over suggests that the month was now September. With the approach of winter, the risk of adverse weather in the Mediterranean increases considerably. Nevertheless the decision was taken to move the ship to the haven of Phoenix (Phenice), a short way along the Cretan coast, because the facilities and general exposure of this port were judged to be much more suitable for a winter stay. Paul attempted to prevent the sailing (v10) by advising strongly against it but the ship's captain and owner were determined to attempt the short journey when weather permitted.

The attempt to reach Phoenix (Phenice)

When a promising day of light southerly winds arrived (v13), they weighed anchor and sailed for Phoenix, towing the ship's boat behind them. Not long after, the weather changed abruptly and the ship was struck by a 'tempestuous wind, called Euroclydon' (v14). The ship could make no headway towards Phoenix and, in an attempt to minimise damage, the crew allowed the ship to run with the wind (v15). The very violent wind blew the ship away from Crete towards the southwest and its extremely turbulent nature soon caused damage to the ship's boat (on tow) and to the ship itself. Ships of that day had only one very stout mast to which the large mainsail was attached; therefore the power of the wind was translated through only one point in the ship – the place where the mast was fixed to the hull and decking structure. When such ships were affected by very strong and turbulent winds, the strains transmitted to the hull were enormous and damage to the basic structure of the ship could occur. No doubt the sailors reduced the sail area as much as possible but, even so, the ship would be driven southwest at considerable speed.

It is recorded that the crew managed to recover the ship's boat with great difficulty when they succeeded in acquiring some shelter on the southern side of a small island called Cauda (now Gavdhos) (vv16-17). This small island is around 50km southwest of Fair Havens. The account now makes it obvious that serious structural damage had been done; v17 reveals that the ship needed to be 'undergirded'. Undergirding is an attempt to strengthen a ship's hull by passing strong cables underneath it and tightening them across the deck. These taut cables help to hold the hull timbers together.

The violent north-easterly wind which carried them to Cauda was obviously a well-known and adverse feature of this area since it had acquired a Greek name, transliterated into English in the AV as 'Euroclydon'. This is assumed to be the the combination of two Greek words **Euros** and **kludon** which mean 'south-easterly' and 'billow'; i.e. 'a south-east (or easterly) wind which raises mighty waves'. Unfortunately, the wind direction described by this word is totally wrong! An easterly or south-easterly wind, no matter how strong, would not have blown the ship from Fair Havens to Cauda but would actually have assisted the journey to Phoenix, albeit dangerously.

Modern editions of the Greek text reveal a different word – 'Eurakulon'. This is mostly understood as a combination of *eurus* (Latin, east wind) or **euros** (Greek, SE wind) + *aquilo* (Latin, north wind), creating a northeast wind. So in newer Bible versions, **Eurakulon** becomes 'Euraquilo', 'Northeaster' or 'Levanter'. I prefer to think it is a local name, possibly derived from '**kulo**' meaning 'to roll down' and '**Eura**' similar to the Greek word for 'wide'. It seems the Greek text that the AV translators used had been corrupted to include 'storm' but the original name

156 / A Passage to Rome

actually described a squally wind rolling down from the Cretan mountains.

It is most likely that this severe north-easterly wind was a southern break-through of the 'etesian winds' which are a common feature of the Aegean Sea region in the late summer and autumn transition months. These winds are generally northerly, although their exact direction may range through the north-west to north-east quadrant. They are generated by the large contrast between land and sea; the wind is then enhanced by the effect of strong low-level atmospheric stability.

In previous chapters, much has been said before about atmospheric *instability* which is the fundamental cause of much cloud and precipitation. The converse of this condition is atmospheric *stability* which occurs, for instance, near areas of high pressure where air sinks towards the Earth's surface (as described in Chapter 4). As the air sinks, it warms due to compression and so becomes increasingly warm as it approaches the Earth's surface. However, there is always some continued interaction between the Earth's surface and the air immediately above

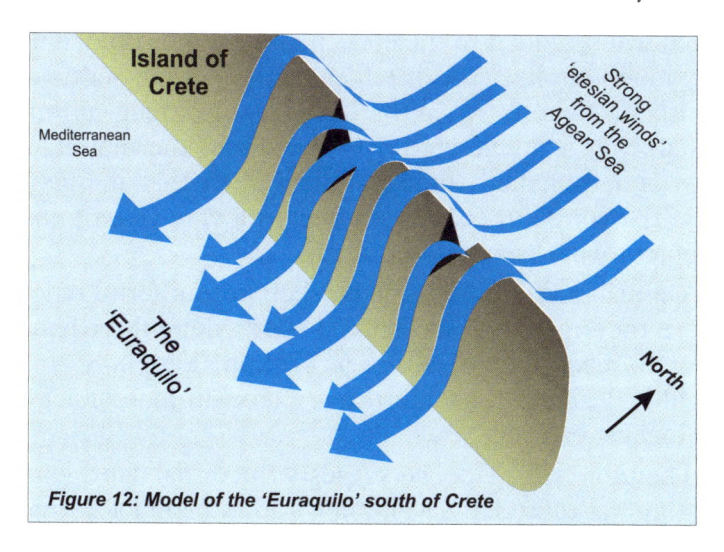

Figure 12: Model of the 'Euraquilo' south of Crete

Divine Weather / 157

it and the effect of this may be to form a 'temperature inversion' in the low-level atmosphere – that is, a layer where the temperature *increases* vertically instead of the normal decrease.

The effect of a temperature inversion is to place a barrier between the interactions near the Earth's surface and those that are going on higher up. A very common example of this effect can be seen in the concentration of smoke pollution at a low level when the smoke is trapped below the temperature inversion. The same happens with fog or even thick drizzly cloud; these are typical occasions when your barometer suggests you should be having fine weather (high pressure) when it is actually cold, miserable and drizzly outside.

Such temperature inversions may also have a marked effect on the low-level wind flow, causing it to be concentrated because it cannot dissipate its energy upwards. The 'etesian winds' are an example of this, with the cold Aegean Sea responsible for forming a low-level temperature inversion that concentrates wind flow beneath it. At times, the general meteorological situation in the Aegean will produce northerly winds in the area which will be added to the etesian effects, thus producing very much stronger winds which can penetrate south to the island of Crete. When this happens, the strong current of stable air is accelerated over the top of the mountain ridge and funnelled through valleys such that it bursts upon the southern coastal sea area as a very violent and turbulent wind (see Figure 12, page 157).

A similar sort of effect can be seen in southern France where the 'mistral' is accelerated south along the Rhone valley to reach speeds as high as 120kph, 75mph. Such a speed is designated as 'Hurricane Force' in meteorology, the highest category.

Therefore the evidence suggests the initial damage to the ship was caused by a well-known and violent local wind feature which probably originated in the etesian wind structure further north.

Cauda to Melita (Malta)

After their rapid journey to the island of Cauda and the frenetic emergency repairs carried out in that area of temporary shelter, there is no respite for the ship and its occupants. A storm soon bursts upon them again; the words 'exceedingly tossed with a tempest' (Ac 27:18) provide a picture of extreme chaos, describing their attempts to stay afloat by 'lightening the ship', even by 'casting out … the tacking', (the ship's gear and rigging equipment). This allowed the ship to stay afloat but it was then carried westwards for 750km (470mi), with the violent weather continuing to inflict yet more damage along the way. The description 'when neither sun nor stars appeared in many days, when no small tempest lay upon us' (v20) showed that the severe weather now affecting them persisted across a wide area of the central Mediterranean. Storm winds, thick and continuous cloud with lashing rain at times, poor visibility and chilly temperatures caused them to give up all hope of survival. These conditions are reported to persist for more than two weeks.

Although there is an implication that the severe weather was a continuation of the 'Euraquilo', this is not possible. The 'Euraquilo' is a class of localised wind which is experienced in a specific area, in this case in the vicinity of the island of Crete. Its intensity depends upon the existence of the Cretan mountains as well as on the specific atmospheric conditions described. In any case the ship's westward progress was actually very slow. It took 14 days to travel 750km west, an average speed of only 2.2 kph, whereas a ship driven by a storm force easterly wind would expect to make very much quicker progress.

The meteorological situation which fits the evidence presented is an intense and slow-moving low pressure

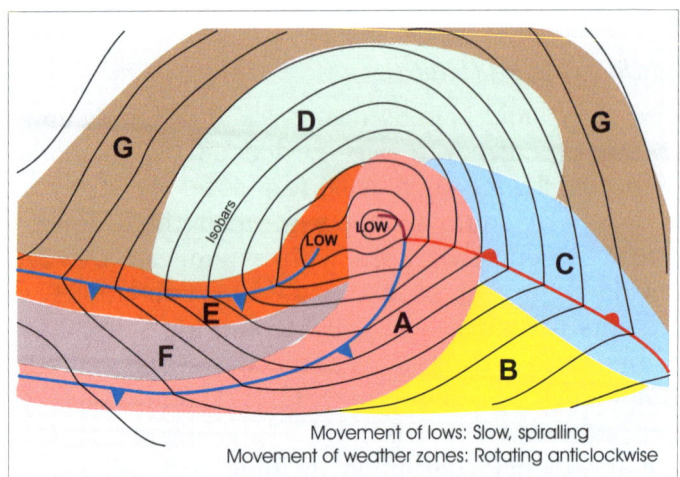

Map 8: An example of weather conditions around an intense low

Movement of lows: Slow, spiralling
Movement of weather zones: Rotating anticlockwise

Zone	Wind	Weather	Cloud, Visibility	Sea
A	Southwest gales; westerly lighter to N of cold front	Heavy rain; Hail, thunder near cold front	Cloudy; Poor or very poor visibility	Very rough Turbulent near colf front
B	Southwest strong to gale	Rain, heavy near low. Much drizzle mist and fog	Cloudy; Very poor visibility	Rough
C	Southwest gales Southeast N of warm front	Rain, heavy near warm front, esp. near low	Cloudy Poor visibility	Rough and turbulent
D	Northeast to east strong and turbulent	Rain or heavy showers, some thundery	Mainly cloudy Moderate visibility	Rough
E	Shifting N-west to N-east, mod to strong, turb.	Outbreaks rain some thundery	Cloudy; Moderate to poor visibility	Rough and turbulent confused
F	Northwest Light to moderate	Rain or showers; some brief dry spells	Cloudy. Moderate to good visibility	Rough
G	Northeast to southeast moderate, gusty	Showers, dry at times	Broken cloud Good, moderate in showers	Moderate

system. As already mentioned in Chapter 7 (the story of Jonah's storm) such weather systems often intensify in the western Mediterranean in autumn and these active features then may be driven south-east by developments in the high atmosphere, such as the penetration of cold air

160 / A Passage to Rome

aloft (an upper trough). The low pressure system will then become slow-moving over the sea to the south of Italy and Greece, where it will intensify even further as very warm desert air is drawn into the vortex circulation and moistened considerably by the warm waters of the Mediterranean Sea. Storm force winds will spiral into the low centre to rush upwards in the vortex region. Latent heat will be released to intensify the process and violent precipitation (including hail and thunder) will be generated.

An active low like this may be slow-moving but it will not be completely stationary. Often the movement of the low centre will be in a series of uneven spirals (imagine the movement of the base of a spinning top) and this will cause considerable alterations in wind direction and variations in weather for a ship drifting on the sea in its immediate vicinity. Map 8 suggests some of the weather variations that are likely to occur around such an intense low complex.

As the grain ship drifts within the area affected by this intense low complex, the combination of ship and vortex movements will cause the hapless vessel to be beset by rapidly changing wind and severe weather conditions. Sudden shifts in wind direction will produce unpredictable blows and strains on the ship's structure, threaten to capsize it and drive it along in many different directions. For the crew, howling wind and lashing precipitation will arrive from all directions, greatly increasing the danger of loss overboard and making shelter impossible. The ship will plunge uncontrollably as the sea is whipped up into large, turbulent and damaging waves. Such an irregular pattern of movement would explain why an average speed of only 2kph was recorded over 14 days of constant storm force winds.

It was at the height of the storm that Paul addressed all on board, telling them of a vision he had received and assuring them they would all be saved. They would be 'cast

Divine Weather / 161

upon a certain island' (Ac 27:26). Soon after (reportedly 14 days after leaving Cauda), they saw land. The crew wanted to abandon ship at once but Paul intervened again, telling the Centurion Julius that all must remain aboard if they wished to survive. He encouraged all to eat, so that their strength would be maintained. The meal was preceded by breaking bread and thanking God for deliverance.

Subsequently, it was possible to run the ship aground (vv39-44). As predicted, all were saved but the continuing storm broke the ship up. Paul and his companions had arrived in very dramatic fashion on the island of Malta (Melita).

Section 3: Malta to Rome

Paul, his fellow prisoners, the soldiers and the ship's crew spent the winter on the island of Malta, receiving help from the local population. When winter ended, the journey recommenced in another Alexandrian grain ship that was bound for Italy. No problems are reported on the first leg of the journey to Syracruse in eastern Sicily, where three days were spent (Ac 27:12). The following verses contain a peculiar expression: '… we fetched a compass and came to Rhegium.' Most other biblical versions translate the Greek word '*perielontes*' as 'we circled around' which is a more literal translation indicating a track which followed the coastline. Presumably, this circuitous track was necessary because of light or contrary winds.

The next day's south wind was ideal to take the ship to Puteoli, its destination in the Bay of Naples (now called Pozzuoli). Although a good deal of the grain would be destined for Rome, the port at Rome was not yet able to accommodate ships of this size. Therefore, although not stated explicitly, the rest of Paul's journey to Rome was by land, a distance of around 200km. This overland journey is confirmed (v15) by the fact that some Christian followers came to meet him at Appii Forum, some 80km south of Rome.

In Rome, total freedom did not come to Paul. He was kept under house arrest and guarded constantly by a soldier. However, his friends had free access to him and he spent the next years evangelising and converting many to the Christian faith.

Comment on the whole story

At first sight, this vivid story describing Paul's journey to Rome could be described as a straightforward account of a very eventful and dangerous maritime journey. The details are recorded clearly and the role of the weather in the story is paramount. In every case, the behaviour of the weather is comprehensible in meteorological terms and well within the range of normal for Mediterranean weather phenomena. The whole account tends to confirm that the weather of Paul's time was very similar to that of today.

Although the first leg of the journey was relatively uneventful, the careful description of each day's sailing gives a valuable insight into the knowledge and skill of the masters of these cargo ships. In the dramatic second leg, the cataclysmic weather that finally destroyed the ship has been shown to come from two meteorological sources. The occupants of the ship were extremely unfortunate to be affected initially by the damaging 'Euraquilo' which was followed shortly after by a major central Mediterranean storm. The final part of the journey once again demonstrates the art of sailing in the region.

However, there are significant spiritual dimensions. Paul's warning against the attempt to sail to Phoenicia (Ac 27:10) showed precognition from some source. Then during the storm, at the time of deepest despair when all thought that death was imminent, Paul stood to address all on board and told them that he had received a message from God (Ac 27:21-26). They would all be saved and cast upon an island. This prediction soon arrived in the shape of a very rocky landfall. When the ship's crew attempted to leave the ship, Paul advised the Roman centurion that everyone must remain on the ship; only in that way would they survive. Paul also directed them all to eat, so that their strength would be maintained. The meal was preceded by breaking bread and thanking God for deliverance. Although in the end the ship broke up in the violence of the weather, as predicted, no one was killed or injured as they struggled ashore.

While over-wintering on the isle of Malta, various other miracles are recorded. Paul was bitten by a viper but suffered no ill effect. A number of people received God's healing through the prayers of Paul in the name of Jesus Christ and his laying-on of hands. This is of course in accordance with the General Commission of Jesus in Mark's Gospel (Mk 16:15-20), a teaching of empowerment for all Christian believers.

Thus the hand of God appears in the account of Paul's journey to Rome. Once again God saved His followers from death and destruction. Just as God used Noah, Moses and many others in the Old Testament to carry out His work, Paul is used here for similar purposes. Paul's vision at the time of greatest danger guaranteed rescue for all on board, rescue without injury. The account of the meal together is a wonderful moment of pseudo calm, with that note of thanksgiving to God linking the story to the concept of grace before a meal. The protection of Paul from the viper's venom is also a dramatic moment, linked with the references to healing which took place as they over-wintered on Malta.

The spiritual teaching element in this exciting account is clear. It is an echo of so much of Old Testament teaching. It is an everyday illustration of the vivid teaching of Jesus Christ as recorded in the Gospels. God saves and protects His people. God uses His people to carry out His works on earth. His direct relationship with His people is summed up in that moment of prayerful thanksgiving before the meal on the ship.

10

The Unseen God

God in the cloud

Throughout the Bible, the hidden presence of God is often expressed through weather imagery. Cloud is the most common element of weather to be used for this purpose. In many accounts, dense cloud shrouds the presence of the Almighty; sometimes, especially at night, fire is reported within the cloud and storms may also occur, usually linked to manifestations of divine anger. On occasions, direct communication is established by means of a voice speaking from the cloud.

Early biblical 'God in the cloud' references

In the Bible, the first references to cloud appear in Genesis 9, when God is setting out the details of His covenant with Noah (Chapter 5). In this case, the cloud referred to is natural atmospheric cloud, part of the requirement for the formation of a rainbow as discussed earlier. The rainbow was to act as a periodic reminder of God's covenant with Noah and, through him, with all God's people.

However the use of cloud as an obscuring agent is an important element in the Exodus story, part of which has already been reviewed in Chapter 6. In the first 'cloud' references of this type, as the Israelites started the Exodus from Egypt, God guided them '…by day in a pillar of a cloud, to lead them the way; and by night in a pillar of fire, to give them light.' (Ex 13:21 – also Psalm 105). When they were pursued by the Egyptian army, God's cloud was interposed between the tribe and the army, so that the Israelite movements were concealed (Ex 14:20). Finally,

God's cloud was a contributor to the confusion of the Egyptian army at it was disabled and destroyed beneath the waters of the 'Red Sea'.

The manna from heaven

In fact the book of Exodus provides an almost complete range of the use of 'God's cloud'. Exodus 16 recounts the well-known story of the 'manna from heaven'. When the Israelite people were worrying about starving in the wilderness, God spoke to Moses, saying that He would 'rain down bread from heaven (v4 – here, 'rain' is used figuratively). Subsequently (v10), the 'glory of the Lord appeared in the cloud'. The use of the word 'glory' gives the description an additional meaning.

The Hebrew word '*kabowd*' is used many times in the Old Testament, often in the phrase 'glory of the Lord'. This word is used in the Bible to mean glory, honour and beauty. Linked to God in this way, it describes these qualities in Him and emphasises His perfection and authority. The story paints a picture of the people looking with awe at a cloud which demonstrated in some way the presence, power and perfection of God. Some examples suggest brightness or fire in the cloud.

When the life-giving manna was provided (vv13-14), it was delivered with the dew – more weather involvement. The morning evaporation of the dew left the solid grains of manna on the ground, which had to be collected before they melted away in the sun. It seems therefore that the writers of Exodus wished to emphasise the gentle and subtle delivery of this special food for God's people. The concept of dew is one of gentleness and invisibility; water droplets that form on the ground directly from physical cooling and the consequential condensation of water vapour from the air. By contrast, the earlier reference to 'rain' suggests a totally different mechanism, less gentle and distinctly visible. However, it is suggested the figurative use of the word rain was probably to indicate God's forthcoming generosity.

Needless to say, there have been many attempts to identify what manna really was. Described in the Bible as 'like coriander seed' and tasting of 'wafers made with honey' (v31), it has been suggested *inter alia* that manna was associated with a substance exuded by the bark of tamarisk, with a species of lichen which grows on sandstone or with resinous gums which are produced by some desert shrubs. None of these proposals have been accepted as fitting totally the biblical descriptions.

The Ten Commandments

The delivery of the Ten Commandments (Ex 19-20) is filled with weather imagery based on God's glorious presence in a 'thick cloud' (Ex 19:9-11) covering 'Mount Sinai'. This is God's cloud at its most dramatic, intended to demonstrate God's all-pervading power. The cloud descends upon the mountain. It is not only thick and extensive but accompanied by 'thunders and lightnings' (v16). There is also dense smoke and the description suggests the appearance of a volcano; the mountain 'quaked' (v18). There is the sound of a very loud trumpet, heard by all the people below. It was at this point in the story that 'the Lord came down upon mount Sinai' (Exodus 20) and enunciated the Ten Commandments in a mighty voice.

Thereafter, Moses 'drew near unto the thick darkness where God was' and was apprised of a detailed set of laws which the AV describes as 'divers laws and ordinances' (Ex 20:22 – 23-33) – these are 'divers' indeed and extremely comprehensive! In Exodus 24, Moses ascends the mountain, seeing the 'glory of the Lord like a devouring fire on the top of the mount' and receives the famous 'tables (tablets) of stone' upon which were written the Ten Commandments.

In the following chapters, Moses receives many more detailed instructions on conduct and worship, including specifications for the construction of the tabernacle and the Ark of the Covenant which it was to contain. The tabernacle was a special place that would be constructed at every campsite. It was to be a sanctuary for God, a meeting place where He could talk to Moses. Events during the remainder of Exodus and in Leviticus (16:2,13), Numbers (9:15-42:17) and Deuteronomy (1:33, 5:22, 31:15) included not only the guiding 'pillar of cloud' which was fiery at night, but also the presence of God in a cloud which came to cover the 'tabernacle' on a number of occasions.

References from the rest of the Bible

Similar usage of 'God in the cloud' imagery appears in a number of other Old Testament books. There are examples in 1Kings 8 and 2Chronicles 5 ('the glory of the Lord filled the house of the Lord') and in Nehemiah 9, where the guiding pillar of cloud is again at work. Ps 78:14 is a eulogy of praise for God's role in the 'Red Sea' crossing and refers to God's cloud. There are also references in Psalms 57, 68, 97, 99 and Isaiah 4, while Isaiah 19 provides a variation with 'the Lord rideth *upon* a swift cloud' – a vivid image which suggests swift retribution for the unfortunate Egyptians!

In the New Testament, it is notable that the use of cloud imagery is extended to include Jesus Christ. Firstly however, there is the traditional image of God in the clouds, appearing in the synoptic gospels (Mt 17:5, Mk 9:7, Lk 9:34-35) in that dramatic scene when Jesus was acknowledged and blessed by a voice from the cloud saying 'This is my beloved son (in whom I am well pleased). Hear him'. In Paul's first epistle to the church at Corinth, there is also a brief reference to God's role in the 'Red Sea' crossing (1Corinthians 10).

Later in the synoptic gospels, Jesus refers several times to his Second Coming and is reported to use cloud imagery in the descriptions. '...they will see the Son of Man coming in a cloud with power and great glory' (Mt 24:30, Mk 13:26, Lk 21:27); also, 'ye shall see the Son of man sitting on the right hand of power, and coming in the clouds of heaven.' (Mt 26:64, Mk 14:62). Revelation 10, 11 and 14 are concerned with the Second Coming and describe angels and Jesus Christ appearing with 'glorious' cloud imagery. The prophesy (Re 14:14) reads 'And I looked, and behold a white cloud, and upon the cloud one sat like unto the Son of man, having on his head a golden crown, and in his hand a sharp sickle.' This provides a sharp and powerful image of a kingly Jesus, returning to bring justice to the world.

Back in the book of Acts, cloud imagery is used in a slightly different way. In the description of the Ascension of Jesus, the account reads '...he was taken up; and a cloud received him out of their sight' (Ac 1:9). This imagery is repeated in Re 11:12, when 'two witnesses' were brought back to life and '...ascended up to heaven in a cloud'. These images have meaningful links with the Old Testament 'taking up into Heaven' of Enoch and Elijah (Chapter 7).

Mountains and clouds

Many 'God in the cloud' stories are associated with cloud forming upon mountains – a common enough event in the area covered by the Bible accounts. The effect of hills and mountains on cloud formation and precipitation has already been mentioned earlier in the book; in particular, the Figure 8 (atmospheric interactions) shows how the flow of air over a mountain range is a mechanism to produce cloud and precipitation. However, the situation is more complicated than this simple diagram would imply, because the formation of cloud and the occurrence of precipitation are concerned not only with mechanical lifting of air but also with humidity distributions and the degree of stability or instability of the atmosphere. This is why the cloud that forms above or upon mountains can be of various types. For illustrative purposes, the following sections describe four discrete types briefly:

Stability, precipitation and the föhn effect

If moist stable air is lifted over a mountain range and descends the other side (as shown in figure 13, page 172), cloud forms, extends across the ridge, and then dissipates on the lee side. Rain or drizzle may affect the windward side of the ridge and the effect of the rain is to extend the base of the cloud downwards to cover even more of the high ground. Meanwhile, the lee side receives much drier air and is described as being in a 'rain shadow'.

In addition, especially if the ridge is high, lee areas will experience a marked föhn effect, which means that the descending air will become much warmer than it was before the lifting process started. For instance, moist air at 10 DegC at sea level lifted to 5,000ft is likely to be at least 15 DegC when it descends the lee side of the mountain to the valley below. The reason for this is a disparity in the rate of cooling and warming. As the air is lifted on the windward side, it cools due to decrease of air pressure and expansion. However the rate of cooling is offset as condensation (cloud) forms and latent heat is released.

By contrast, when the air reaches the ridge and begins to flow downwards towards the lower ground, it warms due to compression and, this time, there is no offset in the rate of change. Thus the air becomes progressively much warmer than it was when it was on the other side of the ridge. This is a dramatic effect experienced in many parts of the world where there is stable airflow across a substantial mountain area. The name originates in the European Alps where high mountains often cause marked föhn effects.

Standing wave clouds

This is an atmospheric variation of the above. In this case, the structure of stability and airflow pattern sets up an oscillating wave motion downwind of the mountains. If the air is sufficiently moist, condensation occurs in the top part of each airflow wave and 'standing wave clouds' are generated. These clouds persist in the one place while often powerful currents of air flow through them. Sometimes, a particular atmospheric humidity structure causes a series of standing wave clouds to be formed above each other, as shown in Figure 14, page 172. This is only experienced with airflow over higher mountains where the lifting effect can be spread upwards through a considerable depth.

Instability cloud and showers

If the atmosphere is unstable, then the mechanical lifting of air by the mountain can greatly boost convective air flows and form deep cumulus clouds or even the larger cumulonimbus (Figure 15, page 173). ('Unstable' means that the lifted air, though cooled, is still warmer than its surroundings and so continues to rise due to buoyancy.)

The precipitation from these clouds is convective in nature (larger raindrops, heavier precipitation) and the cloud base is likely to build downwards as the air below is moistened by evaporation and subsequent re-condensation. The increase of air temperature during the day will strengthen the convective process – this explains why the heaviest showers often occur in the mid to late afternoon. With the deepest convection, the formation of cumulonimbus clouds may result in the showers turning to hail; lightning and thunder may also be generated.

Figure 13: How the fohn effect works

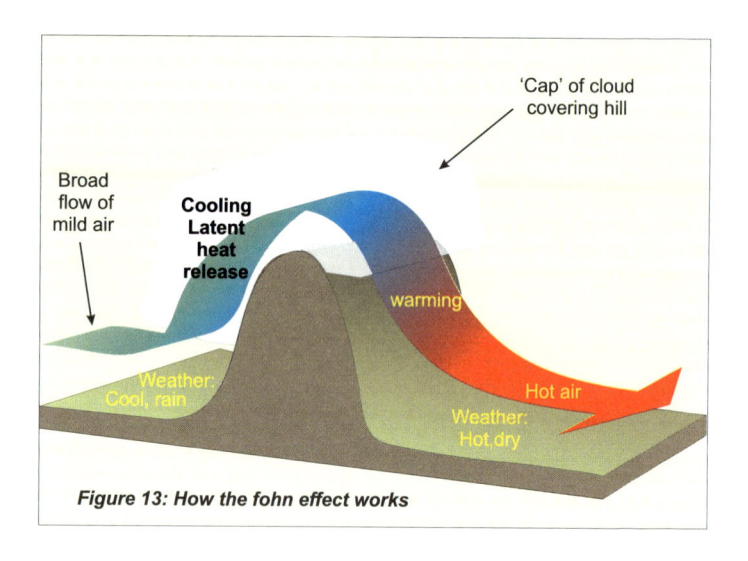

Banner cloud

This is a striking cloud formation that demonstrates a different cloud mechanism. In this case, the cloud appears usually as a triangular-shaped 'banner' which extends from the *downwind side* of a high mountain peak. The cloud appears to be stationary and attached to the mountain.

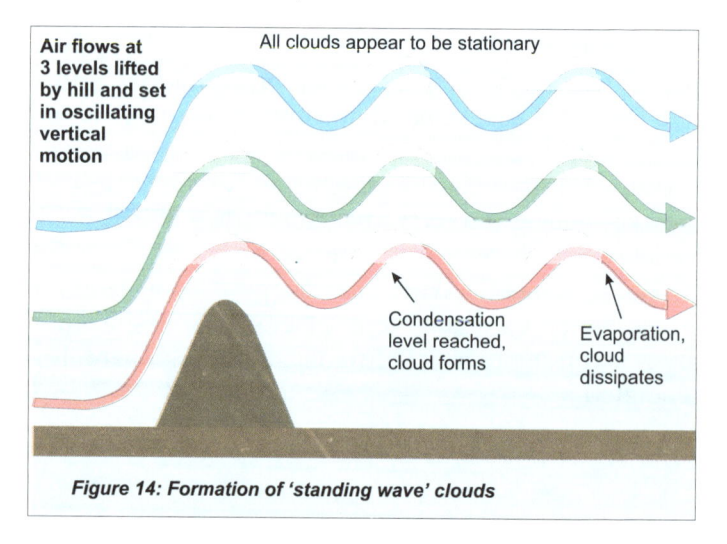

Figure 14: Formation of 'standing wave' clouds

Figure 15: Mountains and convective clouds

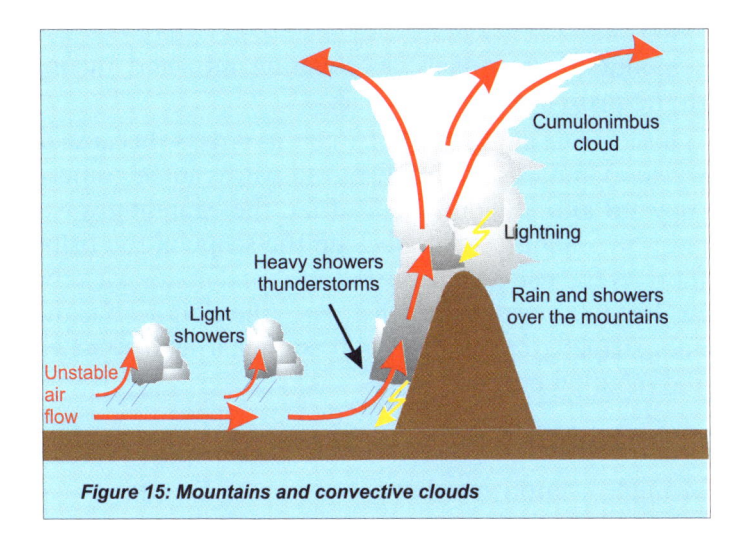

This is normally only seen on the highest mountains with precipitous slopes and crags. In this case, the prevailing airflow over and around the jagged mountain causes reduced pressure at the lee side of the mountain. Figure 16 shows how a strong prevailing flow of dry air over the mountain may result in a flow of air up the steep lee side of

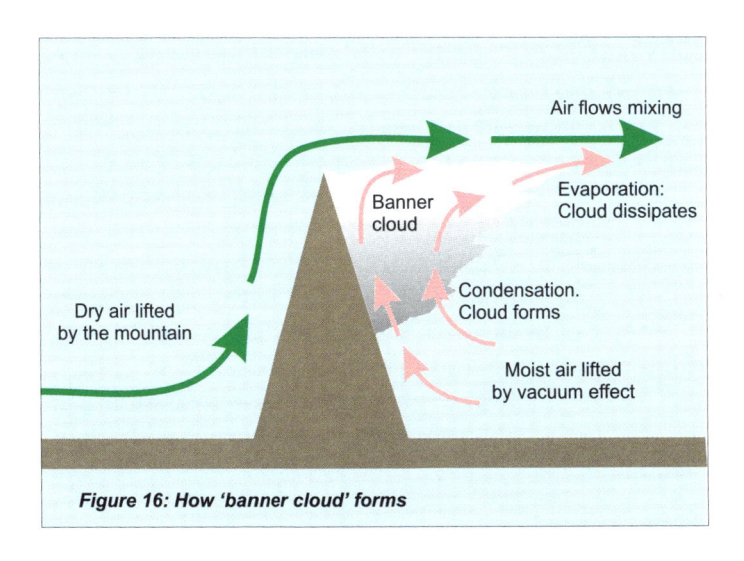

Figure 16: How 'banner cloud' forms

Divine Weather / 173

the mountain, eventually accelerating into and mixing with the main flow over the peak.

This lee-side air will of course cool as it rises (because of expansion) and, if sufficiently moist, will at some point in its upward journey form cloud. Like the 'standing wave' cloud, this 'banner' cloud takes up the shape of the rising airflow. As the rising air is carried away and mixes with the prevailing flow, evaporation dissipates the cloud. Thus the banner-shaped cloud appears to be stationary and attached to the mountain.

The link with God's presence

It is quite unsurprising that the writers of Scripture used clouds in this way. From earliest times, mankind has been able to gaze up at these mysterious formations in the sky, seeing many shapes and colours, manifestations which are seemingly alive in their patterns of movement and change. Many of the clouds present a convincing appearance of solidity but when they descend to the ground (e.g. rolling in as fog or blanketing higher ground), these seemingly solid entities are found to be gaseous and ephemeral. Within the cloud, observers find themselves shrouded by a clammy blanket of water droplets, dank and cold, with visibility and light levels reduced considerably.

It would also be observed that cloud frequently capped hills – a perceived meeting of mystery with reality. When such hills were ascended, entry into the cloud base would take the climber from a world of solid, sharp and reassuring reality to a mysterious, chilly environment, obscured, dull and shadowy. The symbolism of climbing upwards towards God's imagined domain coupled with the sudden replacement of reality with an ephemeral world would transmit a powerful message of mystery. It is easy to appreciate why biblical writers would seek to associate an unseen God with obscuring cloud, especially with cloud that shrouded high ground.

In addition, cloud has long been recognised as a strong link with the maintenance of life. It is only the prior presence of cloud which brings life-giving rain – regarded by spiritual beings as a great and essential blessing from God. At the other end of the spectrum, cloud can be the precursor of disaster, bringing the dangers of lightning, thunder and hail, with their attendant destruction and risk of injury or death.

So it was that the mystery of God's presence could conveniently be shrouded by clouds in all their diversity, ranging from the gentle beneficence of shade and watering to the awesome torrents and terrifying lightning and thunderclaps which were the images associated with God's anger and destruction of evil.

There is perhaps one significant variation in the way the New Testament cloud imagery is presented. Throughout the Old Testament, God is obscured by the cloud. The New Testament references are similar – God was within the cloud when He spoke the blessing of Jesus (e.g. Mt 17:5). By contrast, the association of Jesus with clouds is different. When Jesus speaks of his own return in the Second Coming, he says 'they shall *see* the Son of Man coming in a cloud with power and great glory' (Lk 21:27); likewise the references from Revelation described the returning Jesus as one who would be visible – 'Upon the cloud one sat like unto the Son of Man' (Re 14:14). By this variation, the biblical writers differentiated between God and Jesus. No one knew how to picture God (indeed, it was considered inappropriate to try) whereas Jesus could be made clearly visible and recognisable as a man.

There is one more strand to this discussion. Re 14:14 echoes Da 7:13 – 'I saw in the night visions, and, behold, one like the Son of man came with the clouds of heaven, and came to the Ancient of days, and they brought him near before him'. This suggests a manifestation of human form, to be *seen* in association with cloud imagery. Some Bible commentators have identified this verse positively as a prophecy of the coming of Jesus. Others (generally more recent writings) have suggested the term 'Son of man' is used to contrast this vision with those presented previously – that of four beasts; the 'Son of man' is a poetic description of a vision recognisably in human form. The imagery is of beasts from 'the great abyss' (the source of evil) and the human form coming from above (from God). According to the writers of the Gospels, the term 'Son of man' was adopted by Jesus in some of his sayings.

He who makes the weather

Manifestations of God's power and greatness

There are many occasions in the Bible when elements of weather are used within fulsome eulogies of praise. These prayers of adoration illustrate and emphasise God's mighty power and greatness. In 2Samuel 22 David praises God – 'And He made *(inter alia)*… thick clouds of the skies'(v12): 'The Lord thundered from heaven… He sent out…lightning and discomfited them' (vv14-15). In the Psalms, David urges everyone to praise God: 'Sing unto the LORD with thanksgiving; sing praise upon the harp unto our God: Who covereth the heaven with clouds, who prepareth rain for the earth, who maketh grass to grow upon the mountains.' (Ps 147:7-8). Similar eulogistic references are found in a number of other Psalms, several Proverbs, Job 37, Jeremiah 10 and 51. These eulogies use a whole range of 'weather words' as God's power and glory is praised. For instance God is thanked and praised not only for the creation of clouds but also for nurturing rain and showers, gentle dew, mists and purifying winds. In other passages, writers acknowledge and praise God's power and majesty in descriptions of dense clouds, lightning, thunder, hail, snow, whirlwinds and frost.

All but one reference of this type appear in the Old Testament. The single New Testament reference is in Matthew's Gospel that refers to God's power over the weather: '…for He maketh His sun to rise on the evil and on the good, and sendeth rain on the just and on the unjust'. (Mt 5:45)

Weather imagery and the glory of God

Earlier chapters in the book have referred to highly poetic descriptions of the glory of God (e.g. Chapter 7 Ezekiel), which were often expressed by weather imagery. While most of these descriptions are found in the Old Testament, the dense poetry of the Book of Revelation describes a number of scenes of glory using weather terms. In Re 4:3, a scene of glory is described thus: 'And He that sat was to look upon like a jasper and a sardine stone: and there was a rainbow round about the throne, in sight like unto an emerald.' In this description it is the shape of a rainbow that is envisaged rather than its colours. The image presented is that of an over-arching band of shimmering colour which was surrounding the glory of the Lord God as He sat upon a heavenly throne. The colour of the arc was that of a precious stone, emerald green.

The God of nurture

Gentle dew, life giving rains

One of the first comments made in this book referred to the fact that water was essential for life. This is obvious to all of us, since every day we must replenish water losses from our own bodies; without water, we do not survive long. For their sustenance, the people of biblical times depended largely on local fishing and agriculture; an imbalance in normal water supplies could have serious implications for supply of food and drink. In particular, a dearth of water could cause crop failure and reduce fish stocks. So it was that God was thanked and praised for the provision of the 'right amounts' of water.

The delivery of water by dew has elements of both gentleness and mystery. Even although we know it to be a consequence of cooling and condensation of water vapour from the air, there is still something magical about its silent materialisation. In the Bible, there are references to the beneficial occurrence of dew in the Old Testament and they are invariably positive and respectful. We have already seen that the manna from heaven was delivered with the dew.

There are a number of other similar biblical references to dew; somewhat surprisingly, they are exclusively in the books of the Old Testament. In Genesis 27, in a fatherly blessing of Jacob, Isaac wished 'God give you the dew of heaven'. In Deuteronomy, God is blessed by Jacob for 'His dew'. Job praises the Lord for His dew in Deuteronomy 38. The book of Daniel mentions 'the dew of heaven' a number of times with great respect. Zechariah shows God's beneficence '…the heavens shall give their dew; and I will cause the remnant of this people to possess all these things' (Ze 8:12).

Of course agriculture requires more water than would be delivered by dew alone and so the provision of rain at the appropriate times is a great blessing. There are several references in Leviticus and Deuteronomy to God's promise of '…rain of your land in due season' (De 11:14). Joel refines this to '…gives you the former rain moderately…and the latter rain in the first month' (Joel 2:23). The 'former rain' (not too heavy!) fell later in the year for the early planting. The 'latter rain' was required for the ripening of the crop. In the New Testament, Ac 14:17 makes a similar reference to the blessing of rain at the right time: '…(He) gave us rain from heaven, and fruitful seasons, filling our hearts with food and gladness.'

Interestingly, the word 'showers' is sometimes used instead of 'rain'. '…I will cause the shower to come down in his season' (Ez 34:26); in a Psalm of praise, David writes 'Thou waterest the ridges thereof abundantly: thou settlest the furrows thereof: thou makest it soft with showers'. Examination of the Hebrew texts reveals the use of seven different words for rain or showers. The most common is the word '*mawtawr*' – rain, which may also be hail. When the AV translation is 'shower', the most common Hebrew word used is *'geshem'*. This is derived from a similar word that means to shower, possibly violently. However, some of the texts using this word imply great variability: 'For he saith to the snow, Be thou on the earth; likewise to the *small rain*, and to the *great rain* of his strength.' (Jb 37:6). Here *'geshem'* is used for both small and great rain. Also, Zechariah links the Hebrew word with 'bright clouds' – '...so the Lord shall make bright clouds, and give them showers of rain...' (Ze 10:1).

The texts using *'geshem'* usually have implications of convective showers. Shower precipitation can be very variable – everything from a brief sprinkling to a veritable downpour. The link with bright clouds brings a picture of sunshine and showers, with the well-developed cumulus or cumulonimbus clouds shining brightly in the sunshine. Two of the other words used for rain refer specifically to the 'former' early rain of autumn and the 'latter' spring rain; two more are used only once, with links to arrows and 'throwing water'.

The New Testament Greek also reveals a range of words that have been translated as rain, although the distinction is not quite so apparent. '**broche̅**' is rain but may also be shower according to the definition! '**huetos**' is 'rain, especially shower'! There are also Greek words for the 'early' and 'late' rain. 'Shower' only appears once in the AV New Testament. '...There cometh a shower...' (Lk 12:54). The Greek word used '**ombros**' is a violent shower or a thunderstorm.

It is certain, therefore, that the biblical writers of both Old and New Testaments recognised the difference between rain and showers; in addition to the different Hebrew and Greek words used, the texts often give additional description which makes this apparent.

The wind of nurture

The other meteorological element which is linked with God's nurture, rescue or saving actions is wind. Although wind commonly appears as a mechanism for destruction (as examined in the next chapter), there are a number of occasions in the Bible stories when wind is used for beneficial purposes.

Earlier chapters have already presented most of these stories. The Creation story (Chapter 3) used wind to tame the waters and create the Earth. Wind dried up the effects of the Flood for Noah (Chapter 5). Wind saved the Israelites at the beginning of the Exodus (Chapter 6). Wind is used to save in the stories of Elijah, Ezekiel and Jonah. In the book of Isaiah, there is the story of wind being used to divide the waters of the River Jordan so that the Israelites could cross (Is 11:15).

In the Bible, it is often possible to link wind with '*ruach*' that mysterious Hebrew word which has been presented and discussed in several earlier chapters of the book. It is a word that may be translated as wind, air, breath, spirit, soul, life force or power.

Pictures of God

The examples given in this chapter show how the writers of the Bible attempted to give their readers pictures of God. Of course, these are pictures that cannot be seen, so cloud is used extensively as a suitable and convenient obscuring agent. The meeting of cloud with high ground is, in particular, an important image which allows understanding of a possible God/human interface. In the New Testament, the obscured picture is augmented significantly by the appearance of Jesus Christ *on* not *in* the cloud. This in turn is a powerful visual teaching of the link between God and Jesus Christ.

Weather proves to be very useful in praising God's greatness and glory; almost every weather element is used for this purpose. God's nurture of His people is emphasised by His delivery of the means of life, using normal weather processes.

11

The God of Storms

Storms have long been defined as violent disturbances of weather, always associated with very strong winds and usually accompanied by other powerful manifestations of weather, such as heavy precipitation (rain, sleet, snow, hail), lightning and thunder. Strong winds blowing over the oceans are responsible for creating large and dangerous sea waves; to a lesser degree, this happens also on large inland seas or lakes. In desert or other very dry regions, strong winds generate sandstorms or dust storms. In scientific meteorology, the word storm is used rather more narrowly. A thunder*storm* is the occurrence of lightning discharge and consequential thunder. A *sandstorm* or *dust storm* is the severe reduction of visibility by sand or other solid particles lifted by strong winds. *Storm Force* is a wind speed range in the Beaufort Wind Scale equivalent to a mean speed of 55-63 mph. A *storm surge* is the result of wind effects interacting with the astronomical tide – depending upon the wind direction, this may enhance or diminish the tidal flow.

Most of the biblical stories examined in previous chapters included storms (in the wider sense) as an important element within them. Powerful storm elements were important components of the Creation (Chapter 3) and in the Flood (Chapter 5). The Exodus account reports that God used storm elements dramatically to help the Israelites in their flight from the Egyptian army. The stories of Elijah, Ezekiel, Jonah and Paul are pervaded with storms of various types. The stories of Jesus, presented in Chapter 8, include storms in a number of the accounts.

There are many other references to storms throughout Scripture. Of the various storm elements, wind is the most commonly used weather element; over one-quarter of the weather-related references are associated with some concept of wind and many of these refer to powerful storms. This rest of this chapter analyses these references and gives examples.

Storms of destruction

Storm stories usually focus on destruction of some type, although this may be part of an action to save – for instance there are many examples of God's protection of His people by the destruction of their enemies. Occurrences of land-based storms may destroy crops, houses or other property. Often there is injury or death among animals or people. Sea-based storms are associated characteristically with danger or damage to ships. The outcome may well be shipwreck, injury and death.

The other common usage of storm elements is figurative. The description of a storm is an indication of the devastation to come by another source – losing a military battle, for instance.

Multiple weather elements

In today's reality, storms usually combine a number of weather elements – strong winds, thick cloud, poor visibility, reduced temperature, rain, sleet, snow, hail, lightning and thunder. Certainly, lightning, thunder and hail are very dramatic manifestations of the weather. Their occurrence is often combined with strong and very turbulent winds because these phenomena are associated with powerful convection and strong atmospheric uplift. Such conditions produce the large and awesome cumulonimbus clouds with their anvil-shaped tops which are the breeding grounds for atmospheric electrical activity and violent precipitation. If this very deep convection is imposed on a broad-scale situation of very strong winds (as they often are in the vicinity of a deep low pressure system), then the weather elements will be even more violent and extensive.

All these weather elements have appeared in the storms described in the well-known events of earlier chapters. In the rest of the Bible, a typical example appears in 1Samuel 12 when the prophet Samuel warns the people of Israel and their new king Saul that they must give up their wicked ways and be totally obedient to God.

In the story, the prophet drives home his message in a most dramatic way; he demonstrates the power of God by calling down a storm upon their crops at harvest time: 'So Samuel called unto the Lord and the Lord sent thunder and rain that day: and all the people greatly feared the Lord and Samuel.' (1Sa 12:18). Although only thunder and rain are mentioned here, lightning is an essential precursor to thunder; also, powerful gusty winds accompany active cumulonimbus cloud activity and the 'rain' would be very heavy. Crop destruction would occur. This event would be regarded as very mysterious since 'harvest time' in the Middle East region is in July and normally no rain falls in this month; this is confirmed by current weather statistics which shows many years of zero rainfall in the months of July and August.

An even more severe storm is apparently prophesied by Ezekiel (Ezekiel 38). This refers to God's judgement of Gog, the Chief Prince of the land of Magog, who will attack Israel from the north with a great army. The relevant verse, quoting God's words, reads: 'And I will plead against him with pestilence and with blood; and I will rain upon him, and upon his bands, and upon the many people that are with him, an overflowing rain, and great hailstones, fire, and brimstone.' (Ez 38:22). Here, the violent storm weather elements are added to impositions of 'pestilence and blood', recalling the imagery of the destruction of Sodom (Genesis 19) and the fifth 'plague' of Egypt (Chapter 6). The intention is to communicate a picture of unremitting misery, using fatal illness and disease accompanied by an extended period of cataclysmic weather. In this case, it is judged to be a figurative picture to warn the invaders that the conduct of war will be totally against them and they will perish in great tribulation.

A number of other references use similar storm imagery to warn of destruction by natural forces or to illustrate figuratively the destruction which will be visited upon those to whom the words are directed.

The winds of destruction

Biblical descriptions of destruction by wind alone generally involves the *east wind* or the *whirlwind*.

The east wind

Throughout the Bible, the east wind invariably symbolises destruction by power and extreme dryness. Sometimes the words 'east wind' are used but other passages refer to 'winds from the wilderness' – that is from the desert or arid mountain regions to the east of Egypt and the eastern Mediterranean lands. The mechanism to produce strong easterly winds was discussed in Chapter 6 in connection with the plague of locusts and the division of the 'Red Sea'. Such winds are always extremely dry and their effects are very unwelcome, withering and breaking down growing crops by their strength and strong evaporation effects.

An early biblical reference to destruction that concerned wind appears in Genesis 41. In this reference, Pharaoh dreams that the east wind destroys healthy crops, which are replaced by 'blasted' ears of corn. In the Bible, 'blasted' is the word used to describe the effects of strong easterly winds upon plant life. This dream was part of a warning about a famine to come. Similar references to the east wind are in 2Kings 19, Isaiah 37 and Ezekiel 17.

Other examples of destruction by the east wind alone use its power in various ways. In the book of Job, the troubles of the upright and moral Job begin with the death of his sons when a 'strong wind from the wilderness' is said to have demolished the house and killed the young men. The book of Job is a complex book in which its unknown writer presents a series of poetic and often rhetorical dialogues by Job, three of his friends, God and Satan. The dialogues are filled with weather imagery, often used within figures of speech; these will be discussed in the next chapter.

The 'destroying wind' is also used symbolically. The book of Jeremiah provides several examples. Je 4:11-12 refers to 'A dry wind of the high places in the wilderness…not to fan nor to cleanse', a description of the unpleasantly dry and cold east wind. Later in Jeremiah there is reference to 'a destroying wind' (Je 51:1). The 'wind' in this verse is generally interpreted as the invading host of Medes and Persians. The strong winds of destruction also appear in the poetry of Revelation 6 and 7.

Haggai presents a variation. Here the Governor of Judea and the Chief Priest are to be given a prophecy to encourage them to rebuild the Temple in Jerusalem. This was the second Temple; the first, built by Solomon, was destroyed by the Babylonians in the sixth Century BC. It seems that Israelites had disregarded God's earlier request to rebuild and so and He had '…smote you with blasting and with mildew and with hail in all the labours of your hands; yet ye turned not to me, saith the Lord' (Hg 2:17). In this case, the incitement was not only the destroying 'blasting' of the east wind interspersed with damaging hail but also destruction of the plants by mildew, a destructive fungal infection which occurs as a result of excessive dampness. Such events would not occur together, since 'blasting' is associated with excessive dryness, hail with a certain degree of moisture linked with deep atmospheric instability and mildew with still, hot, humid conditions. God is pointing out that although *all* these hardships were imposed His instructions continued to be ignored!

The whirlwind

Apart from Elijah's dramatic departure from Earth to heaven, the Biblical whirlwind is connected invariably with destruction. Powerful dust-whirls are a common sight in desert areas and their mechanism has already been discussed in Chapter 7 (Elijah). Dust-whirls, although they can never be as large and powerful as tornadoes (where moisture condensation adds considerable extra energy as latent heat) are nevertheless frightening phenomena which can cause serious damage or even loss of life. In appearance, the progress of these inverted cone-shaped spiralling entities are redolent of God's mysterious pillar of cloud and the vacuuming effect of the cone tip near the ground is reminiscent of a living and feeding organism. Material sucked into the vortex is lifted high and carried away to be scattered elsewhere. Also, the sudden drop in air pressure as the vortex passes can cause explosion effects in buildings; the air pressure differential is so great at that moment that the air trapped inside the building explodes outwards through doors and windows. Such damage is not uncommon.

In the Old Testament Bible stories, there are many occasions when God promises to protect His people from their enemies. The book of Isaiah gives an example: 'Thou shalt fan them, and the wind shall carry them away, and the whirlwind shall scatter them' (Is 41:16). This text follows God's promise to give great power to the Israelites, such that they will be able to 'thresh the mountains and make them small' (v15). The results of this will then be winnowed (like grain is thrown up into the air to separate the chaff). God will then send whirlwinds to 'scatter them'. If God can give the Israelites such great power, then they will have no problems with their enemies, who may expect to be treated similarly!

Jeremiah provides an example of the whirlwind as retribution against the wicked: 'Behold, a whirlwind of the LORD is gone forth in fury, even a grievous whirlwind: it shall fall grievously upon the head of the wicked.' (Je 23:19). Here the image is of an angry God creating powerful whirlwinds – the words 'grievous' and 'grievously' emphasise that the result will be catastrophic. 'Falling upon the head' provides an image of stunning, cranial damage, and even death.

When (in Je 23:19) the Hebrew word for 'whirlwind' is examined, an interesting fact is revealed. The Hebrew word *ca'ar* may be translated as 'whirlwind' or 'storm, tempest'. This word is derived from a primitive root which means 'to rush upon, (by implication) to toss' – which still implies a dual meaning. Whirlwinds and storms are of course very different meteorological phenomena. The whirlwind, though violent, is very localised while the storm or tempest is a very strong wind that affects a large area.

Inevitably, those biblical commentators who have addressed this point are divided. Some choose 'whirlwind, others choose 'tempest' but no further conclusions can be drawn from the Hebrew word alone. However, some further help is available towards at the end of the text in the Hebrew word used for 'fall grievously'. This word *'chuwl'* is another primitive root that means 'to twist and whirl'. This gives further evidence for choosing 'whirlwind' and it is suggested here that the image of a whirlwind is much more incisive than that of a wide-area storm. The dramatic image is that the wicked are plucked away, carried high in the spiralling air and dashed to destruction elsewhere; the good are left uninjured and unaffected in the surrounding calm. By contrast, a tempest would affect everyone.

Rain and flood

The link between rain and flooding was discussed in Chapter 5. Heavy and prolonged rain is a consequence of the mass uplift of warm and moist air (though convection can also be involved) – this is why the heaviest rain is experienced in the tropics. While flooding can be caused directly by heavy rain there is always some element of drainage involved. The rainfall drains to lower ground and collects there. Rain falling over high ground (where it is often enhanced by mountain effects) then swells streams and rivers and this excess of water may flood the plains below. This is a periodic happening in many low-lying areas of the world. Some tropical parts are flooded regularly to great depth in this way.

Apart from the story of the Flood in Genesis, there are not very many other references to destruction by flooding; many in fact refer back to the Flood as a warning. The book of Joshua refers several times to 'the flood' but this is considered to be a poetic reference to the River Euphrates, across which Abraham was brought to live in the land of Canaan. Flood references in the Psalms are linked variously to the Genesis Flood, the 'Red Sea' crossing or the subsequent Jordan crossing stories.

Like the other weather elements, flood is used figuratively, often referring to an overpowering army. In Jeremiah, a prophesy against the Philistines warned them: 'Behold, waters rise up out of the north, and shall be an overflowing flood, and shall overflow the land, and all that is therein; the city, and them that dwell therein.' (Je 47:2). This is generally interpreted to refer to the Chaldean forces attacking from the north, flooding south like the overwhelming waters of the river Euphrates.

Fire and lightning

The word 'fire' appears many times in the Bible. Many of these occurrences describe the physical combustion of materials, whether deliberately or accidentally started. However there are some references to 'fire' from the sky or from the clouds that could suggest natural lightning discharges and associated weather.

In the early parts of the Bible, there are a number of occasions when God is said to destroy with 'fire'. The first reference is in Genesis 19, describing the 'fire and brimstone' which destroyed Sodom and Gomorrah. Subsequent references in Leviticus, Numbers, and Job has 'fire' coming down from heaven 'consuming' or 'devouring' people who had displeased or disobeyed God – e.g. 'And there went out fire from the Lord, and devoured them, and they died before the Lord.' (Le 10:2). These are powerful images of swift retribution which can be interpreted variously as actual ground-strike lightning events which carried out the destruction or warnings of retribution which would occur with devastating suddenness. A similar fate awaits the bodies of soldiers sent to arrest the prophet Elijah in 2Kings 1. The captains of these bands (of 50) are scornful and challenging about Elijah's assertion that he is a 'man of God'. In response (3 times) Elijah calls for retribution for these impudent sinners 'And there came down fire from heaven, and consumed him and his fifty.' (2Ki 1:10). Such a story demonstrates the power of God.

Psalm 11 warns even more dramatically of the fate for the wicked: 'Upon the wicked He shall rain snares, fire and brimstone, and a horrible tempest: this shall be the portion of their cup.' (Ps 11:6). Here, 'rain' is used figuratively and the word 'snares' means sudden judgements upon the unwary. The judgements will be delivered along with destroying and injurious fire, the choking brimstone and a high intensity 'horrible tempest'. The image of a lightning ground-strike certainly fits the image of a 'rain or snares' with its danger of sudden injury and death. Brimstone may refer to the inflammable resin of the cypress tree or to the sulphurous deposits that are common in areas where there are, or have been, active volcanoes. This material melts as it burns brightly and emits poisonous fumes – another injurious hazard! Finally, there is no doubt of the weather connection in the 'horrible tempest' – the image is of terrible destruction by the effects of high winds. However the Hebrew words used here imply a more frightening image still: *'ruach'* is followed by *'zal'aphah'* which can be translated as 'the spirit of terrors'. So these few words leave 'the wicked' in no doubt as to their fate. The judgements will scythe down upon them with the certainty of terror, pain, injury and possible death!

Destruction by other means
Drought as a weapon of destruction
It has already been observed that a number of Biblical references to rain are linked to God's nurture and beneficence towards His people. However, lack of rain is obviously a very destructive force in the eastern Mediterranean lands which depend on adequate winter rainfall to carry them through a totally dry period each summer. Any diminution of the winter rain will cause a problem in the following year, with all sorts of agriculture affected detrimentally.

The meteorological word for a serious lack of rain is 'drought'. It occurs as a result of normal winter weather patterns being changed in such a way that rain-bearing weather systems (low surface pressure, weather fronts, atmospheric instability and moisture) cannot occur. Instead, surface pressure remains relatively high and the sinking air warms, dries and prevents cloud. The superficial reasons for such an anomaly may be seen in broad-scale atmospheric processes (Appendix 2), particularly in the behaviour of the high-level wind flows, but the fundamental reason for the change will be much more difficult to find. Factors like *el Nino*, global warming and pollution are likely to be relevant.

The AV has a small number of references that use the word 'drought' but there are many other references which express the lack of rain in another way. The earliest reference of 'drought' was noted at the beginning of Chapter 1 in the translated words of Jacob the shepherd when he was complaining to his uncle Laban – '…in the day the drought consumed me…' (Ge 31:40). However, Haggai 1 gives another example of destruction by drought.

Like the earlier Haggai reference above ('Wind'), the prophecy was a message from God about the inadequacy of the Israelites. The people were poor because they had not honoured God; their work on the fertile land had been reduced to mere survival instead of progress. Because of this, the story tells how God imposed a drought on the land: 'And I called for a drought upon the land....' (Hgg 1:11). This was a warning to galvanise the people into action, to prepare to rebuild the Temple. It seems that God's inducements eventually worked – the Temple was completed in 516BC!

The previous verse in Haggai is an example of drought expressed in a different way: 'Therefore the heaven over you is stayed from dew, and the earth is stayed from her fruit.' (Hgg 1:10). It will be recalled how 'dew' was often written about as a most gentle and life-giving blessing from God. Therefore the lack of dew implies a withdrawal of God's blessing – a serious warning. Similar terminology was used in the story of Elijah (Chapter 7) when an extended drought was imposed on the land.

Withdrawal of rain carries the same message and there are many examples. In Deuteronomy, God points out the retribution that will befall the Israelites if they are not faithful to Him. This retribution includes drought over the land: 'And then the Lord's wrath be kindled against you, and He shut up the heaven, that there be no rain, and that the land yield not her fruit; and lest ye perish quickly from off the good land which the Lord giveth you. (De 11:17). Another reference mentions 'showers' as well as rain. 'Therefore the showers have been withholden, and there hath been no latter rain...' (Je 3:3). The meteorological difference between showers and rain was discussed in Chapter 2; an analysis of the biblical usage of showers and rain in the last chapter ('The gentle dew, the life-giving rains) indicated that the biblical writers were very well aware of the difference between the two types of precipitation.

Negative effects of cloud

Retribution and judgement are also associated with clouds in Lamentations (La 2:1, 3:44), in Ez 32:7, Joel 2:2 and Ze 1:15. Here, cloud is used to cut off light, offering a picture of gloomy, dark days that imply trouble, hardship, depression and strife – the link between darkness and evil again.

Lamentations provides two examples: (1) 'How hath the Lord covered the daughter of Zion with a cloud in His anger, and cast down from heaven unto the earth the beauty of Israel, and remembered not His footstool in the day of his anger!' (La 2:1). (2) 'Thou hast covered thyself with a cloud, that our prayer should not pass through.' (La 3:44). Lamentations is, as the title suggests, a series of five dirges, funeral songs, which express the deep sorrow of the Israelites at their situation. It is the early 6th Century BC and the Babylonians have razed the city of Jerusalem to the ground, completely destroying the Temple. The Israelites are devastated and disconsolate; their laments express the ways in which they see that God has rejected them.

The imagery of cloud is used twice to suggest a mechanism of separation. In La 2:1, the cloud is likened to the barrier of anger which separates the people from God's love and nurture. 'The daughter of Zion' is a reference to the city of Jerusalem and the 'footstool' is considered to be the Ark of the Covenant. The Hebrew words used for 'footstool', *'regel'* + *'Hadom'* first appear in 1Chr 28:2 when King David declares the intention to build a solid and permanent resting place (the Temple) for the Ark of the Covenant. The Ark is considered to be a footstool for God who hovers above it as the pillar of cloud in the tabernacle. *'Regel'* + *'Hadom'* appear twice more in the Psalms in the same context (Ps 99:5, 132:7).

In La 3:44, the imagery of a layer of cloud is used to describe a barrier through which the prayers of the unfortunate Israelites cannot pass. Weather imagery is used here to indicate a barrier of God's anger against His people; a more modern interpretation would suggest that the cloud layer represents sin which prevents the establishment of relationships with God.

Biblical destruction reviewed

Earlier chapters of this book presented some of the major weather destruction stories of the Bible. These involved the whole range of violent weather elements. There are many other lesser-known descriptions. There are storms of destruction which use multiple weather elements, specific destruction by the dreaded 'east wind' or by the violent whirlwind. There is heavy rainfall causing flooding and destruction or 'fire' from the sky in the frightening form of lightning ground-strikes. It is also noted that destruction can take a less dramatic but equally effective form; drought causing death by desiccation; cloud blocking out essential sunlight.

Many references are not in fact direct accounts or stories of destruction. Rather they are prophecies of misfortune, punishment that is predicted to befall a population if they do not conform to a particular plan of God. Equally often, the stories which involve weather are themselves figurative images to powerfully indicate other serious misfortunes which are predicted to affect those to whom the prophesies are directed. Again, it is seen that the writers of Scripture recognised that the use of weather imagery is a very accessible way of communicating a powerful message or teaching.

12

Expressions and Depictions

Weather appearing in figures of speech

Quoted speech in the Bible abounds with what is defined in language as 'figures of speech' – verbal illustrations which use comparison to create an imaginary picture; many of these figures of speech use weather elements for this purpose. Today, our own words are similarly rich in figures of speech; their use enriches our communication and paints exciting and vital comparison pictures for our listeners. Like those whose speech is quoted in the Bible, we too use weather imagery at times. We observe people 'running like the wind' or moving 'like lightning'; we see with regret others who are 'under a cloud', even although they protest they are 'white as snow'. Others may be seen 'looking like thunder' at difficult or embarrassing times.

Teaching

A doctrine supported by weather imagery

The beginning of the 'Song of Moses' (Deuteronomy 32) is an excellent example of several figures of speech expressed in weather parameters. Moses has been given the wisdom of life in God's laws and now he seeks to communicate them to the people. Before he starts, he intones a brief introductory prayer: 'Give ear, O ye heavens, and I will speak; and hear, O earth, the words of my mouth. My doctrine shall drop as the rain, my speech shall distil as the dew, as the small rain upon the tender herb, and as the showers upon the grass.' (De 32:1-2). Four similes are used here, each one referring to a weather element. Moses' discourse shall 'drop as rain, distil as dew, as the small rain, as showers upon the grass'. Here is life-giving water again. The mention of rain is immediately modified to show that it is of the gentle variety, the sort which wets but does not damage – the 'small rain'. The mention of showers brings an image of sunshine too; water and sunshine are the ingredients that the grass needs to grow and be succulent. We all know our lawn grows very quickly on warm days with a mixture of sunshine and showers. With this prayer, Moses is asking that his teaching discourse will be received gently, in such a way that it will be fully assimilated by his listeners as a life-giving discourse.

Weather in proverbs

Proverbs are often brief sentences of succinct teaching, and a number use weather imagery. Three examples show the range of usage. Pr 11:29 says 'He that troubleth his own house shall inherit the wind…' What sort of 'trouble' is not actually defined by the Hebrew word used here, whose English translation is 'trouble' and 'disturb'. However biblical scholars have suggested variously that there are implications within the text of bad behaviour within the family (fights, quarrels), ruinous extravagance, cheating and dishonesty, general dissipation and unfair treatment of servants. Such a person, we read, 'shall inherit the wind'. Here, 'wind' is used as something elusive, an invisible force which passes quickly and leaves nothing of itself behind. The Hebrew word used for 'wind' is once again that mysterious word *ruach*, with its range of meanings spanning the factual to the mystical. Thus the teaching is delivered in a powerful comparison with the disappearing wind – the person generating 'trouble' in his own house shall be left with nothing, destitute. This shall be a warning to him and all who read the proverb.

In Proverb 26 weather is used in a different way, namely to emphasise the incongruity and inappropriateness of the possession of 'honour' by someone recognised as a 'fool'. The proverb states 'As snow in summer, and as rain in harvest, so honour is not seemly for a fool.' (Pr 26:1). In fact the two weather analogies are quite different. In summer, snow does not occur in the eastern Mediterranean lands, but rain, though rare, is not impossible; under certain unusual weather conditions, an isolated heavy shower may be generated. The comparisons intended are therefore of total incongruity (snow) and inappropriateness (rain); any rain that occurs at harvest time is detrimental to the gathering in of the harvest.

These two weather comparisons are linked to the concept of the 'fool' having 'honour'. This is judged to be both inappropriate and incongruous. The 'fool' (the Hebrew word translates as stupid fellow, a dullard; there is also a sense of arrogance) would misuse honour (*kabowd* – this is the same word used for the 'glory of the Lord' (Chapter 10)), his folly would be strengthened and the situation made worse. Thus the use of the two weather analogies in the one sentence is a highly economical and effective way of delivering this teaching.

The final example given here is rather more simple. A verse in Proverb 28 states 'A poor man that oppresseth the poor is like a sweeping rain which leaveth no food.' (Pr 28:3). The weather image is that of torrential rain and high winds. While rain (water) is essential for life and growth, a violent weather episode such as this can have precisely the opposite effect. Planted seed may be swept away by the torrent, along with the fertile topsoil. Alternatively, the ground may become waterlogged and unsuitable for the planted crop. In hilly areas, fast-flowing torrents of rainwater can sweep away property, animals and man. Small farmers often use the fertile ground of dried up riverbeds in the dry seasons, even constructing their houses there; when freak storms occur, there is total destruction.

Against this picture of destruction and raging torrent, the oppressor is placed; specifically the poor man who has become an oppressor. This sort of person is judged to be much worse than the rich oppressor, not least because his own experience of poverty should engender compassion and fellow feeling for those in his debt. However it is a sad fact of human nature that this fellow feeling is frequently absent – the formerly oppressed now armed with power, wield this with ferocity against their former fellows. Perhaps this behaviour is a reaction against their former tribulations; the emotional strategy may be an attempt to assuage their anger by transferring past misery to someone else – of course this does not work and is an example of the so-called 'lose-lose' situation. The oppressor loses because their intention fails; the oppressed lose because of the misery imposed upon them. The ferocity of the oppressors' actions is well described by the analogy of rampaging and destroying water, leaving sterility behind.

Word pictures

A vision from Isaiah

A brief sentence in Isaiah 60 paints a vivid and meaningful word picture in the form of a figure of speech. The text is: 'Who are these that fly as a cloud, and as the doves to their windows?' (Is 60:8). This verse appears within a prophecy which biblical scholars have long linked to the establishment of the Christian faith. The prophet speaks with a sense of awe as he sees a huge influx from all directions. This verse describes a vision of the conversion of vast multitudes, flowing from paganism to the glory of the Messiah. The multitudes are so numerous that their flowing movement is reminiscent of the motions of a fast-moving cloud in the sky, incessantly changing shape as it moves; perhaps each individual in the multitudes is associated with each water droplet in a swirling cloud. It is obvious that all those who read or heard the prophecy would be able to visualise the scene by association with their everyday observations of the mystery of clouds. The second description in the sentence is of a large flock of doves, again a swirling entity when vast numbers are involved, returning to their dovecotes – this is said to be a characteristic behaviour of doves in advance of a storm.

Whiter than snow!

Comparisons to the whiteness of snow are made a number of times throughout the Bible. The first biblical reference is from Exodus, where the comparison is made with the appearance of leprosy: '…behold, his hand was leprous as snow' (Ex 4:6). Similar pictures are presented in Numbers and 2nd Kings as descriptions of leprosy. In Lamentations, snow is used for an illustration of past purity, to describe what the Nazarites of Zion used to be like; in this case, the translation uses the grammatically comparative: 'Her Nazarites were purer than snow, they were whiter than milk…' (La 4:7). Nazarite is the name given to people who were venerated and very distinguished in that society. The description of past purity is reinforced by a second comparison to the whiteness of milk. Ps 51:7 also uses the comparative: 'Purge me with hyssop, and I shall be clean: wash me, and I shall be whiter than snow'. However the Hebrew word used here *(laban)* is translated elsewhere merely as the positive 'white as snow' (e.g. Is 1:18) so the translation in the Psalm may be described as a poetic enthusiasm!

In the New Testament, Mark uses the snow comparison to give a glorious picture of the transfiguration of Jesus: 'And his raiment became shining, exceeding white as snow; so as no fuller on earth can white them.' (Mk 9:3); this compassion with snow extends to the superlative – nothing can possibly be whiter! Similar terminology is used by Matthew when God's angel visits the tomb of the risen Jesus, but there is the added weather analogy of lightning in the picture: 'His countenance was like lightning, and his raiment white as snow' (Mt 28:3). In this case, the depiction is of a dazzling figure; his clothing was brilliant white but significantly, his face shone even brighter; the description 'like lightning' evokes an image of great power as well as light and purity – a most meaningful and vivid picture of a being clearly sent by God.

An expression of the ephemeral

It is not easy to express the ephemeral, but scriptural writers found that they could make use of the wind effectively for this purpose. In the book of Job, The main character Job laments 'O remember that my life is wind: mine eye shall no more see good' (Jb 7:7). As already stated, Job is a complex book in which its unknown writer presents series of poetic and often rhetorical dialogues. The discussion at its simplest level is an attempt to understand the suffering of the righteous and the innocent. The righteous Job has not sinned, yet has suffered terrible disasters in which he has lost all – health, children, wealth and possessions. He and his friends struggle to find a rationale for this situation. In the quotation above, the writer expresses the hopelessness and depression of Job's life by having his character speak a metaphor; Job's 'life is wind', the Hebrew word *ruach* (wind) is used here to portray insubstantiality, emptiness, sorrow.

In Jeremiah, 'wind' is used to express a similar idea. 'And the prophets shall become wind, and the word is not in them: thus shall it be done unto them.' (Je 5:13). Once again the Hebrew *ruach* is used here but this time with an extended interpretation. In one sense, the words of the prophets of the disobedient people of Israel will be 'as wind' – untrue, meaningless. Another other sense of *ruach* emphasises how these prophets are not <u>filled</u> with the *'ruach';* to be a true prophet, it is necessary to be filled with God's Holy Spirit. This is confirmed by the succeeding part of the sentence – 'the <u>word</u> (God's Spirit) is not in

200 / Expressions and Depictions

them'. This concept of the 'word' becomes very important in the Gospels, where Jesus Christ is identified as 'the Word' (Jn 1:1-14)

The New Testament tends not to use 'wind' in the same way and the Greek word for wind '**anemos**' is often employed to describe normal atmospheric wind. However Ephesians provides us with an example of a more ephemeral use; 'That we henceforth be no more children, tossed to and fro, and carried about with every wind of doctrine, by the sleight of men, and cunning craftiness, whereby they lie in wait to deceive' (Eph 4:14). The phrase 'every wind of doctrine' is very evocative; in this sense, the picture is of variable and gusty winds carrying a helpless person successively in many directions.

In all the examples presented in this section, weather parameters are employed in an effective and often succinct way of projecting word pictures for the readers of the Bible.

Situations

Retribution

There are many situations in the Bible which involve retribution. Isaiah refers to God's punishment of the people of Ephraim (the land occupied by one of the 12 tribes of Israel), who were dissipated and drunken. 'Behold, the Lord hath a mighty and strong one, which as a tempest of hail and a destroying storm, as a flood of mighty waters overflowing, shall cast down to the earth with the hand.' (Is 28:2). In this verse, the word 'one' refers to a force or a power of God whose effects will be similar to various intense weather events – a tempest of hail, a destroying storm, a flood; those weather events will produce great destruction and death similar to the powerful entity which God will send to carry out just retribution.

Another common method of destruction or threat of destruction is the use of 'scattering to all winds'. One of Ezekiel's prophecies of destruction includes this term:

'And all his fugitives with all his bands shall fall by the sword, and they that remain shall be scattered toward all winds: and ye shall know that I the Lord have spoken it.' (Ez 17:21). This was to be the punishment of Israel for breaking God's covenant. Not only was there to be much death and destruction by the sword but there was to be no chance for the remnant to regroup or survive elsewhere; they were to be individually 'scattered' in all directions, each to be alone and ineffective. The phrase 'to all winds' is often used as a poetic way of expressing the more prosaic 'in all directions'.

Finally, there is the strong wind or the whirlwind with its frequent link to 'blown away like chaff'. Of course this would be a totally comprehensible image for an agricultural community. Winnowing – separating the grain from the lighter chaff – is part of the harvest procedure; to do this in the traditional way, wind is required. David pleads for God's protection in Psalm 35 by giving him victory over his enemy in battle. 'Let them be as chaff before the wind: and let the angel of the Lord chase them' (Ps 35:5); the light and helpless chaff is carried way in God's wind and David is safe. Similar descriptions are found in Job, Jeremiah and Daniel.

Redemption

God's redemption, forgiveness and nurture are spoken about lovingly in many biblical verses. Sometimes, mankind's feelings for that situation can be expressed poetically by the use of gentle and nurturing weather images. So it is beautifully expressed in 2Samuel – If God's people are obedient to Him then: '… He shall be as the light of the morning, when the sun riseth, even a morning without clouds; as the tender grass springing out of the earth by clear shining after rain.' (2 Sa 23:4). Here there are three weather-related images: First the 'light of the morning' that magical time of dawn when the darkness of the night is banished, almost imperceptibly at first, by the effects of the rising sun. Secondly, the scene is kept simple and pure by the absence of cloud, so the black of the night is replaced by the strengthening blue of the sky and then by the dazzling full orb of the flaming sun, projecting light and heat on to the surface of the Earth. Truly a life giving force, tenderly and gently applied. The third image is of tender and lush grass nurtured by life-giving rainwater and the energy of the sun – the 'sunshine and showers' picture once again, that situation which gardeners know will generate fastest plant growth. God's beneficence will cover his people with equivalent gentleness, freshness and nurture.

By contrast, God's blessing to His people on the first day of Pentecost is expressed in very dramatic weather-related terms: 'And suddenly there came a sound from heaven as of a rushing mighty wind, and it filled all the house where they were sitting. And there appeared unto them cloven tongues like as of fire, and it sat upon each of them.' (Ac 2:2-3). The situation in these verses is the delivery of God's Holy Spirit to each one of His people, in fulfilment of the promises made in the New Covenant (Prophesied in Jeremiah 31). The sound is of a mighty wind, that roaring screaming blast that we have all experienced in a storm. The Greek word used is 'pnoēs', a word linked with respiration and derived from a word which means 'to breathe hard'. There was also the drama of 'tongues of fire' which touched each person – actually the 'tongues' were not fire or lightning but entities that were like fire. A description of a situation when sight and sound combined dramatically to indicate a delivery of great power to each of God's people. In the following verse, the power was obviously received because '... they were all filled with the Holy Ghost, and began to speak with other tongues, as the Spirit gave them utterance.' (Ac 2:4).

Setting the scene with weather imagery

Previous chapters in this book shown how many biblical scenes are described by reference to weather events or imagery. It is common to find weather in figures of speech and some of these have been presented earlier in this chapter. In the many references that remain, all the elements of weather appear, often poetically expressed. Gloom and depression is heightened by being placed in dark, cloudy, rainy days. Cold is accentuated by mention of frost, ice and snow. Tribulations are increased by an excess of wind or rain, bringing destruction and flooding. The 'east wind' and the 'whirlwinds' continue to be villains of the piece! On the other hand, serenity and happiness are often placed among lushness and fertility, fed by the life-giving water of rain or dew, gently nurtured by light winds and balmy conditions. Clouds are often spoken of with awe, as they float past with their ethereal beauty. The following examples indicate the range of scene-setting weather-word descriptions:

A green and pleasant land

The scene is of a green and pleasant land in Deuteronomy 11. 'But the land, whither ye go to possess it, is a land of hills and valleys, and drinketh water of the rain of heaven:' (De 11:11). This brief verse shows us a scene of serenity and fertility. 'Rain of heaven' is a particularly delightful phrase that refers again to that essential provision of life-giving water. The scene is of gentle and nurturing rain, watering every part of the land. The 'land of hills and valleys' is an excellent topography for varied agriculture. This land is of course Canaan, even more famously (but not meteorologically) described as the 'land of milk and honey'.

A wet and miserable situation

The book of Ezra presents us with a very different example of scene-setting imagery. This was the time that the Jews had returned to Judah after captivity in Babylonia. It is reported they had transgressed God's law and intermarried with other races. This was now a great problem and the men met to decide what to do; it is a miserable scene taking place at a cold and wet time of the year (the ninth month – December). The scene is set by this verse: 'Then all the men of Judah and Benjamin gathered themselves together unto Jerusalem within three days. It was the ninth month, on the twentieth day of the month; and all the people sat in the street of the house of God, trembling because of this matter, and for the great rain.' (Ezra 10:9). We can almost feel the desolation, misery and depression that beset this meeting!

The case of the snuffling asses

Jeremiah involves 'wind' in two interesting descriptions of the behaviour of wild donkeys. 'A wild ass used to the wilderness, that snuffeth up the wind at her pleasure…' (Je 2:24). The image of that animal, head high, nostrils wide, snorting noisily to clear the airways and then drawing in the air from all directions is easy to picture. In this case, it is likely the ass was seeking to detect the nearest location of a mate. Many animals have a much more developed sense of smell in comparison with human beings and are capable of sophisticated and remote detection by scent.

The second example is: 'And the wild asses did stand in the high places, they snuffed up the wind like dragons…' On this occasion, there was a great drought in the land and the animal's considerable olfactory sense was being employed to detect water and food – to no avail. However the verse presents the same picture of the animal straining its head upwards and sampling the air comprehensively. The use of the word 'dragons' is an interesting example of the biblical translation problem and is a fascinating diversion.

The dragon is of course a mythical fire-breathing animal. The Hebrew word used is a derivative of another word which has a rather wide-ranging meaning – a sea or land monster! Within the meaning, there is also an implication of elongation and hideousness. So the word can be translated more or less as any dangerous or unattractive land or sea animal. While some early Bible translations retain the word 'dragons' most modern Bible translations substitute 'jackals'; certainly this is an animal whose disturbing howling coupled with its fierce and scavenging behaviour makes it deeply unattractive. It is noted that the Revised English Bible (1989) prefers the word 'wolves'. However a review of the biblical commentaries and dictionaries reveal other arresting proposals. In additions to jackals, there are suggestions of sea serpents, whales, crocodiles, hippopotamuses, pythons or boa constrictors; these studies take account of the context of other occurrences of *'tanniym'* in the Old Testament (about 30 occurrences). It would seem that no definitive conclusion can be reached.

In the New Testament, 'dragon' appears only in the book of Revelation, where its usage indicates the mythical, fire-breathing beast representing Satan and evil.

After the shipwreck

After the drama of the apostle Paul's shipwreck on the island of Malta (as told in Chapter 9), Paul and his companions survived because of help received from the local population. The initial words of Acts 28 review that post-shipwreck situation with admirable brevity, setting the scene for the details that were to follow: 'And when they were escaped, then they knew that the island was called Melita. And the barbarous people shewed us no little kindness: for they kindled a fire, and received us every one, because of the present rain, and because of the cold.' (Ac 28:1-2). One can picture that scene – the pouring rain, the howling wind, the soaked and exhausted crew and passengers being ministered to by the 'barbarians' of Malta, receiving the heat, shelter and sustenance without which many may well have perished.

Which way the wind?

The final example in this section comes from the Old Testament book Song of Solomon. This verse deals with the onset of wind for special beneficial purposes, but there are interesting translation and weather anomalies associated with it. The text is a simple prayer of entreaty, spoken by a young and apparently attractive lady. She prays: 'Awake, O north wind; and come, thou south; blow upon my garden, that the spices thereof may flow out. Let my beloved come into his garden, and eat his pleasant fruits.' (SS 4:16). Taking the text at a literal level, the young lady wishes her lover to come to a perfect situation, private, comfortable, fragrant and with delicious fresh fruits to eat. She judges that the wind from a particular direction will establish all these ideal conditions and generate the perfection she desires for her lover.

However it is accepted that the garden and the fruit may be a figurative reference to the physical allures of the young lady herself. The Song of Solomon is a lengthy love poem in which the aspects and attributes of human love are likened time and again to the natural surroundings described. At a deeper level, most Bible interpreters now take the poem in its entirety to represent the love of Christ for the Church and for the individual souls which comprise it. The poem's emphasis on all aspects of human love show that divine love and human love are not to be viewed apart; indeed the biblical teachings on marriage concur.

Whatever interpretation is applied, the process must start with the actual biblical text, and it is here that we find the translation anomalies referred to above . The problem is rooted in the phrase 'Awake, O north wind; and come, thou south;' which many other Bible translations give as 'Awake, north wind, and come, south <u>wind</u>' – this is from the NIV Bible. It is immediately obvious that the two texts disagree in a fundamental way. The words of the AV may be interpreted as an invitation to the north wind to start blowing (although the comma after 'come' complicates matters) while the NIV appears to urge the opposite – the invitation is for the south wind not the north wind. In the one translation, the young lady may be praying for a north wind, in the other, a south wind. Most biblical interpreters accept the latter (south) interpretation but there are those who say that she is asking for both – first a north wind, then a south wind!

A study of the Hebrew text does not resolve the issue. The word *'teyman'* is used for 'south (wind)'. This word means south, towards the south, on the right hand. There were no compass directions in these days; directions were indicated by an observer facing east, towards the rising sun. The wind directions were 'forward' (east), 'back' (west), 'right hand' (south) or 'left hand' (north). In the definitions of *'teyman'* there is no suggestion of the word 'wind' and some studies note that 'wind' is what is defined as an 'inserted word' by the translators. Of the 22 other occasions of *'teyman'* in the Bible, only one (Ps 78:23) adds the word 'wind' in the same way. All others refer to the direction south. Another Hebrew word *'darowm'* also means 'south'. On the single occasion it is translated as 'south wind' (Jb 37:17), 'wind' is noted as an inserted word. None of this suggests a definitive interpretation.

Also the question of the comma after the word 'come' cannot be resolved by examination of the Hebrew text. No such punctuation appears and the inserted comma is a translator's device to assist with interpretation. Also, the Hebrew word translated as 'come' has a range of meanings, for instance it may mean 'go' as well as come. Literally, the Hebrew phrase is: 'Come (or go) south (to the south, the southern quarter, the right hand) – no occurrence of 'wind'. However it is possible to approach this difficulty of translation in another way – by considering what weather conditions are likely to be associated with north or south winds. The question which may be asked is: 'Which wind (north or south) would be more likely to create the desired situation for the young lady's garden?'

Firstly, the location must be established. The text mentions a number of locations in Judah, including Jerusalem, so the location is positively established in that eastern Mediterranean country (now Israel). Secondly, the season is relevant. The text informs us that there are ripe fruits on the trees, so the time of year must be within the summer quadrant. In this region in summer the characteristics of the north wind are clear, dry, cool by night and hot by day. The south wind is hot and dry by night, extremely hot and very dry by day with a risk of dust haze which thickens to blowing dust/sand with any significant wind increase. Therefore the meteorological evidence points to the fact that a burning and dusty south wind would not be conducive to the perfection required in the young lady's garden; the relatively less hot, clear and dry north wind would be more likely to create a pleasant situation. Considering the question of a request for both winds, there seems no sense in replacing the cool dry north wind (possibly a shade chilly at first) with the burning and dusty south wind later in the day; this proposition is considered unlikely.

So it is proposed here that the addition of meteorological considerations to the straight text of the traditional AV wording (especially with 'added comma' deleted) provides strong evidence for the prayer being a request for the *north* wind to come, not the *south* wind. The sensible picture is of the young lady praying in the still of the early morning, asking for the clear, fresh north wind to 'awake' and blow gently on her garden by flowing southwards across it. It is noted that this interpretation still applies if the depiction is figurative; the young lady would hardly be calling for her lover to luxuriate in her personal allures if these were being presented burning hot, dry and dusty!

13

Real Meteorology!

This chapter examines the occasions in the Bible when weather wisdom or embryonic meteorology is revealed. It is tempting to think that the people of Biblical times were completely ignorant of meteorology, the modern science of weather. While it is undoubtedly true that their 'scientific' knowledge must have been extremely scanty, the tenets of weather lore show us that event sequences had been noted and interpreted in quite a number of cases. This, after all, is what science is all about – observation, analysis, conclusion, application.

It has already been said at the beginning of this book that those in weather-sensitive industries build up a knowledge of the way the weather works. Such knowledge may well be a matter of life and death (for the mariner, for instance) or a matter of economic success or ruin (e.g. in agriculture). So it does not surprise that many examples of weather lore known around the world are rooted in marine or agricultural culture. Often, these are only valid for the areas in which they have been formulated; in addition, they normally apply for short time periods ahead. We will see the reason for this when we examine specific examples from the Bible.

A few of the references given in the following section may have been noted in earlier chapters but they are now examined with a sharper meteorological focus.

Weather observations
Diurnal (day-night) variations
Chapter One of this book commenced with the story of the Jacob the shepherd complaining about the weather he commonly experienced. He found it far too hot during the day and suffered for the cold at night! His words show an appreciation of daily weather patterns in dry and arid regions. The sun, unobstructed by clouds, shines with full force upon sparsely covered rocky ground that becomes very hot and raises the low-level air temperature to very high levels. Although convection currents will undoubtedly develop, the dryness of the air will prevent condensation as the air rises and cools – therefore, no cloud. At night, the clear skies allow maximum radiation of heat from the ground; the surface becomes very cold and this cools the layer of air in contact with it. The unfortunate Jacob, lying, it would seem, with inadequate bedding in his flimsy tent, could not sleep because of the cold. The writers of this story about Jacob (Genesis 31) revealed weather awareness linked directly to personal weather observation and used this in the complaining words of Jacob; however there is no suggestion of explanation for this large daily temperature range.

The gentle dew
A rather more focused weather observation appears in Exodus: 'Israel then shall dwell in safety alone: the fountain of Jacob shall be upon a land of corn and wine; also his heavens shall drop down dew' (De 33:28). In describing the ideal conditions that God will provide for His people, this statement includes the gentle and life-giving water provided by the dew. The Hebrew word *'tal'* is a specific word meaning 'dew or night mist' and *'shaamayo'* the word for 'his heavens', meaning the sky, the abode of the stars. These words are important links to the physical process because most occasions of dew formation occur when there is rapid night-time cooling; this means

little or no cloud present. Thus the Hebrew words in this verse present a correct physical picture of a night when significant dew will be deposited.

A verse in Proverbs makes a similar observation about dew but there is a significant difference: 'By His knowledge the depths are broken up, and the clouds drop down the dew.' (Pr 3:20). In this case it is stated to be the clouds which drop down dew. In fact, the presence of cloud normally inhibits dew formation because cloud reduces the loss of heat from the ground and so reduces the chance of condensation in the low-level air. The same Hebrew word for dew is used in this verse but the word translated as 'clouds' is defined as 'a thin cloud, a thin vapour, possibly the firmament of stars'. Of the 23 occasions this particular word is used in the Bible it has been translated in the AV either as 'cloud' or 'sky', occasionally as 'heaven'. Some Bible translations change the word 'cloud' to 'sky' but others retain 'cloud'.

This discussion illustrates the translation problem once more. If the writers of Pr 3:20 meant to describe a cloudless sky then their observation accords with meteorological fact; if they thought dew was a form of precipitation from clouds then this is an incorrect understanding. Because the translation of the Hebrew word does not suggest thick cloud, it is suggested the former judgement is the more likely.

Spring is sprung!

The Song of Solomon offers a brief observation on the variation of the seasons in the Eastern Mediterranean region. 'For, lo, the winter is past, the rain is over and gone; the flowers appear on the earth; the time of the singing of birds is come, and the voice of the turtle is heard in our land;' (SS 2:11-12). The young lady's lover wishes her to come away with him now that the summer has arrived. (Biblical texts speak only of summer and winter; spring and autumn are usually referred to as agricultural seasons linked to planting and harvest.) Winter is rightly observed as the wet and sometimes cold time of the year. In summer, no rain falls on this land but in spring and autumn transition months there are likely to be occasional showers, possibly of a thundery nature. Certainly the main rain and unpleasantness of winter will have gone by spring-time but if the prediction in the quotation is for total dryness, this could be rather optimistic!

Weather by direction

The book of Job provides the final weather observation of this section. 'Out of the south cometh the whirlwind: and cold out of the north.' (Jb 37:9). This is part of a long statement by Job which points out that God is in control of everything. So it is ordered by God (and accords with reality) that whirlwinds are generated in very hot desert areas which are to the south of the Eastern Mediterranean lands. Such weather manifestations will normally arrive from the southern quadrant.

The second part of the verse specifies that God brings cold weather from the north, which again is in accordance with reality. Earlier in the book we have examined the reason for a general decrease of temperatures as one travels north. In this verse, the Hebrew word used for 'north' actually means 'scatterings'; thus the observation is that the north wind not only brings coldness but also 'scatters' the clouds and dissipates them. The scientific actuality is not 'scattering' in the sense of driving apart but the reduction of cloud elements by dissipation as the air becomes progressively drier. As the air becomes drier, condensation in rising air becomes less and less likely and the consequential cloudless nights impose maximum cooling.

This biblical observation about the effect of north winds accords with earlier observations (starting at Genesis) that cloudless nights result in low temperatures.

Weather wisdom; an appreciation of cause and effect

Weather wisdom begins to extend the knowledge acquired through observation by applying a degree of analysis and interpretation. This is the second process in science.

Bright clouds and showers

'Ask ye of the Lord rain in the time of the latter rain; so the Lord shall make bright clouds, and give them showers of rain, to every one grass in the field.' (Ze 10:1). In this verse from Zechariah, 'bright clouds' are linked to 'showers of rain'. The Hebrew word used is clearly linked to storm concepts. The word for 'bright clouds' *(chazizim)* means cloud, storm, lightning flash, thunderbolt, while two separate words are used for 'shower' and 'rain'. This is a promise of blessings from God but it is rather surprising that thunderstorms are implied; such weather is not usually welcomed by farmers. Perhaps the 'bright clouds' (cumulus shower clouds) and (moderate) rain showers of the AV translation is the best interpretation of what is promised as a blessing!

Showers are mentioned with a different association in the book of Job: 'They are wet with the showers of the mountains, and embrace the rock for want of a shelter.' (Jb 24:8). The writer of this verse shows an appreciation of shower intensification on mountains. Convectively unstable airflows are forced to rise by mountain terrain and so this is often the first place that cumulus clouds and showers form. For this reason, showers are likely to be heavier and more frequent in mountainous areas throughout the day. This is a common occurrence that can be observed in many areas of the world.

In both these cases about showers, the writers have linked showers with 'bright clouds' (either bright by reflection or perhaps by lightning) and with the enhancing effect of mountains.

Wind waves

Biblical writing proves that there has long been some understanding of the link between wind and sea waves. The 'Red Sea' story in Exodus includes the words 'Thou didst blow with thy wind, the sea covered them;' (Ex 15:10). Psalm 107 establishes the link more positively: 'For He commandeth, and raiseth the stormy wind, which lifteth up the waves thereof' (Ps 107:25) and subsequently 'He maketh the storm a calm, so that the waves thereof are still' (Ps 107:29). In the description of Jesus calming storm in both Matthew and Mark's Gospels, the scene described an onset of very strong wind which resulted in high waves, placing the boat in great danger of foundering (Chapter 8). However the clearest statement comes from John's Gospel: 'And the sea arose by reason of a great wind that blew' (Jn 6:18).

What actually happens is that an airflow across a completely calm sea will generate low-level frictional effects and there will be a resulting energy transfer to the sea. The fluid of the sea reacts by setting up what is apparently a wave motion on the surface but what actually develops is a series of travelling rotations in the water, each flowing around a horizontal axis. The larger the surface wave motion, the larger the rotation embedded in the sea. When the diameter of the rotation exceeds the depth of the water, for example when the wave approaches the shore, the rotation is destroyed and the surface wave is seen to 'break'.

In Ps 107:29, the stilling of the waves is described; calm wind equals waves stilled. In reality, just as it takes time for the energy of the wind to be absorbed by the sea and waves to develop, so a sudden calming of the wind will not result in a calm sea for some time. The energy will gradually dissipate and the waves will become lower and lower but occur a greater distance apart. Such sea waves are defined as 'swell' and these low waves can sweep across vast distances of ocean, slowly dispersing their energy.

Modern wave forecasting for shipping takes swell into consideration and wind waves are added to the effects of swell to produce a composite wave forecast. The motions are complicated and the combination of the two classes of wave requires complex calculations.

Certainly the biblical writers of these verses appreciated the 'cause-and-effect' of wind and waves; no doubt those who sailed on the sea could make estimates of the effect of various winds upon the waves.

Early meteorology

This section introduces the third and fourth processes of science – conclusion and application. Even in of the older Old Testament writings, there is a clear indication of weather conclusions being drawn.

Conclusions and application

Organisation by nature

Ecclesiastes is another complex book in the 'Wisdom Literature' section of the Old Testament. It is a rather sceptical philosophical discourse which identifies its writer as '...the Preacher, the son of David, King in Jerusalem' (Ecc 1:1). This suggests the author was Solomon, son of David, but most modern Bible commentators now reject this. In Ecclesiastes 1, the emphasis is in the pointlessness of human existence; the writer describes aspects of the Earth's workings to show that nature continues by its own rules and mankind's existence does not impinge on this.

The examples based on weather start with: 'The wind goeth toward the south, and turneth about unto the north; it whirleth about continually...' (Ecc 1:6). These words communicate a picture of a wind that is rarely still; the speed and direction change constantly. The final part of the verse applies a suggestion of organisation: '...and the wind returneth again according to His circuits'. In other words, it is accepted there is a pattern of organisation, which is not understood by mankind.

The following verse speaks of the behaviour of water: 'All the rivers run into the sea; yet the sea is not full; unto the place from whence the rivers come, thither they return again.' (Ecc 1:7). Although not explained, there is some understanding here of the cycle of condensation and evaporation; the sea is not full because some of the water is returned to land by cloud and rain, so the rivers are refilled. This is nothing to do with any action of mankind. The writer of Ecclesiastes considers his point is proved!

These two examples illustrate at least the beginnings of understanding about some workings of the weather. The observations have been made, they have been analysed and now we see some conclusions drawn. There is a water cycle that involves weather, driven by unseen forces of nature; the ever-changing wind is organised by these same forces. Mankind is not involved.

That north wind again

Job and Proverbs provide brief examples of a more focused understanding of wind. Examining the verse from Job first: 'Fair weather cometh out of the north: with God is terrible majesty' (Jb 37:22). The first half of this verse positively links the north wind with fair weather. The term 'fair weather' can cover a number of meteorological descriptions – e.g. fine, sunny, clear, dry, settled. This is a more comprehensive forecast than the example which was examined in the 'Observations' section earlier in this chapter – north wind = cold. The problem with this verse comes when the second half is read '…with God is terrible majesty'. What does this mean? What is the link with the statement about weather?

To explain this, it is necessary to return to the Hebrew text once again. There it is found that 'fair weather' is a translation of *'zaahaab'* which is translated as 'gold' and has implications of shimmering, splendour and (the weather link) clear skies. In fact 'gold' is given in the AV margin

Divine Weather / 217

translation as an alternative. Most other Bible versions opt for the 'gold' concept: 'Out of the north comes golden splendour...' (Jb 37:22) – this is the RSV translation. Commentators argue this variously. Some say it referred to physical gold located in countries to the north; some prefer the golden splendour which probably derives from the Septuagint (Greek translation) which suggested 'clouds shining like gold' and some stay with the more prosaic 'fine weather' imagery. In any event, commentators suggest that the link between the two parts of the verse is one of undeniable properties. The intention is to suggest there is absolute certainty that fine weather (or gold) comes from the north; equally the 'terrible' (fearful, awesome, reverential) majesty of God is certain and unquestionable.

The second 'north wind' example also has problems – but these are of a different nature: 'The north wind driveth away rain: so doth an angry countenance a backbiting tongue' (Pr 25:23). Taken at face value, the first half of this verse has meteorological reality. If the day is wet, the imposition of a north wind will drive the rain away. The rainy day – that is a situation of thick cloud and mainly continuous rain – will be associated with an extensive weather feature, like a front or a low pressure trough. In the vicinity of these features, there is mass uplift of moist air which produces these weather conditions. We have already discussed the characteristics of a north wind for the biblical lands. This brings dry, clear and cool conditions. Simply stated, a rain-producing weather system affecting any area will be driven away south as the cool, dry, clear north wind undercuts it; this is likely to enhance the rain (greater uplift) for a time but the following weather will be drier and clear. Pr 25:23 compares this certain action to the effect that an angry face will always have on someone who is indulging in 'backbiting' – unkind slander. A slanderer will invariably be warned and discouraged by the sight of an angry frown denoting considerable disapproval.

The problem comes with the AV margin note once again. Referring to the words 'drive away rain' an alternative translation 'bringeth forth rain' is suggested. This is completely the opposite! A review of the Bible translations shows a spread of opinion. Some retain the concept of driving away rain; some accept the opposite alternative. The biblical commentators are also divided in their opinions, most acknowledging and commenting upon the dual meaning. The Hebrew text uses *'tsaaphown'* for north and *'ruach'* for wind. The Hebrew *'tsaaphown'* is one of four words that may be used for north; its translation includes the concepts gloomy, hidden and unknown and, directionally, it is attributed to the northern quadrant rather than due north. In this sense, *'ruach'* is used to mean airflow. The two words together imply a wind from the northern quadrant, north-west to north-east.

Although a north or north-east wind will arrive in the biblical lands after a long continental track – and so be dry, clear and cool, the wind from north-west is totally different because its track takes the air across the waters of the Mediterranean Sea. In Israel, north-west winds are relatively moist as a result of this track and such winds can bring showers to the area. Therefore the alternative translation 'bringeth forth rain' is also meteorologically compatible and may be used as a comparison to reinforce the teaching of the verse. However, from a meteorological point of view, it must be said that the absolute certainty of showers from a north-west wind cannot be supported. There are many other factors in a weather situation which determine what weather is experienced with a specific surface wind direction; it is quite possible for some north-west winds to be associated with completely dry weather.

Theories of clouds and rain

There are two examples which comment specifically on the rainfall mechanisms associated with cloud. Ecc 11:3

commences with the phrase: 'If the clouds be full of rain, they empty themselves upon the earth...' This can be interpreted as an over-simplistic view of the workings of precipitation but it deserves deeper examination before that judgement is made.

At the beginning of Ecclesiastes 11, the writer urges the rich to be generous, and the section which starts with v3 introduces the idea of 'what is to be, must be' – thus the reference to clouds and rain: 'If the clouds be full of rain, they empty themselves upon the earth...' Although the statement is over-simplistic (and incorrect) from a weather science point of view, it has a poetic truth.

After clouds are formed by the effects of rising air and condensation, precipitation mechanisms take place within the cloud and these may culminate in rainfall from the cloud (or they may not). Two major mechanisms are recognised. The first is coalescence, where colliding water droplets amalgamate to form bigger droplets; eventually the heavier droplets may fall through the cloud becoming larger and larger until they fall out the bottom as rain. The second is the rather more complicated supercooled water/ice crystal process which was explained in Chapter 6 (Hail Formation). This is an important mechanism for all types of precipitation. Either or both of these mechanisms may result in precipitation from the cloud; if this is not evaporated in the air below, it arrives as rain, sleet, snow or hail.

It may be that the writer of Ecclesiastes was merely pointing out that clouds which are ready to rain will do so; however a simplistic picture of punctured clouds emptying out their water can also be implied by the words 'emptying themselves'. Recourse to the Hebrew shows that the word used has also a translation 'pour out' and this is preferred by some Bible versions. 'Pouring rain' is a more acceptable image – these are words we use today to describe heavy rain. Certainly the writer of Ecclesiastes recognised the

220 / Real Meteorology!

link between clouds and rain; it is not possible to gauge understanding beyond this.

For the second example, we return to the book of Job. Here there is a rather sophisticated comment about rain: 'For he maketh small the drops of water: they pour down rain according to the vapour thereof' (Jb 36:27). The power of God is again the subject of Job's discourse; the previous verse starts: 'Behold, God is great!...'. The Hebrew word used for 'vapour' is also translated as mist, fog, so this verse presents a succinct poetic picture of God's complete power over all natural things. God's clouds are assembled from 'vapour'. The rain which then falls will come from these clouds. In the following verse, God's beneficence to mankind is acknowledged as His clouds '...do drop and distil upon man abundantly'.

In passing it should be noted that there is a scientific problem with the word 'vapour'. Science defines 'water vapour' as an invisible gas – this has been the terminology used in the weather explanations throughout this book. By contrast, the popular, non-scientific definition is mist, steam – in fact water vapour which has condensed. For this verse from Job, it seems clear that the popular translation was the understanding of the time.

Even so, the description of precipitation formation in v37 is close to reality. It is the rising of moist air from low levels which forms clouds. These clouds may precipitate if the precipitation processes within them are strong enough – in other word they behave '...according to the vapour thereof'.

Here is the weather forecast.....

References to biblical weather forecasting rules are confined to the Gospels of Matthew and Luke and are the reported words of Jesus Christ. These are examples of the final scientific process – application.

The famous red skies

This first example is a piece of weather lore known in many parts of the world: 'He answered and said unto them, when it is evening, ye say, it will be fair weather: for the sky is red. And in the morning, it will be foul weather to day: for the sky is red and lowring. O ye hypocrites, ye can discern the face of the sky; but can ye not discern the signs of the times?' (Mt 16:2-3). Obviously, this was a well-known piece of weather forecasting lore when Jesus spoke these words, because he used these words to drive home a challenging answer to a dangerous question.

The question had come from the Pharisees and the Sadducees. 'The Pharisees also with the Sadducees came, and tempting desired him that he would shew them a sign from heaven. (Mt 16:1). This question was a form of challenge to Jesus; as highly religious Jews both Pharisees and Sadducees were opposed to the teachings and actions of Jesus. In his reply, Jesus pointed out that 'signs from heaven' were already present and challenged them to open their closed minds so that they could see them. Jesus strengthened his reply with a rhetorical question that emphasised the inconsistency of their position – if they could see and understand weather signs in the heavens, why could they not see 'the signs of the times?' (The teaching, preaching and miracles of Jesus).

In the modern English language, the weather saying has become: 'Red sky at night, shepherd's delight. Red sky in the morning, shepherd's warning'. In both night and morning cases, the red sky normally referred to is caused by the presence of very high cirrus cloud, a cloud of ice crystals which is seen during the day as white and wispy. The colour of the cloud changes to red when the rays of a low sun in the opposite part of the sky are refracted by the ice crystals of the cloud.

The key to the difference between an observation of red cirrus cloud at night and in the morning is linked to the normal movement of weather patterns – west to east. Red cirrus cloud in the evening will be east of the observer, lit by the setting sun in the west. Because weather systems generally move from west to east, this cloud is expected to continue moving away east to leave a fine night behind (delighting the shepherd!). Red cirrus cloud in the morning will be located to the west of the observer (lit by the rising sun in the east). Such cloud may well be the forward edge of an approaching weather system, so a warning of bad weather is given.

This saying may work for mid-latitude regions in both northern and southern hemispheres because in both zones the upper wind flows which drive weather systems are often in the westerly quadrant. The saying does not work in the equatorial zone or in the highest latitudes. Over the region of the biblical lands, upper winds are quite commonly in the western quadrant, although wind speeds vary greatly. Higher latitudes (e.g. 45-65 Deg) are much more likely to experience upper winds from other directions.

In a way, this weather saying suffers the same problems as your domestic barometer, which may advise fine and settled weather in the depths of freezing fog! First of all, the saying will only work with an observation of existing cloud. Weather systems can move very quickly and the associated cloud may be may be well out of the ground observer's range when the morning observation is made. For instance, a day which later turns very wet and windy may have started calm and cloudless; the weather system responsible may have been too weak or too far west to be noticeable in the morning. On the other hand, the red cirrus cloud may be present but lighter upper winds and other developments well away from the area can easily delay the movement of the weather system or cause it to move elsewhere; in this case the warning may be premature or completely wrong!

Divine Weather / 223

Then there is the general problem of upper winds not in the westerly quadrant. If the upper winds are easterly (this happens periodically), the weather system will arrive from the east and the saying does not work at all; the morning cloud will thicken from the east and cannot be turned red (sun also in the east). Finally, there is the question of cloud type; the red cloud may not be cirrus but innocuous altocumulus or high-level stratocumulus. Seen in the early morning, it may look the part but deteriorating weather will not follow!

Nevertheless, the sequence of events has obviously worked sufficiently well to become a piece of weather lore that has survived for the last 2000 years and more.

'Do-It-Yourself' weather forecasting

The example from Luke's Gospel is an identical message about discernment, delivered this time to the 'people' but with a different piece of comparative weather wisdom. 'And he said also to the people, When ye see a cloud rise out of the west, straightway ye say, There cometh a shower; and so it is. And when ye see the south wind blow, ye say, There will be heat; and it cometh to pass. Ye hypocrites, ye can discern the face of the sky and of the earth; but how is it that ye do not discern this time?' (Lk 12:54-56). The same fundamental question – if they could see and understand weather signs in the heavens, why could they not 'discern this time?' (The teaching, preaching and miracles of Jesus).

In this case, there are two weather predictors. The first is the 'cloud in the west' – this predictor has all the same problems of the 'red sky in the morning'. Will the cloud move east? This will be dependent upon the atmospheric wind patterns. Will the cloud develop to produce showers? This depends upon a whole range of atmospheric conditions which will determine what sort of a cloud it is and how it develops. The Greek word used here is '**ombros**' which is a word associated with storms and thunder; so the writer of this verse was referring to the appearance of a convective type of cloud, cumulus or cumulonimbus. This part of the weather statement has echoes of the cloud in Elijah's story (Chapter 7 – the end of the drought).

The second predictor is that of observed wind direction – the southerly wind will bring heat. In the land where Jesus ministered, the southerly wind meant air from the desert, which invariably would be very hot, dry and dusty. General characteristics can be attached to winds from other directions too. The dreaded east wind with its unwelcome desiccating character; the fresh and relatively cool north wind; the balmy and more moist west wind from the Mediterranean Sea. One problem associated with such predictors is that they take no account of the track of the air. The wind often does not blow in a straight line, so an airflow arriving from a particular direction may have taken a curved track beforehand and so acquired unexpected characteristics. This happens commonly.

However, of the winds from the four directions, the most reliable predictor of heat is probably associated with the south wind. Even a curved track upwind still brings the air from desert regions.

A brief comparison of biblical weather forecasts with their modern equivalent

The fundamental task remains the same. Observe, analyse, conclude and apply this knowledge to make a prediction. In the examples given above, it has been pointed out that the prediction rules used were prone to error from a variety of sources. For the modern weather forecaster, these sources are still alive and well today! Whatever prediction business you work in, there is going to be percentage of error. The difference is that the modern meteorologist is now armed with several significant advantages over the biblical forecaster:

- The way the atmosphere works is now largely understood.
- Scientific observations of many weather parameters are available for all parts of the world, not only near the surface but to great atmospheric depth.
- Advice is available from very large computers, because it is possible to approximate atmospheric processes by mathematical equations.
- There is constant international co-operation between meteorologists both in operational forecasting and research.

This means that the modern-day weather forecaster can predict specific weather parameters in any part of the globe for a significant time period ahead – currently in the order of 10 days; it is possible to give rather less specific weather trends for even longer periods. As a result of continuing research and development work, accuracy continues to improve.

Although fundamentally the same task, weather forecasting, like many other sciences, has come a very long way since biblical days.

14

Patterns of Weather Usage

The review procedure (Appendix 1) identified 496 Bible verses that contained one or more valid weather words. This brief chapter reviews this single verse data as a whole. A simple statistical procedure is employed to see if meaningful patterns of usage emerge. To do this, each verse is allocated to one of six 'Event Categories' and also noted within a 'Location Category'. The categories are as follows:

Event categories

1. Use of weather events as a divine force of destruction
2. Use of a weather event as a divine force of preservation or creation
3. Weather events, imagery or concepts demonstrating the power of God
4. Weather used within figures of speech – similes, metaphors
5. Normal weather described. Weather used for scene setting
6. Weather wisdom and early meteorology

Location categories

A	The Law	Genesis – Deuteronomy
B	History	Joshua – Esther
C	Poetry	Job – Song of Solomon

D	Major Prophets	Isaiah – Daniel
E	Minor Prophets	Hosea – Malach
W	The Gospels	Matthew – John
X	The early Church	Acts
Y	The Epistles	Romans – Jude
Z	The Apocalypse	Revelation

The result of the categorisation

The basic numerical data produced by the categorisation of all 496 verses is shown in Table 1 on page 230:

Comparison of verse frequencies in Old and New Testaments

The tabulated figures reveal that there are 406 weather-related verses in the Old Testament and 90 in the New Testament. This represents an 82/18% split. Considering the overall text sizes of Old and New Testaments (approximately 77/23%), it can be seen that there is no significant bias of data towards either Testament.

'Event category' totals

All the following analyses are based on Table 1. Figure 17 on page 232 looks at the distributions totals for the categorised events. In addition, each frequency bar is split to show distributions within the Old and New Testaments.

The tallest column shows that, by a significant margin, the greatest frequency of weather verses appear in the 'Mystery of God' (3) category. This result is unsurprising since it is reasonable to expect a bias towards the Mystery of God throughout the Bible. In earlier chapters of this book, we have often seen examples of the mystery of God expressed with the aid of weather imagery. The different shading within the column indicates how many verses there were in each Testament. Of the total of 165 verses,

128 (77%) are located in the Old Testament; this figure is the same which was calculated for the proportional size of the Old Testament – the suggestion here is that 'Mystery of God' verses are not concentrated disproportionately in any Testament.

It is interesting to note how frequently 'Figures of speech' (4) occur; Figure 17 shows this category to have the next highest frequency of usage. Listening to today's speech around us, we will find it rich in figures of speech; as already discussed in Chapter 12, many of today's figures of speech use weather comparisons. It seems that the people of biblical times were similar to us in this respect – some things do not change! The spread in the Testaments have a slight bias towards the Old Testament; however a split of 83%/17% is not significant; the implication is that figures of speech appear with similar frequency in both Testaments.

'Destruction' (1) and 'Nurture' (2) are next in the decreasing frequency totals. In some ways it is surprising that the occurrences of these categories lag so far behind; we know that many of the most well-known Bible stories involve descriptions of destruction or saving actions as vehicles of teaching. Looking at the Testament splits, it is here we can see a significant difference. Almost all (96%) occasions of 'Destruction' and 'Nurture' that involve weather appear in the Old Testament.

Categories 5 and 6 show the smallest frequencies; the smallest being recorded in 'Meteorology' (6). This is not unexpected because 'Weather Wisdom', as an activity of man, is unlikely to appear in the earlier parts of the Bible, which is very much focused on the activities of God. Also, the normal processes of human development would suggest a concentration of weather wisdom in the later writings of the Bible. It is with some surprise therefore that we find the preponderance (albeit only 57%) of weather verses involving weather wisdom actually appear

TABLE 1

Use of weather events or language:	A - The Law	B - History	C - Poetry and wisdom	D - Major Prophets	E - Minor Prophets	W - Gospels	X - Acts	Y - Epistles	Z - Revelation	Total
1. a divine force of destruction	15	13	15	27	12	0	0	0	3	85
2. a divine force of preservation or creation	29	7	7	9	2	0	1	1	0	56
3. demonstrating the power of God	36	13	51	23	5	20	1	7	9	165
4. figures of speech — similes, metaphors	3	1	36	34	12	7	1	8	1	103
5. used simply for scene setting	8	6	11	10	1	8	8	0	0	52
6. Weather wisdom and early meteorology	0	0	17	3	0	10	5	0	0	35
Total	91	40	137	106	32	45	16	16	13	496

in the Old Testament! This will be examined in more detail in the following section.

Patterns from the 'Event Categories'

The Event Categories split naturally into two parts; 1, 2 and 3 are directly linked with the actions or attributes of God, while 4, 5, 6 are linked to the activities of mankind, in speech, scene-setting or proclaiming weather wisdom. For this reason, the bar charts now presented display these ranges of values together.

The power and mystery of God

Figure 18 (page 232) reveals the spread of verse occurrences in the first three event categories and in relation to their position in the Bible. The popularity of the 'Mystery of God' references are confirmed by significant totals throughout the Bible. The largest concentrations appear in the 'Poetry' category, with good numbers also shown in the 'Law' and 'Major Prophets'. The New Testament shows a significant Mystery of God frequency in the Gospels; this may refer to God the Father or, generally later in the Gospels, to Jesus the Son.

As already seen in Figure 17, 'Destruction' is confined largely to the Old Testament with the highest concentration the 'Major Prophets'. The New Testament eschews weather destruction by God, except in Revelation, where 3 verses can be found. The same applies to 'Nurture'. This is concentrated in the Old Testament, especially in the 'Law'. There are only two occurrences of nurture in the New Testament, one in the 'Early Church', one in the 'Epistles'.

The contributions of humanity

Figure 19 (page 233) presents a similar display using the frequencies of Categories 4, 5 and 6. It is immediately obvious that the patterns presented for these categories are dissimilar to Categories 1, 2 and 3. Obviously, the

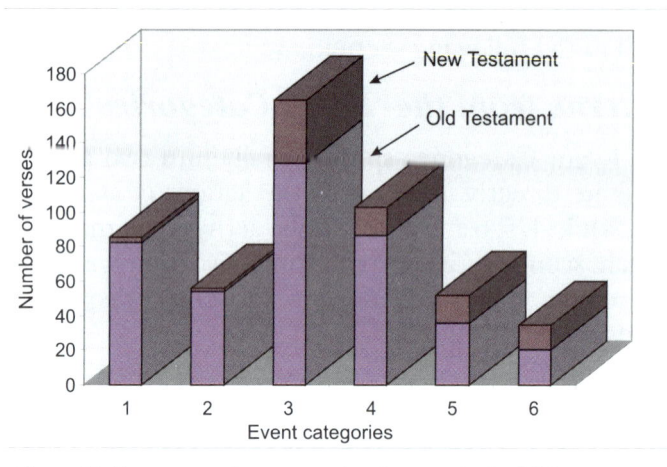

Figure 17: Frequency of weather-related verses in the Bible

activities of mankind are much less consistent than those of God!

Category 4 shows that figures of speech abound, especially in 'Poetry' and the 'Major Prophets'. Few appear in 'Law', 'History', the 'Early Church' and the 'Apocalypse'. This pattern confirms that figures of speech

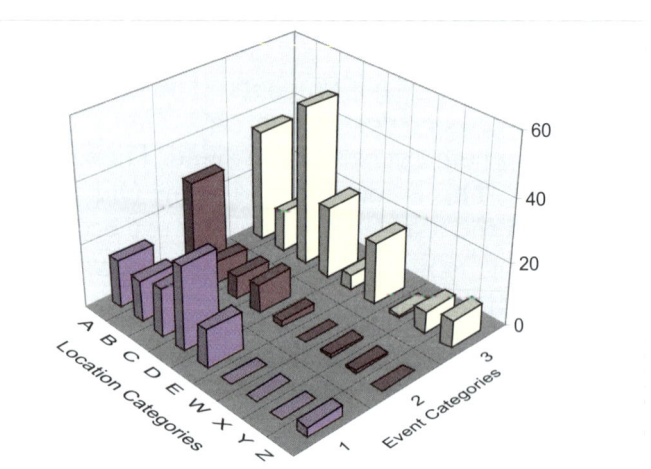

Figure 18: The power and mystery of God (Event Categories 1,2,3)

232 / Patterns of Weather Usage

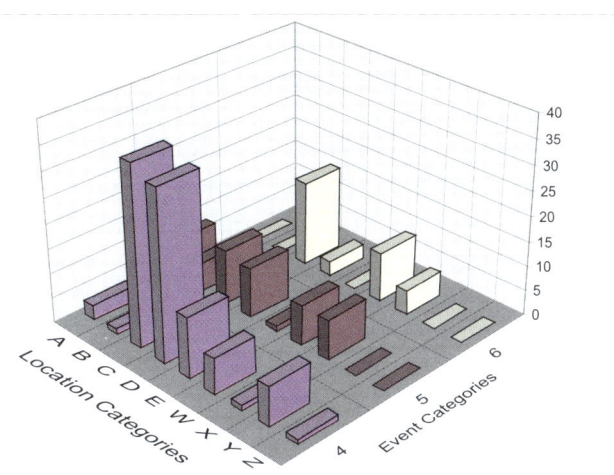

Figure 19: The contributions of humanity (Event Categories 4,5,6)

will be common when there are many occasions of the spoken word of humanity.

Normal weather descriptions and scene-setting texts (Category 5) are spread across most of the locations but none appear in the 'Epistles' or the 'Apocalypse'. Perhaps the texts of these location categories do not concern themselves with much everyday normality!

Turning to 'Weather Wisdom', the surprise Old Testament preponderance noted from Table 1 is revealed to occur in the 'Poetry' category. In fact most of these are within the book of Job. As expected, there is a significant occurrence of 'Weather Wisdom' in the Gospels and the book of Acts but this total does not exceed the Old Testament frequencies. Total text sizes of these categories are similar (the Gospels are rather larger but account repetitions may suggest an offset) so the larger occurrences of weather wisdom in 'Poetry' can be accepted as real.

Here, the assumption that man's knowledge (in this case, of the weather) would develop and become more sophisticated over the years must be questioned.

Divine Weather / 233

Examining the 'Weather Wisdom' verses one by one, it is revealed that the most scientific occurrences appear in the Gospels, with the words of Jesus – Mt 16:2-3 and Lk 12:54-56. These specify simple but valid weather forecasting rules – see Chapter 13 'Here is the weather forecast...' section for the full discussion.

However, some of the references from the Old Testament 'Poetry' category also express aspects of weather wisdom in a sophisticated way (e.g. Chapter 13 'Conclusions and application' section). This is a particularly fascinating result because these texts are significantly older than the Gospels. In seeking the likely dates for these writings, biblical commentators almost invariably commence their assessments by emphasising how difficult it is to be positive about dating! Most of the 'Poetry' books are placed in the 800-500BC span.

This result could be another confirmation that mankind's progression of knowledge does not progress smoothly upwards but is subject to discontinuity at times. The quite sophisticated understandings of weather processes in the time of Job (800-500BC?) may not have been superseded for many hundreds of years.

15

In Conclusion...

God and his activities

Our journey through the Bible has shown us how the writers of the Bible often turned to weather descriptions, images and concepts to communicate their messages. Because weather is so familiar to humankind, its full range of elements is available to illustrate and communicate meanings, some remarkably complex and fine. Warning, retribution and dramatic teaching is often communicated in stories or illustrations of violent and frightening weather; ferocious storms, powerful winds, lashing rain and hail, lightning, thunder, flood – though these may also be used for saving actions against the enemies of God's people. At the other end of the scale, fine, balmy weather is used effectively to envision nurture, safety and well-being; sunshine, light showers, light winds, the gentle dew – the essentials of life.

The mystery and awesome power of God is also expressed frequently in weather terms. In particular, the presence of God, unseen within an enveloping cloud, provided the people with an effective 'picture'. The lowering of clouds on to higher ground is linked with a powerful image of God descending to Earth, perhaps to become accessible to certain chosen individuals. The images of God 'in the cloud' and Jesus visible 'upon the cloud' are a significant realisation; here is an illustration which shows how Jesus can be pictured overtly, God cannot.

The life and activities of mankind

The popularity of figures of speech involving weather is a valuable indication of the link between the people of biblical times and ourselves. Such figures of speech are quite common throughout the Bible – especially in those books where there are many reports of the spoken word. It is fascinating to see that the figures of speech used by the biblical characters are similar to those used by many in the world today. Similarly, the inclusion of weather in general scene setting is another common characteristic found in most books of the Bible and in many of today's writings.

However one focus of interest for this book is the degree of weather understanding which was demonstrated by the biblical writers; also, the fact they used weather as an illustrative mechanism shows a confidence in the weather appreciation of their readers. In considering the knowledge that is demonstrated by biblical texts, Chapter 13 described three stages which indicated the level of understanding. Firstly there is weather observation – a process which meteorologist and non-meteorologist alike participates in every day. It is obvious that the people of biblical times did likewise and some of the observations showed considerable skill. Next there is a process of analysis – an appreciation of cause and effect. This part of the process is found in many parts of the Bible, though not in the earliest parts. Some of the texts show considerable powers of analysis and presentation.

Finally there is the link to scientific meteorology through clear statements of weather wisdom. This is the final process which leads to basic rules for the behaviour of weather. While the most sophisticated examples are found in the New Testament (reported words of Jesus Christ in the Gospels), there is a surprising number of exmples from many hundreds of years earlier; these are found in the so-called 'poetic' books which span from Job to Song of Solomon. Although most of the examples are found in the book of Job, the other poetic books – Psalms, Proverbs,

Ecclesiastes and Song of Solomon provide at least one example each of weather wisdom verses. This is a surprising result since the advance of human knowledge with time would suggest a concentration of weather wisdom examples in the New Testament.

So has this book come up with anything new…?

The words of the Bible have been evaluated many times over the centuries and the conclusions of biblical scholars and commentators abound. Many of these opinions were taken account of when the weather-related texts identified by this review were examined from a meteorological point of view. It is suggested here that this unique approach of this book has allowed confirmation of accepted biblical views in many cases and extensions of these views in others. In a few cases, new interpretations have been able to be advanced.

Here is a reminder of some examples:

1. Taking the words of the writers of Genesis in the Flood story (Genesis 6-9), an atmospheric science approach would not suggest the limited flooding explanation which has been adopted by some commentators is particularly likely.
2. Meteorological considerations do not indicate a wholly scientific explanation for the Plagues of Egypt (Exodus 1-13); many previous conclusions depend on unlikely atmospheric assumptions.
3. The events of the 'Red Sea' (Sea of Reeds) crossing, (Exodus 14), may be better explained by the involvement of a tidal element from the Mediterranean Sea. This suggests a crossing on the southern shores of the Mediterranean.
4. Considering the story of Elijah's approaching storm (end of the drought, 1Kings 18), the

  combination of meteorological considerations and the careful translation of the Hebrew text suggests that the 'cloud as small as a man's hand' can be positively identified as a huge cumulonimbus cloud in the far distance.

5. Weather considerations suggest that the young amorous lady in Song of Solomon 4:16 would probably be calling for the north wind, not the south wind as most translations suggest.

6. Meteorological logic can be applied meaningfully to parts of the stories involving Jesus and the Sea of Galilee (The Gospels). Some previous explanation attempts are considered unlikely.

7. The considerable weather knowledge of biblical sailors is revealed by the meteorological view of Paul's sea journey to Rome (Acts 27-28). The AV translation error of the 'Euraquilo' wind is revealed and alternative explanations proposed.

The Bottom Line

The frequent use of weather in the Bible, spanning from the distant past of the Creation to the future of the Apocalypse, is an incredible demonstration of the communication of complex ideas in a succinct and comprehensible manner. Christians believe that the Bible is inspired by God; one important inspiration of the many writers who wrote the text of the Bible was to make full and effective use of the weather in all its moods.

  It works! The people of biblical times understood.

  So do we.

Postscript

Should we pray for the weather we want?

People do! A fine day for the wedding, the christening, the village fete; the best conditions for that sporting event you hope to win; plenty of snow for the skiing holiday you and the family have been looking forward to so much. Of course people want their important occasions to be perfect so it is not surprising that their petitions to God will include special weather requests.

Personally, I cannot remember an occasion when I prayed for particular weather. I suppose it is because I am a meteorologist and I know how the world's weather must keep itself in balance all over the globe. As explained earlier in this book, the global weather system is a complex engine, each specific weather event a part of the whole, all linked together. If God grants my petition for fine weather (and this is an alteration from what had been 'scheduled' to happen) then someone else gets the bad weather I didn't want! What if they had been praying for fine weather, too? Well, if God grants their petition as well as mine, the bad weather then goes somewhere else again. The point is, someone somewhere loses out!

However, one of the most obvious examples of prayer and weather in the Bible is that 'end-of-drought' story involving Elijah (Chapter 7). Elijah kept praying and eventually the rain was delivered. Should we take that as justification for our personal weather petitions? Not quite, because God had already revealed that he would deliver rain and end the drought (1Ki 18:1). At the end of the contest for supremacy, Elijah knew (1Ki 18:41) that rain was coming and his subsequent prayers were much more likely to be those of adoration and thanksgiving, rather than of petition.

Nevertheless there are many places in the Bible where people are urged to make petitions to God. Indeed sometimes God Himself calls for prayer; in Je 29:12 God says through His prophet '…ye shall go and pray unto me, and I will hearken unto you.' In Mk 11:24 Jesus teaches '…What things soever ye desire, when ye pray, believe that ye receive them, and ye shall have them.' This does not imply any restriction and I do not believe there is one, apart from our attention to Christian teaching which should keep us ever alert to the dangers of selfishness and indifference towards other people and situations.

So, although I make no 'weather petitions' personally, I see them as no different from any other petition to God. As a Christian, I do believe God always hears our prayers. I do believe he always answers them – in his own way and in his own time. I am certain God always knows best – this is why many of my prayers are not specific petitions but thanksgiving for past, present and future gifts – beautiful weather included!

J.M.

Appendix 1

Methodology used to Identify and Categorise Weather-related Bible Texts

1. Primary Bible source.

The King James Authorised version (AV) was chosen as the primary Bible source. All 66 Books of the Old and New Testaments were reviewed. Books from the Apocrypha were not included since AV Bibles have not included any part of the Apocrypha in 20th Century editions. Editions of the AV before the 20th Century commonly included some books of the Apocrypha and a number of today's Bible editions do likewise. (The Apocrypha is the name for a group of books that span the several hundred-year period between the end of the Old Testament and the beginning of the New Testament.)

2. Identification of 'weather words'

Potential 'weather words' were extracted manually from 'Cruden's Complete Concordance to the Old and New Testaments' (Lutterworth Press 1930). This single volume work contains 225,000 references of word occurrences in the AV Bible. The complete word list was reviewed and note made of every word that could reasonably be used in a weather-related sense.

This examination produced a total of 116 words. These are listed in Table 2 on the next page.

Air	dried	hailstones	sea, -s	thunderbolts
blew	drop	heat	season, -s	thunders
Blow, -ing, -n	drought	hot	shower, -s	vapour, -s
Bloweth	dry	ice	sky, -ies	warm, -ed, -eth
Bow	dust	light, -s	snow	warming
Cloud, -s, -y	fine	lightning, -s	spring	water,-ed,-ing
coast, -s	fire	mist	star, -s	waterest
Cold	flash	Mountain, -s	still	waters
Cool	flood, -s	night, -s	storm, -y	waterspouts
dark, -en	flow, -ing	pool, -s	summer	wave, -s
Darkened	forecast	pour, -ed	sun	weather
Darkeneth	foreknow,-n	rain, -ed, -y	tempest	wet
Darkness	Foreknowledge	rainbow	tempestuous	whirlwind, -s
day, -s	frost	red	thunder, -ed	wind, -s
desert, -s	frozen	river, -s	thundereth	windy
Dew	hail	roar, -ing	thunderings	winter

Table 2: 'Weather Words' extracted from Cruden's Complete Concordance

Divine Weather / 243

3. Concordance search of 'weather words'

Using the concordance search facilities provided by Bible study computer programs and AV Bible text datafiles, occurrences of every weather word were sought and noted. The above list of 116 weather words generated over 8,000 biblical references. Each verse was displayed for assessment.

On examination, references were either rejected (because they had no conceivable weather-related link) or accepted as a weather-related event. For instance, it was possible to accept all occurrences of 'frost' and 'wind' because these words referred to weather-related events on every occasion. However many of the weather words can be used in a non-meteorological sense. For instance, although some instances of 'bow' referred to 'rainbow' (and so were chosen) many others proved to be 'bow' as in 'bow and arrow' and were not relevant to this study. Still others proved to be 'bow' as in 'bow down before you'. Similarly, although many occurrences of 'hail' did indeed refer to frozen ice pellets falling from the sky (accepted), many others were found to be the greeting 'Hail!' All instances of 'non-weather' verses were rejected at this stage.

At the end of this procedure, there were 1,307 occurrences of relevant and accepted biblical weather words.

4. Verses and passages

Many of the 1,307 weather words occurred in the same verse. Sometimes it was the same word repeated; for instance the word 'cloud' often appeared two or more times in the same verse. Other weather words frequently appear together; 'thunder' and 'lightning' are invariably partners in life and often appear together in the same biblical sentence. It was found that a total of 496 verses contained the 1307 weather words.

Each verse reference was then checked for adjacency. Where this occurred, the Bible text was examined to see whether two or more verses could be combined into a passage which dealt with a single weather event or a series of weather events which were part of the same story. This was done where appropriate. A total of 388 passages of variable length were gathered in this way.

5. Final grouping

Some of the passages are part of well-known Bible stories that involve weather in some way. 31 of the 388 passages were grouped together into 12 major Bible stories and these are presented in Chapters 3 to 9, starting with the Creation and ending with the Apostle Paul's highly eventful sea journey from Jerusalem to Rome. The remaining 357 passages were categorised and examples are presented in Chapters 10 to 13. For completeness and to investigate patterns of usage, Chapter 14 presents a separate statistical analysis all 496 single verses.

Appendix 2

Broad-Scale Weather Processes

The key process for the existence of the Earth's weather is differential (unequal) heating. This differential heating causes complex atmospheric motions, not only in the wind at or near the surface but throughout the atmosphere to great height. The air (wind) flows vertically as well as horizontally; most winds have a vertical as well as a horizontal component. Because of this, there are many variations in temperature and humidity all through the atmosphere. The accumulation of all these parameters determine broad-scale weather processes.

As a fundamental starting-point, Figure 20 (page 248) shows the very simple global convection currents which would be generated in the Northern Hemisphere on a stationary sphere.

In this model (remember the laboratory beaker experiment which demonstrated convection currents?) air rises from the hottest part of the globe near the Equator and descends at the coldest part, the North Pole. Near the surface, air flows southwards to replace the rising air near the Equator. The large convection current circulation is then completed by the transfer of air at high levels northwards from over the Equator to the North Pole.

This is not what happens on Earth, because upon this extremely simple scheme of basic movement there is imposed a considerable disrupting force – the rotation of the Earth. The speed of this rotation is almost 1700kph at the Equator. The effect this has on the freely flowing air in the Northern Hemisphere is to deflect it markedly to the right, from an Earth point of view. (The opposite happens in the Southern Hemisphere). So the air which has risen to high levels over the Equator does not flow due north but, due to that deflection, turns east and starts to wind its way around the hemisphere in a vast spiral which edges northwards. Very soon, this introduces another complication.

Because the spiral of rotation becomes ever smaller as the air travels north (the diameter of the Earth becomes smaller) the 'conservation of angular momentum' comes into play. This is the physical law which allows the performing ice skater to increase his or her spin by drawing both arms tightly in towards the body. You can demonstrate this effect to yourself by spinning around on an office chair and extending and retracting your arms and legs! The effect is very marked (and great fun!).

Just like the ice skater increases spin by reducing the radius of his or her mass, so on Earth the speed of the upper airflow increases markedly as its spiral tightens. By the time the air reaches mid latitudes, the conservation of angular momentum would have caused it to accelerate to incredible speeds. However the low density of air allows it to dissipate its energy by other means. Basically, two things happen. The flow splits and it also buckles to become a complex system of air motion; this produces sufficient dissipation of energy to reduce airflow speeds to some degree.

Figure 21 on page 248 gives a schematic indication of the sort of flow splits that may occur.

In the high atmosphere, the flow split north of the Equator sends some of the high-level air back towards the surface of the Earth in the 20-30 DegN and DegS areas. At low levels, some of this air flows north and produces a convergence of low-level air in middle and northern latitudes. These northern convergence areas become zones of rising air. By the mechanism discussed earlier in the chapter, the areas of sinking air will be generally cloudless and very dry while the zones of uplift will be unsettled, cloudy and potentially wet. It is notable that almost all the world's deserts are to be found under these zones of descending air, around 20-30 DegN and DegS. Check your atlas and you'll see!

The buckling in the upper airflow is a mechanism to extend the circumference of the circling air. This results in the formation of huge atmospheric air waves, generally in mid-latitudes. A representation of what happens is shown in Figure 22, page 249.

This wave-shaped upper airflow extends right around each hemisphere and is constantly changing. While the air is rushing along in these flow patterns, the waves themselves are not static

Divine Weather / 247

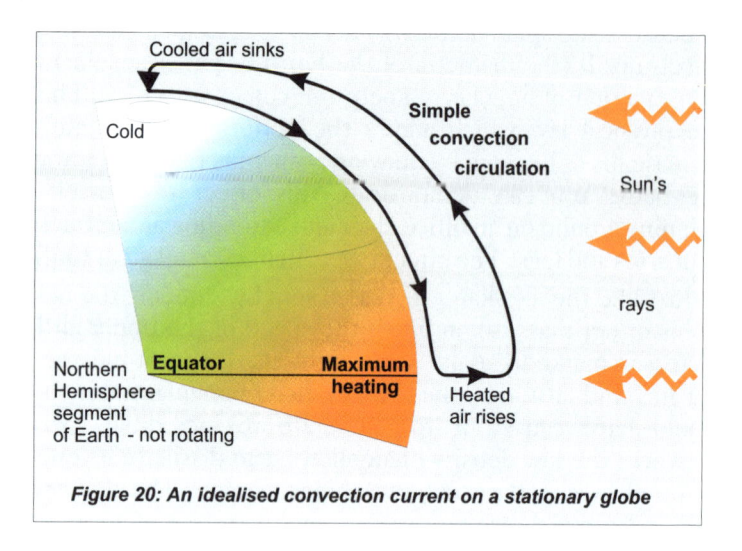

Figure 20: An idealised convection current on a stationary globe

features. They may progress (move east) or regress (move west). The amplitude of individual ridges and troughs may increase or decrease. They may reorganise into a different number of waves around the hemisphere. They may form cut-off whorls. These high atmosphere airflow waves are very important because they represent the beginnings of broad-scale variations in the weather.

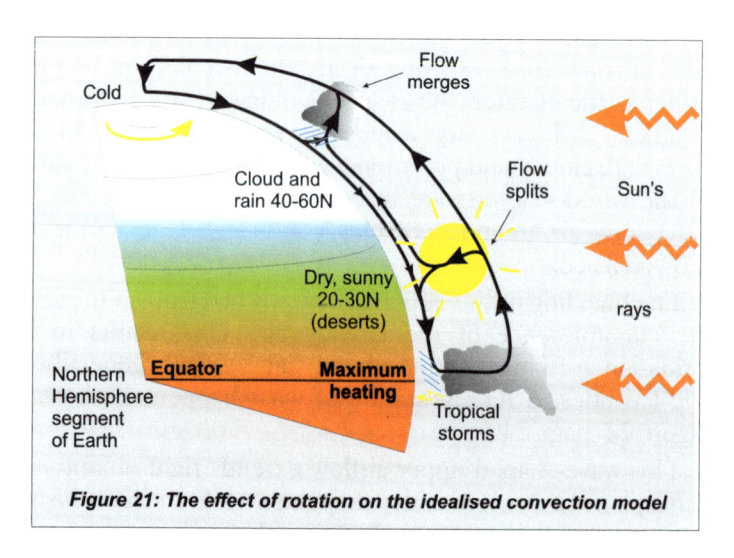

Figure 21: The effect of rotation on the idealised convection model

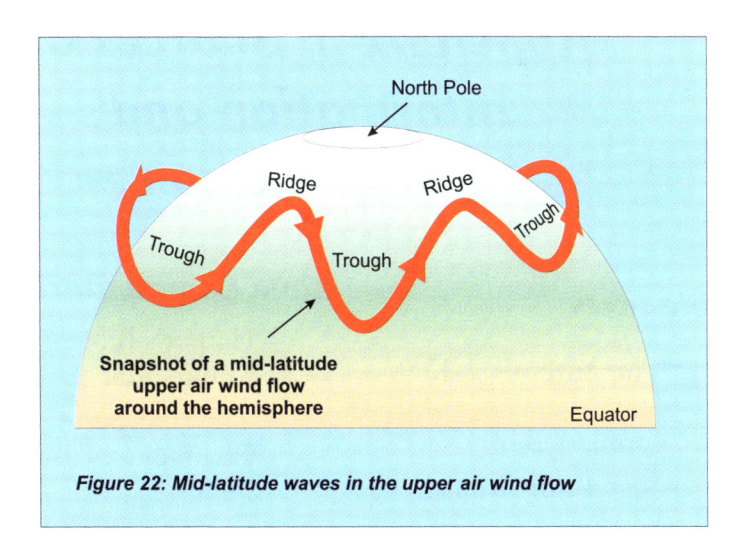

Figure 22: Mid-latitude waves in the upper air wind flow

The aggregation of upper flow splits and waves means that the maximum speed of upper winds does not usually exceed 250 mph (400 kph). These maximum upper winds occur as concentrations of the flow called 'jet streams' that are usually located in mid-latitude and sub-tropical regions. The position, intensity and structure of these jet streams are of great importance in meteorology.

At any point on the Earth's surface, the broad-scale upper pattern overhead at that moment will be the first determinant of what basic sort of weather you will have. In mid-latitude regions, if you are under a trough in the upper flow, you will be in a cold weather regime of some type. Beneath a ridge, the regime will be warm weather of some type. In the zones between, the weather type will be unsettled. However, it is emphasised that the actual weather you experience will be formed from the many other processes and scales of movement which are discussed in Chapter 4.

Appendix 3: Sources of Information and Interpretation

Bible texts

- The Authorised King James Version. 1611 (primary Bible)
- New International Version
- Revised Standard Version
- Good News Bible
- Revised English Bible
- Jerusalem Bible
- Young's Literal Translation
- Derby's Translation
- American Standard
- New American Standard
- New King James
- The Living Bible
- The Septuagint (Bagster 1879)
- UBS Greek Text
- BHS Hebrew Text
- The Interlinear Bible

Bible Commentaries

- Harper's Bible Commentary
- The Interpreters Commentary of the Bible
- The New Jerome Biblical Commentary
- Matthew Henry's Commentary
- Adam Clarke Commentary
- Jamieson Fausset & Brown Commentary
- Wycliffe Commentary
- Keil and Delitzsch Commentary
- Barnes' Notes
- Vincent's word studies
- Seiss' Apocalypse

Bible Dictionaries, Encyclopaedias, General Reference

- Applied Bible Dictionary

- Nelson Bible Dictionary
- Unger's Bible Dictionary
- Vine's Expository Dictionary
- Strong's Complete Dictionary of Bible Words
- Thayer's Greek Lexicon
- Brown Driver & Briggs Hebrew Lexicon
- Modern Greek-English Dictionary
- Classical Greek Dictionary
- International Standard Bible Encyclopaedia
- The Lion Handbook to the Bible
- Nave's Topical Bible
- The Treasury of Scriptural Knowledge
- Cambridge Factfinder
- Encarta Encyclopaedia

Bible Concordances and Search Tools

- Cruden's Complete Concordance
- The NIV Complete Concordance
- Young's Analytical Concordance
- Strong's Exhaustive Concordance of the Bible
- Englishman's Concordance
- PC Bible Study
- Bible Companion Series

Meteorological and Geographical Information

- The World Weather Guide
- The Meteorological Glossary
- The Times Atlas of the World
- Tidal Information: Ports of the World (Lloyds of London)

Divine Weather / 251

Abbreviations

1Ki	1Kings
1Sa	1Samuel
1Th	1Thessalonians
2Ki	2 Kings
Ac	Acts
AV	Authorised Version
cm	Centimetres
Da	Daniel
De	Deuteronomy
Deg	Degrees
DegC	Degrees Celsius/Centigrade
DegE	Degrees East
DegF	Degrees Fahrenheit
DegN	Degrees North
DegS	Degrees South
Ecc	Ecclesiastes
Eph	Ephesians
Ex	Exodus
Ez	Ezekiel
ft	Feet
Ge	Genesis
He	Hebrews
Hgg	Haggai
in	Inches
Is	Isaiah
Jb	Job
Je	Jeremiah
Jn	John
km	Kilometres
kph	Kilometres per hour
La	Lamentations
Le	Leviticus
Lk	Luke
m	Metres
mi	Miles
Mk	Mark
mm	Millimetres
mph	Miles per hour
MSLP	Mean Sea Level Pressure
Mt	Matthew
NIV	New International Version
Pr	Proverbs
Ps	Psalm
Re	Revelation
SS	Song of Solomon
UBS	United Bible Societies
v	Verse
vv	Verses
Ze	Zechariah

Bible references

The following are the main Bible references discussed in the book. The text itself contains many further references (particularly chapters 10-12) which are not indexed here.

OLD TESTAMENT

Genesis

Ch.1 · · · p9, 28ff, 79, 103

Ch.2 · · · p9, 44f

Ch.5 · · · p123

Ch. 6-8 · · p68ff

Ch.9 · · · p87

Ch.31 · · · p12

Exodus

Ch.1-2 · · p89f

Ch.9 · · · p92ff

Ch.10 · · · p101ff

Ch.11 · · · p106ff

Ch.11-13 · p106

Ch.13 · · · p165

Ch.14-15 · p107ff

Ch.16 · · · p166

Ch.19 · · · p167

Leviticus

Numbers

Deuteronomy

Ch.11 · · · p204

Ch.32 · · · p195

Ch.33 · · · p211

Joshua

Judges

Ruth

1 Samuel

Ch.12 · · · p184

2 Samuel

Ch.23 · · · p202

1 Kings

Ch.17-18 · p113ff

2 Kings

1 Chronicles

2 Chronicles

Ezra

Ch.10 · · · p205

Nehemiah

Esther

Job	Jeremiah
Ch.7 · · · p200	Ch.2 · · · p205
Ch.24 · · · p214	Ch.4 · · · p186
Ch.36 · · · p221	Ch.23 · · · p188
Ch.37 · · · p213, 217	Lamentations
Psalms	Ch.2-3 · · · p193
Ps. 11 · · · p190, 196	Ezekiel
Ps. 29 · · · p70	Ch.17 · · · p202
Ps. 35 · · · p202	Ch.38 · · · p184
Ps. 105 · · p215	Ch.1 · · · p124ff
Proverbs	Ch.13 · · · p126
Ch.3:20 · · p212	Ch.37 · · · p127
Ch.25:23 · p218	Daniel
Ch.26:1 · · p197	Hosea
Ch.28:3 · · p197	Joel
Ecclesiastes	Amos
Ch.1 · · · p216	Obadiah
Ch.11 · · · p220	Jonah · · · p128ff
Song of Solomon	Micah
Ch.2 · · · p212	Nahum
Ch.4 · · · p207ff	Habakkuk
Isaiah	Zephaniah
Ch.28 · · · p201	Haggai
Ch.41 · · · p187	Ch.1 · · · p192
Ch.60 · · · p198	Ch.2 · · · p186

Zechariah
Ch.10 · · · p214
Malachi

NEW TESTAMENT

Matthew
Ch.5-8 · · · p133ff
Ch.14 · · · p137f
Ch.16 · · · p222
Ch.24 · · · p141
Mark
Ch.15 · · · p143ff
Luke
Ch.12 · · · p224
Ch.17 · · · p141
John
The Acts
Ch.2 · · · p203
Ch.27-28 · p149ff, 206
Romans
1 Corinthians
2 Corinthians
Galatians
Ephesians
Philippians
Colossians

1 Thessalonians
Ch.2 · · · p141
2 Thessalonians
1 Timothy
2 Timothy
Titus
Philemon
Hebrews
James
1 Peter
2 Peter
1 John
2 John
3 John
Jude
The Revelation

Divine Weather / 255